Responsibility to Protect

Responsibility to Protect

The Global Moral Compact for the 21st Century

Edited by Richard H. Cooper
and Juliette Voïnov Kohler

First published in 2009 by PALGRAVE MACMILLAN® in the United States—
a division of St. Martin's Press LLC, 175 Fifth Avenue, New York, NY 10010.

Where this book is distributed in the UK, Europe and the rest of the world,
this is by Palgrave Macmillan, a division of Macmillan Publishers Limited,
registered in England, company number 785998, of Houndmills, Basingstoke,
Hampshire RG21 6XS.

Palgrave Macmillan is the global academic imprint of the above companies
and has companies and representatives throughout the world.

Palgrave® and Macmillan® are registered trademarks in the United States, the
United Kingdom, Europe and other countries.

ISBN-13: 978-0-230-60902-0
ISBN-10: 0-230-60902-3

Library of Congress Cataloging-in-Publication Data

Responsibility to protect : the global moral compact for the 21st century /
Richard H. Cooper and Juliette Voïnov Kohler [editors].
    p. cm.
Includes bibliographical references and index.
ISBN 0-230-60902-3
    1. Humanitarian intervention. 2. Genocide—Intervention. I. Cooper,
Richard H. II. Voïnov Kohler, Juliette.

JZ6369.R48 2008
172'.4—dc22   2008029267

A catalogue record of the book is available from the British Library.

Design by Scribe Inc.

First edition: January 2009

10 9 8 7 6 5 4 3 2 1

Printed in the United States of America.

Contents

Foreword

Samantha Power*

In September 2004 U.S. Secretary of State Colin Powell appeared before the U.S. Congress to discuss the ongoing slaughter in Darfur, Sudan, then estimated to have taken some 200,000 lives. He used the occasion of his testimony to issue the first formal public finding of genocide in the history of the U.S. State Department. "We concluded—I concluded—that genocide has been committed in Darfur," Powell said, "and that the government of Sudan and the Janjaweed bear responsibility." A year later, in September 2005, 150 countries in the United Nations (UN) General Assembly unanimously affirmed their support for a nonbinding resolution asserting their belief that states bore a "responsibility to protect" populations being slaughtered around the world.

Both moments arose from the seeming emergent consensus that genocide and mass atrocity are monstrous crimes that require governments to act to stop them. The seeds for this idea were planted in the Nuremberg Tribunal in 1945, which took the radical step of holding leaders of a sovereign state accountable for crimes against humanity carried out while in office. Yet Nuremberg only punished those crimes that could be linked to a "crime against peace," the hostile crossing of an international border. The Genocide Convention of 1948, adopted unanimously by the General Assembly (which then had fewer than one-third of the countries it has today), required state parties to take steps to prevent and punish the crime of genocide, defined as "acts committed with intent to destroy, in whole or in part, a national, ethnical, racial or religious group." Little was done to enforce the terms of the Genocide Convention for the next half century, until, in 1993, the International Criminal Tribunal for the former Yugoslavia was established, quickly followed by one for Rwanda. The norm against genocide was finally having its day, but it was being enforced in courtrooms. At last count, 161 individuals from the former Yugoslavia have been indicted (5 of whom remained at large), while 70 from Rwanda have been tried or face trial. The creation of the permanent International Criminal Court (ICC) in 1998 seemed to signal that most of the world's governments supported ending impunity for perpetrators of mass atrocity.[1]

When Secretary Powell issued the State Department's genocide finding and the General Assembly endorsed the responsibility to protect, it reflected a shift from legal accountability to political action. Powerful countries appeared willing to recognize that, as important as punishment was, by definition it only happened *after* the most heinous crimes had been allowed to occur. Although Powell was issuing a legal finding, he was doing so in a distinctly political setting, and, it seemed, he was laying a foundation for robust diplomatic, economic, and perhaps even military or police action. The General Assembly resolution, too, was hailed because it meant that whole governments—not simply national or international prosecutors— were accepting responsibility for protecting civilians. In a remarkably short time, influential UN member states went from ignoring mass atrocities altogether to setting up international tribunals to punish them, to accepting that they had a responsibility to prevent or stop them.

But despite the fanfare surrounding both events and the sense of promise they engendered, the stark reality is that little has been done to stop the slaughter in Darfur. Neither a finding by the U.S. secretary of state nor a spirited affirmation of the responsibility to protect seems to have made a meaningful difference in the lives of Darfur's displaced and threatened. Indeed, when it comes to the cause of civilian protection, state practice deviates dramatically from stated aspiration. For all of the norm fortification that has occurred over the last decade, perpetrators of systematic crimes against humanity around the globe may well take solace from the current international climate. If supporters of responsibility to protect (R2P) are to succeed in actually getting governments to act upon their responsibility, three formidable phenomena must be overcome: long-standing understandings of national interest, the resurgence of "sovereignty" as a deterrent to action, and the "Iraq syndrome."

Create a Domestic Political Interest

The motivations of governments and the individuals who comprise them have not changed. No matter how large or small, how rich or poor, how democratic or undemocratic, states pursue their national interests. The definitions of those interests vary somewhat, but generally governments pursue policies that advance economic welfare (for elites or for the broader populace) or enhance national security. Since stopping crimes against humanity rarely advances economic or security interests, policymakers will seldom see preventive action by itself as a mechanism for promoting the national interest. Indeed, as with Sudan today or Saddam Hussein's Iraq in the 1980s, western governments may see their security interests as being advanced by building close ties with a regime that murders its own citizens.

While this is a reality that must be reckoned with, governments are susceptible to pressure. Democracies, in particular, are far more prone to exercise their responsibility to protect when they are subjected to domestic political pressure. In other words, if the slaughter of civilians does not implicate the "national interest" as it is traditionally defined, it can, occasionally, implicate the domestic political interest of a head of state or an influential political bloc.

In 1995 President Clinton led the charge for North Atlantic Treaty Organization (NATO) action in Bosnia largely because his hesitant response to the tragedy had started to make him look like a weak leader at home. Relentless press coverage, strong editorial support for civilian protection, sustained grassroots and grass-tops pressure, and a worsening situation on the ground eventually caused Clinton to see the costs of inaction as greater than the risks of action. In France and Britain, too, it was public outrage over the Serbs' July 1995 massacre in Srebrenica that prodded the French and British governments to support NATO action. Today, the slaughter in Darfur has ignited a sophisticated, well-resourced, antiatrocity movement in the United States, which has forced the Bush administration to take steps to deal with the issue. Nick Kristof, John Prendergast, Eric Reeves, evangelical Christian groups, student antigenocide chapters, Jewish organizations, celebrities (such as Don Cheadle, George Clooney, and Mia Farrow), and influential members of Congress have made it impossible for Bush to look away, even at a time when the United States is already juggling an unprecedented number of significant national security challenges (Iraq, Afghanistan, Iran, North Korea, Arab-Israeli peace, Lebanon, etc.).

This book includes multiple references to public opinion polls that show strong support for multilateral action in the face of genocide or mass atrocity. This public support is important, but it is not sufficient. The support must be mobilized and rendered politically relevant. Supporters of the new norm must galvanize what has been a relatively passive and apolitical humanitarian contingent into an active bloc. Darfur has suffered greatly because the United States and Canada are the only two countries in which the issue has captured the public imagination. The paradox is that the United States, the western country that is most suspicious of international norms and institutions, is facing greater domestic political pressure to act to protect endangered peoples than western governments that wholeheartedly support the new norm but are disinclined to place their national treasure (in the way of troops, equipment, or funding) on the line in exercising the responsibility that they hail. If R2P is to become an influential international norm, it will be because supporters of the concept understand that governments will rarely exercise their "responsibility" naturally—they will have to be pressured to do so.

Neutralize the "Sovereignty Bloc"

In the 1990s pundits and governments prematurely hailed the "demise of sovereignty." In the wake of the cold war, many were tempted to trumpet the "end of history" and the triumph of western liberalism, which carried with them assumptions about the spread of human rights consciousness and protection. In the first decade of the twenty-first century, however, the sovereignty shield has made a comeback. And because of the military and economic strength of its strongest backers, it is a more potent device than ever. In historical terms the so-called unipolar moment—in which the United States functioned as the world's sole superpower—lasted little longer than an actual moment. Both economically and geopolitically, other rising powers have begun throwing their weight around in international institutions, and each of them are—in different ways—asserting their sovereign right to be left alone, while also insisting that smaller and less developed countries also have the right to be free of western meddling. The most important of these ascendant powers is of course China. From North Korea to Darfur, it is clear that the days when China concentrated on its economic ascent, forswearing an aggressive geopolitical role, have passed. It has begun threatening to use its veto on the UN Security Council and has already begun throwing its diplomatic weight around in the developing world to secure economic advantage. And China is not alone. Russia and Venezuela, the new petro-authoritarian powers, are also becoming important global and regional players, using their oil wealth as leverage to buy off domestic opposition and to entice or bully their neighbors.

The rise of these countries has given developing countries in the south growing confidence to stand up to developed countries in the north. The Group of 77 (G-77) now includes 133 of the 192 countries in the UN, and its agenda frequently mirrors that of China. These countries rarely sit back passively to receive edicts from developed countries within international bodies. Instead of simply venting in the General Assembly, they engage in increasingly sophisticated balance-of-power politics. Suspicious of rich, western countries, they have resurrected the near-reverence for sovereignty that western governments thought had been banished by the carnage of the 1990s. The "southern revolt" has meant that a diminishing number of voices are speaking out on behalf of human rights in the international system.

Indeed, they are joining forces to elect human rights abusers to the Human Rights Council or to blunt human rights resolutions in various UN bodies.

The R2P norm was crafted precisely in order to avoid inflaming developing countries' fears that western countries would trample their sovereignty. Discussions in the 1990s about the "right of intervention" raised hackles among smaller countries that former colonial powers were using humanitarian pretexts to cloak their imperial designs. The new R2P norm very deliberately gave national governments the right of first response. Only when the authorities in the country where abuses are occurring fail to exercise their primary responsibility does a secondary responsibility vest upward to the broader international community.

Since the 150 countries in the General Assembly who signed on to the Millennium Summit consensus document included G-77 countries in the developing world, it is tempting to believe that these countries have begrudgingly accepted that states have to earn the sovereign right to be left alone—in other words that sovereignty can be conditioned on behavior. Yet while they have done so in writing, as Darfur attests, it will be difficult to convince them to do so in fact. Although the day may come when they see China as the country that most threatens their sovereignty and their natural resources, they currently seem pleased to see Beijing flexing its muscles and standing up to western consensus. Supporters of R2P should expect more, not less, pushback in the international system as they try to mobilize support for diplomatic, economic, or military intervention.

Overcome the Iraq Syndrome

A third essential factor behind the reluctance of governments to exercise their responsibility toward civilians can be distilled in a single word: Iraq. We have already seen the pernicious effect of the war in Iraq on the international response to Darfur, and we should expect the Iraq War to undermine responsiveness for a long time to come. In the United States, we once spoke of the "Vietnam syndrome"—the bitter residue that the Vietnam War left in the minds of citizens and commanding generals. This syndrome was said to have been "kicked" by the overwhelming victory of the U.S.-led coalition in the Persian Gulf War of 1991. Then, starting with the Mogadishu firefight of October 1993, we began speaking of the "Somalia syndrome." This mistrust of "small wars," peacekeeping, and nation-building was said to be banished by the Clinton administration, when it used air power to swiftly end the slaughter in Bosnia in 1995 and Serbia's ethnic cleansing in Kosovo in 1999. But it is unclear what it will take to overcome the lasting effects of the current Iraq syndrome.

The Iraq syndrome will infect international readiness to enforce the responsibility to protect in two ways. First, U.S. legitimacy and credibility have been severely eroded by the decision to go to war without Security Council approval, by the failure to find weapons of mass destruction, and by its incompetent and inhumane conduct of the war. The responsibility to protect turns on a threshold question of just when atrocities have risen to a level that warrants outside interference. The ability of the United States to weigh in credibly on these discussions is hugely diminished. Other countries must thus step forward—developing their own intelligence sources and making their own empirical claims, avoiding association with Washington and its "global war on terror." In many circumstances it is hugely challenging to find or develop independent sources of information while mass atrocity is under way. Those carrying out slaughter are not exactly eager to be watched as they carry out massacres. Thus it will always be difficult to develop an international consensus on the nature or scope of violence. Since most countries in the UN (developed and developing) are generally looking for reasons not to act—rather than reasons to act—they will be prone to seize upon the inevitable uncertainty in order to delay or avoid action. The post–Iraq War international climate of suspiciousness will thus make it even harder to mobilize resources in a timely fashion.

Iraq should be a monument to flawed policy choices, poor planning, and what can happen when a country acts on minimal provocation without international support and without proper preparation. Instead, the "lesson of Iraq" in many parts of the world (including the United States) is being boiled down to its simplest and least helpful cliché: don't intervene to help people abroad, you'll end up in a quagmire. President Bush's opportunistic invocation of Saddam Hussein's chemical weapons use against the Kurds has caused many at home and abroad to associate the bungled war in Iraq with humanitarian intervention. Thus the second way the Iraq War has harmed R2P is that, thanks to Bush's misleading framing of the Iraq invasion, the cause of civilian protection has been damned by association. Bush's war had very little to do with Iraqi welfare, and it is important for the war's critics to remember that the tragedy of Iraq is the result of too little—not too much—regard for civilians. The concept of civilian protection must be rehabilitated and disassociated from a war whose architects gave civilians marginal consideration, with catastrophic results.

* * *

Gareth Evans, one of the originators of the R2P norm, writes in his essay in this important book that in these dark times a "candle flickers in the darkness," and R2P is that candle. There is no question that vulnerable civilians in danger of deportation or outright extermination look out from behind barbed wire or from long lines at UN feeding stations and hope that international rhetoric will be matched by international will. They do not read the fine print of UN resolutions. They do not know that states will not be held to their word, or that the Millennium Summit outcome document is just that: a document. As a result, more often than not, civilians who have set their sights on the candle of international promise have seen their hopes shattered.

If the twentieth century was about norm generation, the twenty-first century must be about norm enforcement. This means shaping a different world by first taking stock of the world as it is. It means stating outright that we are embarrassed to treat the worthy explosion of international humanitarian assistance as a substitute for outright protection. The world as it is includes countries that are skeptical of the norm because they fear that R2P will be used as a cover for unwarranted western meddling. Many of these countries care more about national and regional pride than they do about their own citizens. The world as it is also includes countries that offer ostentatious support for the norm, hailing it at international conferences and boasting about their role in its formulation, and yet risk little to ensure that the norm is enforced. As advocates who prod governments to do more and to be more, we must use the candle to shine light on those states that commit atrocities as well as those countries that allow them. Only if we, as citizens, take our responsibilities seriously will we convince governments to do the same.

Notes

* Samantha Power is the Anna Lindh Professor of Practice of Global Leadership and Public Policy, based at the Carr Center for Human Rights Policy, where she was the founding executive director (1998–2002).
1. Only China, Iraq, Israel, Libya, Qatar, the United States, and Yemen voted against the Rome Treaty. Twenty-one countries abstained.

The Responsibility to Protect

The Opportunity to Relegate Atrocity Crimes to the Past

*Richard H. Cooper and
Juliette Voïnov Kohler*

Ｉf reason and conscience ruled the world, extreme forms of violence would not so frequently be the means to an end. The twentieth century and its share of mass atrocities are painful reminders that despite all the decent people who inhabit this planet, mankind too easily resorts to the most destructive patterns to achieve political, economic, or religious gains. On the other hand, drastic improvements have been witnessed in nearly every type of human activity during the last hundred years. Scientific discoveries, technological advances, economic development, as well as social and political changes attest to the ingenuity of mankind. As a result, virtually every aspect of our lives has been affected, often in a positive way. Man has stepped onto the moon. The number of liberal democracies stands at an all-time high. Slavery, a long-time practice, has been abolished. Mortality has dramatically declined, and smallpox has been eradicated. And while all this progress was achieved, too many parts of our world were plunged into the abysses of hell and mass murders. Obviously, such carnage has not been confined to the past hundred years, but this last century has proved extremely deadly in comparison, with hundreds of millions of individuals lost to war or victims of mass atrocities. As we draw a curtain over the legacies of the twentieth century, it is difficult to ignore that mankind continues to be disgraced by its inability to curb such radical forms of violence. Genocide, crimes against humanity (including ethnic cleansing), and war crimes—the atrocity crimes of our times—have gone unabated. And as we enter the twenty-first century, these mass atrocities are still too widespread. Atrocity crimes are man-made, and therefore they can and must be solved by man. With the universal endorsement of the "responsibility to protect," there is hope that the twenty-first century will, at last, relegate atrocity crimes to the past.

On September 16, 2005, the United Nations (UN) General Assembly took an historical yet surprisingly little noticed step toward the abolition of atrocity crimes. At a time of great turmoil in global affairs, world leaders unanimously embraced the responsibility to protect, a new global moral compact to put an end to the most egregious crimes that have repeatedly stained humanity. The consensual text reads:

> Responsibility to protect populations from genocide, war crimes, ethnic cleansing and crimes against humanity
>
> 138. Each individual State has the responsibility to protect its populations from genocide, war crimes, ethnic cleansing and crimes against humanity. This responsibility entails the prevention of such crimes, including their incitement, through appropriate and necessary means. We accept that responsibility and will act in accordance with it. The international community should, as appropriate, encourage and help states to exercise this responsibility and support the United Nations in establishing an early warning capability.
>
> 139. The international community, through the United Nations, also has the responsibility to use appropriate diplomatic, humanitarian and other peaceful means, in accordance with Chapters VI and VIII of the Charter, to help to protect populations from genocide, war crimes, ethnic cleansing and crimes against humanity. In this context, we are prepared to take collective action, in a timely and decisive manner, through the Security Council, in accordance with the Charter, including Chapter VII, on a case-by-case basis and in cooperation with relevant regional organisations as appropriate, should peaceful means be inadequate and national authorities are manifestly failing to protect their populations from genocide, war crimes, ethnic cleansing and crimes against humanity. We stress the need for the General Assembly to continue consideration of the responsibility to protect populations from genocide, war crimes, ethnic cleansing and crimes against humanity and its implications, bearing in mind the principles of the Charter and international law. We also intend to commit ourselves, as necessary and appropriate, to helping states build capacity to protect their populations from genocide, war crimes, ethnic cleansing and crimes against humanity and to assisting those which are under stress before crises and conflicts break out.[1]

Conceptually, the responsibility to protect (also referred to by the acronym R2P) builds on earlier efforts to strike a balance between two fundamental principles governing international relations. On the one hand, the international community is a system of equally sovereign states. Going back to the 1648 Peace of Westphalia, the essence of sovereignty is control by the sovereign over his people and protection of his territory against external interference. Accordingly, what goes on within the boundaries of a state is neither the business of other states nor, by extension, the concern of their people. On the other hand, the international community has increasingly become united in the promotion of mutual goals, while people have embraced the fact that they are bound by their common humanity. Over the last sixty years, the development of international law, actual state practice, and the evolution of civil society have gradually shifted the balance between state sovereignty and human security to the benefit of the latter.

In international law, the primary precursor of the principles enshrined in the R2P doctrine can be found in the four 1949 Geneva Conventions, which form the core of international humanitarian law. According to common Article 1 of these conventions, states "undertake to respect *and* to ensure respect for the present Convention in all circumstances" (emphasis added). The twofold nature of states' obligations—domestic and international—was recently reaffirmed by the International Court of Justice (ICJ) in its 2004 advisory opinion on the "Legal Consequences of the Construction of a Wall in the Occupied Palestinian Territory." Over and above international law, state practice, especially as evidenced by some of the action taken by the UN Security Council during the 1990s, is also an example of the growing recognition that humanitarian crises, even if confined to one state, can be considered threats to international peace and security, thus justifying the involvement of the international community.

Besides state actors, the evolution of society also explains a growing border-free humanism. "Modern life," for a start, has had a profound impact on the way people relate to one another, even at far-reaching distances. The explosion in telecommunication, migration, tourism, and trade has woven human beings into a globalized world where economic interdependence is being upgraded to human interconnectedness. Civil society members—whether driven by secular values or religious beliefs—increasingly focus on ways to alleviate the plight of fellow human beings not only at home, but around the globe. Through research, funding, advocacy, lobbying, and action in the field, civil society has stepped into the international arena and attempts to transcend state borders for the benefit of mankind. The R2P doctrine, for instance, was first conceptualized in 2001 by a group of eminent individuals: the International Commission on Intervention and State Sovereignty (ICISS). Today, people around the world say the UN has the responsibility to protect people from genocide and other heinous human rights abuses, wherever they may take place. Within the UN system itself, civil society is given additional opportunities to have a voice and a role to play: business corporations are mobilized through the UN Global Compact to implement UN values, while the participation of nongovernmental organizations (NGOs) and local authorities alongside state representatives is encouraged.

So that the R2P norm can mature from a noble premise to a fully fleshed doctrine whose implementation has decisive impact in the field, two particular types of challenges need to be addressed. A first challenge lies in gaining deeper acceptance of this norm. Despite its universal endorsement by the international community, R2P remains a controversial doctrine. On one hand, some—particularly among scholars and human rights activists— will argue that the R2P norm is too weak. According to those supporting this point of view, not only does this norm barely go beyond existing treaty law, but it is also not legally binding. In addition, the norm is so vague and can be interpreted in so many ways that the formal agreement reached by the General Assembly should not be seen as overcoming the differences in opinion as to how individual states and the international community as a whole should deal with atrocity crimes. On the other hand, the newly adopted norm is criticized for being too broad and for allowing powerful states to interfere in the domestic affairs of weaker states. This point of view is generally carried forward either by states that suffered foreign interventions in the past (former colonies, for example) or by states that might be the subject of the international community's scrutiny because of the current human rights or humanitarian situation within their borders. Of course, it is by striking a delicate balance between these divergent points of view that the R2P norm generated the consensus of the international community. But this unanimity is fragile, and any effort to give greater legitimacy and weight to this political norm faces hurdles. Three years after its adoption, the implementation of R2P still ignites the same sensitivities. In the spring of 2008—and as this book went to press—the international community was debating whether R2P could be invoked by the Security Council to decide coercive intervention against the Burmese government in order for the international community to assist its people in coping with the humanitarian crisis in the aftermath of Cyclone Nargis.[2]

Yet strengthening the consensus on the R2P norm is just one of the challenges ahead. A second type of difficulty stems from the necessity to move R2P from rhetoric to action. First and foremost, this means ensuring that current state practice matches the R2P commitments made during the 2005 World Summit. In this regard, the situations in Iraq, the Democratic Republic of the Congo (DRC), Uganda, and Darfur are good illustration of how seriously—or not—R2P is taken by states. How are the governments of specific countries implementing their responsibility to protect their populations from atrocity crimes? And how is the international community fulfilling its own responsibility to prevent and stop atrocity crimes in these countries? In addition to making R2P a living and applied doctrine, this norm should be further clarified and developed. The consensual language that was adopted by the General Assembly leaves many questions unanswered. Where does prevention start and end? Given the difficulty of proving that prevention succeeded, what kind of arguments can be put forward to make it the primary response to atrocity crimes? Who decides, and on the basis of what criteria, that a government has failed its own responsibility to protect? Are peaceful measures always capable of stopping atrocities? If not, what are the criteria for the use of force and should the UN Security Council be the sole body having authority to decide it? The challenges faced by the R2P norm, as well as suggestions on how to address them, are discussed in the following chapters.

Roots and Rationale

Section 1 of the book explores in five chapters the origins, objects, and justification for the R2P principle. In Chapter 1, Gareth Evans, who was cochair of the ICISS, takes the reader through a brief history of why and how this policy emerged in 2001 and made its way to the General Assembly where it became official doctrine in 2005. Evans' chapter also discusses the remaining agreements to be reached for this new norm to have decisive impacts in the field.

Chapters 2, 3, and 4 tackle the issue of "will"—and the related issue of "why we should care"—through different angles. Although 150 heads of state or governments embraced R2P three years ago, they did so through a nonbinding resolution, and several governments, including Security Council permanent members, have since expressed reticence in further clarifying and elaborating upon this norm. Another obstacle to an increased acceptance of R2P at the domestic level stems from the fact that most of the executive branches of the UN member states have not yet taken the necessary steps within their own governments to implement this commitment through legislative measures. In the case of the United States, for instance, R2P is on the administration's agenda, albeit in a limited way, but Congress has so far neglected to thoroughly consider whether existing legislation should be amended or new legislation adopted in order for the United States to fully comply with its responsibility to protect. Deeper acceptance of R2P also inevitably raises the issue of support from civil society, for it is individuals that are the primary beneficiaries of this doctrine, and only with the backing of civil society will R2P receive increased legitimacy. An R2P constituency at both the domestic and the international levels can in turn ensure that states carry through the political and moral undertaking they have accepted when they endorsed the principle of R2P. Beyond this political function, civil society has an important role to play in implementing this norm. Knowledge and acceptance of R2P are prerequisites for civil society to play its part in ending atrocity crimes. What kind of argument should be made for the members of civil society to take this cause to heart? Providing answers to this question is the goal of the chapters written by Cherif Bassiouni, Susan Mayer, and Aaron Dorfman and Ruth Messinger.

In Chapter 2, Bassiouni identifies the philosophical doctrine behind R2P. Based on his analysis, the author elaborates on how R2P calls for a transformation of the international community. At the heart of this evolution toward an international community bound by commonly shared values and interests is a strong international criminal justice system. Following Bassiouni's study, Mayer treats another aspect of the issue of will in a pragmatic way, with a particular emphasis on the American point of view. Arguing that atrocity crimes are costly—both in human and financial terms—Mayer analyzes the reasons why individual states and the international community allow such atrocities to take place. Having identified why states generally remain passive in the face of mass atrocities, the author offers insights on how to overcome this obstacle and move toward principled, legitimate, and efficient action to prevent and stop atrocity crimes.

Chapter 4 brings a religious perspective to the discussion. Just as secular values underpin the R2P principle, religious doctrine can provide behavioral guidance as to whether and in what way individuals should act in order to prevent and stop atrocity crimes. The Christian view on R2P is discussed and analyzed in a book edited by the World Council of Churches, The *Responsibility to Protect: Ethical and Theological Perspectives*.[3] According to Hugo Slim, "Christ leaves us in no doubt that we are called to speak and act in order to protect one another and that in matters of protection there are no limits around who we should protect."[4] A Muslim perspective of R2P was offered by Bassiouni to the editors of this book. In a February 2008 *opinio juris*, Bassiouni explains that the moral principle of R2P is, in its essence, part of Islamic law in so far as three groups of individuals are concerned: Muslims, Christians and Jews with whom there is a treaty or who have paid Jizya (a fixed tax for protection), and any other people with whom the Islamic state has a treaty or who are within the jurisdiction of an Islamic state. If the R2P principle becomes international law, it will thus extend the degree of protection currently afforded under Islamic law. A

Jewish argument for R2P is presented in this book in the chapter by Dorfman and Messinger. Through an analysis of formal legal codes and narrative literature, the authors extract the fundamental values that inform Jewish ethics when it comes to preventing and stopping atrocities.

Equipped with a philosophical, secular, and religious understanding of the doctrine of R2P, the book then investigates what precisely is meant by "atrocity crimes" and presents some of the challenges to R2P implementation that result from the nature of the crimes considered. In the final essay of Section 1 of the book, David Scheffer offers an overall view of the five characteristics of the crimes falling within the scope of the R2P doctrine. Scheffer's analysis of crimes against humanity reveals some of the difficulties in applying the R2P doctrine, in particular to "slow motion" crimes. Another challenge stems from the lack of a framework to activate the international dimension of R2P: how do judicial authorities (ICJ, International Criminal Court [ICC]) and political bodies (Security Council) work together?

A second group of challenges facing R2P stems from the very issues this norm is intended to tackle. Genocide, war crimes, and crimes against humanity are generally caused by multiple factors. In some cases, a long history of grievances has long poised relations between groups of people. Yet in other cases, it may be a lack of good governance, damaging international interference—or lack of international engagement—and poor socioeconomic conditions that lead to the unleashing of man's worst behaviors. Moreover, atrocity crimes occur in extraordinarily chaotic situations. Implementing the R2P norm thus requires a deep knowledge of the situation under scrutiny and sound judgment as to what kind of action should or should not be taken. Does R2P provide enough guidance as to how states should actually prevent and stop atrocities? How are the R2P principles actually implemented by states? What are the lessons learned from the international community's action or inaction in the face of atrocity crimes? These types of issues are discussed in Section 2 of the book.

Where the Rubber Hits the Road

Section 2 discusses the R2P situations in Northern Uganda, Darfur, the Democratic Republic of the Congo, and Iraq. The first three situations are the object of an investigation by the prosecutor of the ICC because domestic authorities are unable or unwilling to comply with their responsibility to protect and the international community has had to step in. Iraq, in turn, is not currently the object of an ICC investigation, and one may argue as to whether or not atrocity crimes are actually taking place. The rationale for a chapter on the situation in Iraq stems nevertheless from the huge political controversies resulting from the U.S. invasion and the impact it has had on the definition and acceptance of R2P—and in particular, the use of force for "humanitarian" purposes—around the world.

Section 2 of the book opens with the analysis of an R2P "false friend": the intervention in Iraq. Although the invasion was not primarily aimed at ridding a population of a brutal dictator who had committed atrocity crimes, this argument was put forward by the United States and the United Kingdom as a secondary justification for their action. It is thus not uncommon for people to ask whether R2P, if it had been global doctrine in 2003, would have provided the United States and its allies with an additional justification to invade Iraq or, on the contrary, whether R2P would have made the "humanitarian" argument less convincing. The debate is not only legal. It has immense political ramifications.

Following a methodical analysis of six criteria for the use of force, Kenneth Roth, in Chapter 6, is compelled to affirm that the military invasion fails the test for humanitarian intervention. Turning to the current situation in Iraq, which too raises issues as to what R2P calls for, Roth contends that despite the urgent need to stop the killing, the presence of military troops offers little prospect of making things better. As an alternative, Roth urges international efforts to focus on a political solution to Iraqis' grievances and backs this diplomatic route with a call for the involvement of the ICC.

Chapters 7, 8, and 9 deal with Africa, a continent that, today, carries the heaviest burden in terms of atrocity crimes. The chapter written by Herbert Weiss is a stark demonstration of how mass atrocities might have been avoided in the DRC if so many opportunities to prevent conflict had not been lost. With wars and atrocity crimes having claimed between three and four million lives in the last decade, the DRC is unfortunately a forceful illustration of how ugly things can turn when hatred among groups, lack of good governance, damaging international interference—or lack of international engagement—and poor socioeconomic conditions come together. Based on the DRC's horrifying experience, Weiss pleads for an increased commitment by the international community to the prevention of atrocity crimes since "protection is not only served by prevention, but often it cannot be served any other way."

The reality of atrocity crimes—the terror of being attacked, the long-term suffering endured by victims and their families, especially children, and the resulting destruction of the social fabric of entire regions—is vividly portrayed by Mary Page in her chapter on northern Uganda. With a domestic government failing in many accounts in its responsibility to protect and an international community less than eager to bypass President Museveni's objections to intervention, the most significant response to the

Ugandan humanitarian crisis has come from the ICC. Some critics argue that the pursuit of justice is an obstacle to peace. But a survey indicates that 65 percent of Northern Ugandans favor punishing the leaders of the Lords Resistance Army, and nearly 90 percent of those who had heard about the ICC believed that the Court would contribute to both peace and justice, supporting the view that international criminal justice is rising as a powerful tool to deter perpetrators, stop atrocity crimes, and contribute to the rebuilding of stable societies. Page's concluding remarks, however, emphasize that justice is only one piece of the puzzle and that Uganda will recover from its scars only if significant and sustained efforts are directed at rebuilding this nation.

Of the three African R2P situations analyzed in this book, Darfur is the one that has attracted the most attention on the part of civil society. In the United States in particular, a broad constituency of individuals, human rights organizations, and faith communities are actively pressing the government and the international community to live up to their responsibility to protect. An account of the historical evolution of grassroots human rights activism and a discussion of the key features of successful organizing are the focus of the chapter written by William Schulz. Taking the crisis in Darfur as a backdrop for his illustration and sprinkling it with personal anecdotes, Schulz argues that in the absence of a broad-based constituency committed to fighting atrocity crimes whenever they arise, and pending the day that inaction becomes so stigmatized that no leader will remain passive in the face of atrocities, citizen movements organized to stop particular atrocities are the only alternative.

The R2P situations in the DRC, Sudan, and Uganda all testify to the gaps within the current legal, institutional, and political framework to prevent and stop atrocities in a legitimate, efficient, and sustainable manner. If we, individually and collectively, as citizens or state representatives, let our conscience and reason guide us in fulfilling the promise embedded in R2P, we still need to be fully equipped to do so. The third section of this book, titled "Moving the Responsibility to Protect from Rhetoric to Action: What it Means for Philanthropy, the United States, and the International Community," offers some insights into what can be done to improve our capacity to prevent and stop atrocity crimes.

Moving the Responsibility to Protect from Rhetoric to Action

Civil society is a diverse conglomerate that brings together organizations such as registered charities, NGOs, community groups, women's organizations, faith-based communities, professional associations, trade unions, business associations, coalitions, and advocacy groups. Each member of civil society, just like every individual, has an important role to play in bringing R2P forward. Yet, because collective action gives civil society a greater capacity to induce change, civil society has a commensurate responsibility to help realize the societal transformations that benefit everyone. Some corporations for instance—and those institutions having economic ties to them—have come under increasing fire lately for ignoring whether their activities fuel atrocity crimes.

Chapter 10 puts forward the little known role of another part of civil society: philanthropists. The philanthropic community has played and is called to play a particular role when it comes to R2P. Firstly, the financial support of foundations was crucial to establishing the ICISS. Secondly, a discussion of the role of philanthropy is also interesting in itself because this activity brings together diverse members of civil society: philanthropists influence research, education, advocacy, and projects. In their chapter, Adele Simmons and April Donnellan focus on the role of philanthropy in preventing atrocity crimes. They discuss the added value of philanthropy, and, based on past success stories and an evaluation of what philanthropy is best at, the authors also identify the niches, the specific areas in which foundations and donors can have the most influence.

Chapters 11 and 12 offer two different perspectives of how the United States should act in order to spare populations from atrocity crimes. Although the implementation of R2P is both a domestic issue—which demands a stable society not driven to commit or suffer atrocities—and a foreign policy matter, both essays focus on the latter since the international dimension of the U.S. responsibility to protect is, today, more at stake.

In Chapter 11, Lee Feinstein and Erica De Bruin offer an overview of the U.S. position on the R2P norm as it has evolved over the last fifteen years. Their analysis evidences that the political leadership—both Democratic and Republican—is extremely reluctant to accept any limitations to U.S. "freedom of action" in cases involving the commission of atrocity crimes. The authors also demonstrate how the September 11, 2001, attacks have had an impact on U.S. foreign policy, in particular with the recognition that failed states, humanitarian disasters, and ungoverned areas can become safe havens for terrorists, thus posing security dangers for the United States. Building on the premise that the prevention of atrocity crimes is not just a humanitarian goal, but an important security interest, Feinstein and De Bruin argue that the United States must develop a formal strategy to implement R2P and offer a number of specific recommendations for the administration and Congress to do so.

In Chapter 12, Joe Volk and Scott Stedjan make a passionate plea for pacifism and offer an inspiring vision of a world free of atrocity crimes. Under the presumption that prevention, in particular the prevention of conflict, is the key to successful implementation of R2P, Volk and Stedjan argue that the United States currently does not have the political will needed, and thus is ill-equipped, to prevent or stop mass atrocities. The authors thus put forward ten steps for this country to become an "R2P leader."

Despite their differences, the two essays on U.S. foreign policy are evidence that one country, however powerful and good intentioned, has neither the capacity nor the legitimacy to do it alone. Individual governments, however, have a specific duty to work with others in shaping an international community that will come to grips with mass atrocities. The role of international institutions cannot be undermined and must be contended with. The World Summit outcome specifically refers to the UN as a forum to decide on diplomatic and coercive measures to help protect populations from genocide, crimes against humanity, and war crimes. Although this organization is the main institution to advance R2P, other international bodies such as the ICC need to be upgraded for the international community to live up to its responsibilities. Chapters 13 and 14 turn to the role of the UN and the ICC in realizing R2P.

Too often in popular belief, the UN is expected to be the answer to overwhelming catastrophes, including situations of genocide. Although it is strongly desirable that the UN lives up to these hopes, a quick reality check shows the gap between such lofty aspirations and what this institution is actually capable of accomplishing. In their chapter, William Pace, Nicole Deller, and Sapna Chhatpar provide a detailed survey of what the UN can do, and make concrete suggestions on what this organization could do to better respond to emerging and acute R2P crises. To those who too quickly dismiss the UN as an organization that is incapable of stopping atrocity crimes, this chapter is a wake-up call that demonstrates the challenges and opportunities ahead.

The last chapter of the book addresses the controversial aspect of R2P enforcement. Nowadays, physical coercion against individuals within another state is framed as a military issue. In Chapter 15, Richard H. Cooper and Juliette Voïnov Kohler argue for two shifts in paradigm. First a focus on genocidaires and other perpetrators of atrocity crimes, as opposed to victims. Second, a move away from ad hoc and politically driven military interventions toward sustainable judicial deterrence and enforcement. At the heart of this new approach is a strengthened ICC with the capacity and authority not only to conduct impartial investigations, but to arrest fugitives. The authors suggest the establishment of an International Marshals Service (IMS) to serve as the enforcement arm of the nascent international criminal justice system.

In conclusion, R2P provides the base for a global moral compact that will bring "a new order of things." The desire for peace, justice, and human dignity is written in the hearts and minds of all people, and all people have roles to play in bringing these ideals forward. It all starts with being aware, with education and information. Beyond this minimal requirement for being a responsible citizen of the world, every reader may feel compelled to take a more active social or political role. This book offers many examples of ways in which individuals can become engaged and make a difference: from voting in favor of local, state, and federal representatives that promote the realization of R2P, to lobbying politicians for more specific legislative measures, to funding human rights NGOs, to pressing university pension funds to divest. Both reason and conscience cry out for a mature world in which atrocity crimes are relegated to the twentieth century. It is hoped that this book will spark the many lights that are needed to bring civilization to a higher level where genocide, crimes against humanity, and war crimes are unthinkable human behavior.

Notes

* Richard H. Cooper is the convenor of the R2P Coalition in Oak Brook, Illinois. Juliette Voïnov Kohler is senior program officer at the Global Humanitarian Forum in Geneva, Switzerland.
1. UN GAOR, Sixtieth Session, 8th plen. mtg., UN Doc. A/RES/60/1, paras. 138 and 139 (October 24, 2005), http://daccessdds.un.org/doc/UNDOC/GEN/N05/487/60/PDF/N0548760.pdf?OpenElement.
2. For an analysis of how R2P applies to Burma in the aftermath of Cyclone Nargis, see http://www.responsibilitytoprotect.org/index.php/pages/1182.
3. Semegnish Asfaw, Guillermo Kerber, and Peter Weiderud, eds., *The Responsibility to Protect: Ethical and Theological Perspectives* (Geneva: World Council of Churches, 2005).
4. Ibid., 9.

Section 1

The Responsibility to Protect: Roots and Rationale

I

The Responsibility to Protect

From an Idea to an International Norm

*Gareth Evans**

A Moral Issue that Won't Go Away

"Never again" we said after the Holocaust. And after the Cambodian genocide in the 1970s. And then again after the Rwandan genocide in 1994. And then, just a year later, after the Srbrenica massacre in Bosnia. And now we're asking ourselves, yet again, in the face of more mass killing and dying in Darfur, whether we really are ever going to be capable, as an international community, of stopping nation-states from murdering their own people. How many more times will we look back wondering, with varying degrees of incomprehension, horror, anger, and shame, how we could have let it all happen?

That said, it is important to recognize not only how far we have yet to go with the responsibility to protect but how far we have actually come. First proposed in 2001 as a way of describing the core moral and political issue in the intervention debate, by 2006 the phrase "responsibility to protect" was being routinely used, publicly and privately, by policymakers and commentators almost everywhere whenever the question was debated as to what the international community should do when faced with a state committing atrocities against its own people, or standing by allowing others to do so.

More important still, the concept has now been formally and unanimously embraced by the whole international community in the United Nations (UN) Sixtieth Anniversary World Summit in September 2005. And arguably even more important, given the Security Council's executive authority, it was subsequently reaffirmed by the Security Council in April 2006, and has begun since to be incorporated in country-specific Security Council resolutions.

In just five years—a remarkably short time when set against other movements in the history of ideas—we have seen the emergence of what can reasonably be described as a brand new international norm of really quite fundamental ethical importance and novelty in the international system. In any view that is unquestionably a major breakthrough, and one that, for all the grinding and wearying task of implementation that lies ahead, should regenerate our optimism about the art of the possible in international relations.

Where We Were:
Sovereignty as a License to Kill

To see how far we have come, we have to remember where we were. For centuries, going all the way back to the emergence of the modern system of sovereign states in the 1648 Treaty of Westphalia, the view has prevailed that, to put it bluntly, sovereignty is a license to kill: what happens within state borders, however grotesque and morally indefensible, is nobody else's business. Although the language of the 1945 UN charter is more delicate, it essentially reflects this traditional view, with Article 2(7) providing: "Nothing should authorise intervention in matters essentially within the domestic jurisdiction of any State." The UN founders were overwhelmingly preoccupied with the problem of states waging war against each other, and took unprecedented steps to limit their freedom of action in that respect. But, notwithstanding all the genocidal horrors inflicted during World War II, they showed no particular interest in the question of what constraints might be imposed on how states dealt with their own subjects.

The slate in this respect was not entirely blank. Individual and group human rights were recognized in the UN charter and, more grandly and explicitly, in the Universal Declaration. With the drafting of the charter of the Nuremberg Tribunal in 1945 came the recognition in international law of the concept of "crimes against humanity," which could be committed by a government against its own people and not necessarily just during wartime. Then came the Genocide Convention of 1948, with its apparently explicit override of the nonintervention principle for the most extreme of all crimes against humanity.

It was almost as if, with the signing of the Genocide Convention, the task of addressing man-made atrocities was seen as complete: it was rarely invoked and never effectively applied. And it is only in very recent years—with the establishment of the international criminal tribunals for the former Yugoslavia and Rwanda, and now the creation (over U.S. objections) of the International Criminal Court (ICC)—that any remotely systematic measures have been taken by the international community against individuals committing crimes against humanity.

The state of mind that even massive atrocity crimes like those of the Cambodian killing fields were not the rest of the world's business prevailed throughout the UN's first half century of existence: Vietnam's invasion, which stopped the Khmer Rouge in its tracks, was universally attacked, not applauded. The traditional view of sovereignty, as enabling absolute control of everything internal and demanding immunity from external intervention, was much reinforced by the large increase in UN membership during the decolonization era—the states that joined were all newly proud of their identity, conscious in many cases of their fragility, and generally saw the nonintervention norm as one of their few defenses against threats and pressures from more powerful international actors seeking to promote their own economic and political interests.

The Humanitarian Intervention Debate:
Battle Lines Drawn

With the arrival of the 1990s, and the end of the cold war, however, the prevailing complacent assumptions about nonintervention came under challenge as never before. The quintessential peace and security problem became not interstate war, but civil war, and internal violence perpetrated on a massive scale. With the breakup of various cold war state structures, most obviously in Yugoslavia, and the removal of some superpower constraints, conscience-shocking situations repeatedly arose. But old habits of nonintervention died very hard. Even when situations cried out for some kind of response, and the international community did react through the UN, it was too often erratically, incompletely, or counterproductively, as in Somalia in 1993, Rwanda in 1994, and Srebrenica in 1995. Then came Kosovo in 1999, when the international community did in fact intervene as it probably should have, but did so without the authority of the Security Council in the face of a threatened veto by Russia.

All this generated very fierce debate about what came to be called the issue of "the right of humanitarian intervention." On the one hand, there were those—mostly in the north—who argued strongly for "the right to intervene"; on the other hand, claims were equally vehemently made mostly in the south—about the primacy and continued resonance of the concept of national sovereignty. Battle lines were drawn, trenches were dug, and verbal missiles flew: the debate was intense and very bitter, and the 1990s finished with it utterly unresolved in the UN or anywhere else. This led UN Secretary-General Kofi Annan to make his agitated plea to the General Assembly in 2000, which brought the issue to a very public head and resonates to this day: "If humanitarian intervention is indeed an unacceptable assault on sovereignty, how should we respond to a Rwanda, to a Srebrenica, to gross and systematic violations of human rights?"[1]

The Birth of the Responsibility to Protect:
ICISS

The task of meeting this challenge fell to the International Commission on Intervention and State Sovereignty (ICISS), sponsored by the Canadian government—more particularly, Lloyd Axworthy, its farsighted then foreign minister—and strongly supported by Chicago's MacArthur Foundation. I had the privilege of cochairing the commission with the Algerian diplomat and veteran UN Africa adviser Mohamed Sahnoun, and we presented our report, titled *The Responsibility to Protect*, at the end of 2001.[2]

The objectives of the commission were essentially threefold: to produce a guide to action on responses by the international community to internal, man-made, human rights violating catastrophes that would be intellectually credible and satisfying, not profoundly offending either the lawyers or philosophers; politically credible enough not to be rejected out of hand as a framework for action by either north or south, the permanent five members of the Security Council, or any other major international constituency; and compelling enough in its basic message to be able, in practice, to actually motivate action and mobilize support when a situation demanding such a response arose.

There were several reasons for thinking that we might not be totally deluding ourselves. The commission's membership was strong—with its U.S. member, for example, being Lee Hamilton—and well balanced regionally; we engaged in consultations just about all around the world; the report was succinct but comprehensive in scope, addressing not just the legal and moral dilemmas that have been at the heart of most of the academic and policy debate about coercive intervention so far, but political and operational issues as well; its recommendations had a sharply practical political focus; and, above all, its approach was innovative, bringing to the table some genuinely new ways of thinking about the issue encapsulated in the title of our report. We made, I think it is fair to say, four main contributions to the international policy debate that have been resonating ever since.

The first, and perhaps ultimately the politically most useful, was to invent a new way of talking about "humanitarian intervention." We sought to turn the whole weary debate about the "right to intervene" on its head and to recharacterize it not as an argument about the "right" of states to anything, but rather about their "responsibility"—one to protect people at grave risk: the relevant perspective, we argued, was not that of prospective interveners, but those needing support. The commission's hope was—and so far, broadly, our experience has been—that using "responsibility to protect" rather than "right to intervene" language would enable entrenched opponents to find new ground on which to more constructively engage, as proved in the case after the Brundtland Commission, years earlier, which introduced the concept of "sustainable development" between developers and environmentalists. With a new script, the actors have to change their lines and think afresh about what the real issues in the play actually are.

The second contribution of the commission, perhaps most conceptually significant, was to insist upon a new way of talking about sovereignty: we argued that its essence should now be seen not as "control," as in the centuries-old Westphalian tradition, but, again, as "responsibility."[3] The starting point is that any state has the primary responsibility to protect the individuals within it. But that is not the finishing point. Where the state fails in that responsibility, through either incapacity or ill will, a secondary responsibility to protect falls on the wider international community.

The third contribution of the commission was to make it clear that the "responsibility to protect" was about much more than intervention and, in particular, military intervention. It extends to a whole continuum of obligations: the responsibility, most important of all, to *prevent* these situations from arising; the responsibility to *react* to them when they do, with a whole graduated menu of responses, from the persuasive to the coercive; and the responsibility to *rebuild* after any intrusive intervention—of which the most important is the responsibility to prevent.

The remaining contribution of the commission was to come up with guidelines for when the most extreme form of coercive reaction, military action, would be appropriate. The first criterion was obviously *legality*, and here we saw our task as not to try and find alternatives to the clear legal authority of the Security Council, but rather to make it work better, so there was less chance of it being bypassed. That was followed by five criteria of *legitimacy*: in short, the seriousness of the harm being threatened; the motivation or primary purpose of the proposed military action; whether there were reasonably available peaceful alternatives; the proportionality of the response; and the balance of consequences—whether more good than harm would be done.

The Evolution of an International Norm

It is one thing to develop a concept like the responsibility to protect, but quite another to get any policymaker to take any notice of it. Departmental bookshelves are full of barely opened reports by blue ribbon commissions and panels. The most interesting thing about the *Responsibility to Protect* report is the way its central theme has continued to gain traction internationally, even though it was almost suffocated at birth by being published in December 2001, in the immediate aftermath of 9/11 and by the massive international preoccupation with terrorism, rather than internal human rights catastrophes, which then began.

The concept was first seriously embraced in the doctrine of the newly emerging African Union,[4] and over the next two to three years, it won quite a constituency among academic commentators and international lawyers (a not unimportant constituency, given that international law is the rather odd beast that it is—capable of evolving through practice and commentary as well as through formal treaty instruments).

But the big step forward came with the UN Sixtieth Anniversary World Summit in September 2005, which followed a major preparatory effort involving the report of a high-level panel on new security threats[5] that fed, in turn, into a major report by the secretary-general himself.[6] Both these reports emphatically embraced the R2P concept, and the Summit Outcome Document, unanimously agreed upon by the more than 150 heads of state and governments present and meeting as the UN General Assembly, unambiguously picked up their core recommendations. Its language, though a little wordier and woollier than it needed to be, was quite clear-cut in picking up the core theme of the commission's report.

That this endorsement happened was anything but inevitable. A fierce rearguard action was fought almost to the end by a small group of developing countries, joined by Russia, who basically refused to concede any kind of limitation on the full and untrammeled exercise of state sovereignty, however irresponsible that exercise might be. What carried the day in the end was not so much consistent support from the European Union (EU) and United States—support that, after the invasion of Iraq, was not particularly helpful. Instead, the support that mattered was persistent advocacy by sub-Saharan African countries led by South Africa, as well as a clear—and historically quite significant—embrace of limited-sovereignty principles by the key Latin American countries. Above all, what carried the vote over the line was some very effective last-minute personal diplomacy by Paul Martin, the Canadian prime minister, demonstrating not only Canada's commitment, a model of its kind, to following through on the report that it had commissioned but the clout that middle power countries can have when they try.

A further important conceptual development has occurred since the September 2005 summit: the adoption by the Security Council in April 2006 of a thematic resolution on the Protection of Civilians in Armed Conflict, which contains, in an operative paragraph, an express reaffirmation of the World Summit conclusions relating to the responsibility to protect.[7] We have now begun to see that resolution, in turn, being invoked in subsequent specific situations, as with Resolution 1706 (August 31, 2006) on Darfur.[8] A General Assembly resolution may be helpful, as the World Summit's unquestionably was, in identifying relevant principles, but the Security Council is the institution that matters when it comes to executive action. At least a toehold has now been carved there.

On any view, the evolution in just five years of the R2P concept, from a gleam in an international commission's eye, to what now has the pedigree to be described as a broadly accepted international norm (and one with the potential to evolve into a rule of customary international law), is an extremely encouraging story, and we ought to be encouraged by it.

Unfinished Business

This is just about where the good news ends. We simply cannot be at all confident that the world will respond quickly, effectively, and appropriately to new human catastrophes as they arise. There is much unfinished business to attend to, falling, from my perspective, into four main categories.

Holding the Line Against Backsliding

We cannot, unfortunately, assume that the bridgehead achieved at the World Summit and in subsequent Security Council resolutions will necessarily hold. Some member states—particularly in Asia—were very reluctant to accept this part of the summit's outcome document and continue to fight a rearguard action against it. They have been much aided in this respect by R2P's false friends. Occasional efforts by defenders of the 2003 invasion of

Iraq—notably the UK government—to paint it as justified by R2P principles (as other defenses in terms of possession of weapons of mass destruction or support for international terrorism crumbled away) have not been at all analytically persuasive.[9] But they have succeeded admirably in reinforcing the arguments of R2P opponents that any concession as to the limits of state sovereignty would create an excuse that would be exploited all too willingly by neocolonialists and neoimperialists keen to return to their bad, old interventionist habits of decades past. Those concerned about consolidating R2P as a universally accepted international norm—and one legitimizing close attention by the Security Council to the behavior toward their own people of a number of deeply unsavory regimes—will have to stay on their toes for a good while yet.

Guidelines for the
Use of Military Force

The most sensitive aspect of the R2P concept is undoubtedly the part of it that would allow—and perhaps even encourage—the use of nonconsensual military force in the most extreme cases. The ICISS, as already noted, recognized that this issue had to be addressed, and that the best way to do so would be to try to forge a consensus as to when it was in fact right to fight. It accordingly identified a set of prudential criteria in this respect that, it argued, should be adopted by the Security Council, and its recommendations in this respect were subsequently embraced (albeit generalized to apply to the use of force generally, not just in an R2P context) both by the High-Level Panel on Threats, Challenges, and Change in 2004 and the secretary-general in his own report to the 2005 World Summit (although not adopted by it). No criteria of the kind the commission argued for, even if agreed as guidelines by the Security Council, will ever end argument on how they should be applied in particular instances. It is hard to believe they would not be more helpful than the present totally ad hoc system in focusing attention on the relevant issues, revealing weaknesses in argument, and generally encouraging consensus.

The ultimate policymakers are not the only ones who need to have their heads clear on these issues: those in the advocacy business are likely to be taken much more seriously by those in the decision-making business if able to intelligently distinguish between different cases in the way R2P principles are applied, understanding those that are suitable cases for military treatment and those that are better advanced by less extreme measures. That way, when a case comes along—and Rwanda, Srebrenica, and Kosovo were all clear examples—that can only be resolved by tough military action, the argument for taking it will be much more clearly heard.

To better explain what is meant here, there is no better case study than the current situation in Darfur. Many have been asking whether this is not indeed a proper case for a nonconsensual mission, with a UN-mandated mission if necessary shooting its way in (as is now agreed what should have happened, but did not, in Rwanda). But *is* it such a case? How *does* one apply to this situation the set of guidelines at issue here, and for which the ICISS commission, the High-Level Panel, and the secretary-general all argued? Taking each of them in turn:

Criterion 1: Seriousness of Harm—Is the threatened harm to state or human security of a kind, and sufficiently clear and serious, to justify prima facie the use of military force? In the case of internal threats, does it involve genocide and other large-scale killing, ethnic cleansing, or serious violations of international humanitarian law, actual or imminently apprehended? In the early stages of the Darfur conflict this criterion was unquestionably satisfied; it is probably met again now, and certainly would be if the current African Union (AU)/UN force were to leave: a scenario of mass killings in chaotic circumstances could unfold in short order, combined with many more deaths in the camps from malnutrition and disease flowing from the inability of international relief agencies to maintain a presence.

Criterion 2: Proper Purpose—Is it clear that the primary purpose of the proposed military action is to halt or avert the threat in question, whatever other motives may be in play? This would clearly seem to be satisfied in that the international community has no other strategic interest or ulterior motive for intervening in Darfur; indeed, it would be hard to imagine a region of the world where there is less other motivation than protection of human suffering.

Criterion 3: Last Resort—Has every nonmilitary option for meeting the threat in question been explored, with reasonable grounds for believing lesser measures will not succeed? At the time of writing (May 2008), more could certainly be done short of full-scale armed intervention. Four arrows are still in the international community's quiver—enforcement of ICC indictments; targeted sanctions against a range of senior government officials; wider economic sanctions, including measures to encourage disinvestment (not dissimilar to what the United States has been doing, for better or worse, vis-à-vis the Hamas government in Gaza, including pressure on European banks to cut their financing); and, as a coercive but significantly less extreme military option than a full-scale ground exercise, a toughly enforced no-fly zone. Some of these options have been flagged in previous Security Council resolutions, but none seriously delivered.

Criterion 4: Proportional Means—Are the scale, duration, and intensity of the planned military action the minimum necessary to secure the defined human protection objective? This would likely appear to be uncontentious, in the sense that it could reasonably be presumed that any military intervention would be scaled to the minimum necessary to prevent further large-scale and irreparable harm and the protection of civilians, not necessarily to achieve regime change.

Criterion 5: Balance of consequences—Is there a reasonable chance of the military action being successful in meeting the threat in question, with the consequences of action not likely to be worse than the consequences of inaction? This would be the hardest criterion of all to satisfy in the present circumstances of Darfur. A nonconsensual deployment would be hair-raisingly difficult for a number or reasons: logistical, given the huge size of the contested territory and limited supply points; the risk to civilians ahead of the arrival of the protective international force, with a hostage population of two million or more sitting defenseless in large concentrations; the risk to civilians from the inevitable collapse of humanitarian relief operations if a nonconsensual intervention occurred; the implications for north–south peace, remembering that the killings and displacement associated with this decades-long battle were many times even that of the present Darfur tragedy, and that north–south peace agreement implementation is extremely weak and fragile at best; and the wider implications of a UN mission taking place as a primarily Western-backed enterprise, probably having to have a significant number of white, non-Muslim personnel.

None of this means that the R2P concept is irrelevant—just that it has to be implemented here by means falling short of full-scale coercive military intervention. The point, particularly for those who continue to think that any embrace of R2P means committing oneself to multiple military interventions in highly problematic circumstances, is that R2P is about much more than coercive "humanitarian intervention." Shooting one's way into a resisting country is at the extreme end of the R2P prevention-reaction spectrum, and only to be contemplated as a last resort and when all five criteria of legitimacy are satisfied. Having those criteria on the table, understood and accepted as framing these debates, would make for a more principled and less ad hoc, *realpolitik*-driven international order.

Building Available Capacity

If R2P is not to remain more theoretical than real, we must somehow solve the problem of capacity, ensuring that the right civilian and, as necessary, military resources are always there in the right amounts and with the appropriate capability. The experience of the AU mission in Darfur was a classic demonstration of the problem—too few troops, too poorly equipped, and too immobile to effectively perform even the limited civilian protection task required by their present mandate. The UN is currently feeling desperately overstretched, with more than eighty thousand military and fifteen thousand civilian personnel deployed worldwide,[10] but with the world's armed services currently involving some twenty million men and women in uniform (with another fifty million reservists, and eleven million paramilitaries, according to the International Institute for Strategic Studies [IISS], which somehow manages to keep count of these things),[11] it hardly seems beyond the wit of man to work out a way of making some of that capacity available when and where it's needed to prevent and react to man-made catastrophe. Again, it is important for those of us in the advocacy business to be conscious of these issues, to know what kinds of resources, both military and civilian, need to be available, when, where, and how, and to campaign for change accordingly.

Generating the Political Will to Act

This ever-recurring problem is probably the largest and most difficult piece of unfinished business. We have to get to the point where—when the next conscience-shocking mass human rights violation comes along, as it inexorably will—the reflex response of both governments and the public around the world will be to talk immediately about R2P and find reasons to act, not to pretend that it is none of our business.

None should underestimate the scale of this problem of mobilizing political will. All the other ingredients can be there—the knowledge of what's happening or about to happen, the acknowledgement of general responsibility, even the capacity and resources to act. But still there can be, and often is, a reluctance by governments—and the intergovernmental organizations in which they sit—to jump the final hurdle. The problem of finding the necessary political will to do anything hard, expensive, or politically sensitive is just a given in public affairs, domestically and internationally.

That said, the evident absence of such will should not be a matter for lamentation but mobilization. For every Indian Ocean tsunami that generates a massively sympathetic international human response and an outpouring of material support, there is a Pakistani earthquake, just about as horrendous in its human consequences, that does not. We have to live with these vagaries in the human psyche and our various body politics and work on ways of overcoming them. Political will is not hiding in a cupboard or under a stone somewhere waiting to be discovered; it has to be painstakingly built.

All politics is, in a sense, local. The key to mobilizing international support is to mobilize domestic support, or at least neutralize domestic opposition. The key to mobilizing that support, through the media and from decision makers themselves, is to have not just a good organization, good lobbying techniques, and good contacts, but above all good arguments, intelligently and energetically advanced; they may not be a sufficient condition, but are always a necessary one for taking difficult political action.

Those arguments may be *party interest* arguments designed to consolidate a government's vocal domestic base (always an important element in the Bush administration's interest in Sudan, such as it has been), *national interest* arguments (much easier to make now in relation to "quarrels in far away countries between people of whom we know nothing," in Chamberlain's terms, because of what we do know now about the capacity of failed states, in this globalized world, to be a source of havoc for others), *financial* arguments (in terms of a million dollars worth of preventive action now saving a billion dollars worth of military intervention later), or even *moral* arguments (given that however basic politicians' real motives may be, they always like to be seen as acting from higher ones).

When we say that R2P is the responsibility of the international community, that means *all* of us. It is other sovereign states with the capacity to help and support those with the will to protect their own people but the inability to do so. Those who have a role here are not just the Security Council permanent five and the other major players. They include the middle powers—like Canada, which has done so much to advance the R2P cause, and my own country, Australia—and indeed any government that is seen as consistently principled and having a mind of its own and that has ideas, and creativity, and the energy and stamina with which to pursue them.

Beyond individual states, R2P is very much the responsibility of the intergovernmental organizations, above all, the UN, but also all the other global organizations and agencies with preventive or reactive roles; the regional organizations, including the EU, the North Atlantic Treaty Organization (NATO), and the AU; and the courts, particularly the new international criminal courts, the new instruments of not just retributive but deterrent justice. Within the UN the crucial players are the secretary-general, with his persuasive authority and his own formal capacity under Article 99 of the charter to bring to the attention of the Security Council any matter that, in his opinion, may threaten international peace and security; the Security Council with its unique executive authority; and within the Security Council, the permanent five—who don't always have the capacity to make things happen, but certainly can ensure they do not, as was the case, so tragically, with Rwanda in 1994.

The responsibility to protect is also the responsibility of nongovernmental organizations (NGOs), the media (not least CNN's cameras), and civil society more generally. It is to prevent through all the strategies of community reconciliation, government capacity building, and economic empowerment that so many international NGOs are implementing on the ground; it is to analyze, to warn, and to alert in the way done by my own International Crisis Group and organizations like Human Rights Watch; and, in the case of both international and domestic NGOs, it is to mobilize and ring alarm bells when the occasion demands. And ultimately the responsibility to protect is that of all of us as individuals—whether we be government officials, with all the temptation and opportunity in the world to claim that a problem is someone else's business, or ordinary members of the public, who can make our voices heard if we *want* them to be heard.

Making Idealism Realistic

At the core of the task of all those who want the R2P principle to prevail is the reality that there is a role for morality in the foreign policy of every country in the world, from the greatest to the smallest. It is true that a foreign policy built almost entirely and self-consciously around some sense of moral mission can be equally misguided, as we have seen all too clearly in the United States, with the neoconservative democracy, human rights, and regime change agenda—all now in tatters—in Iraq, Iran, and North Korea.

In the December 2006 issue of Vanity Fair, one of the fiercest original supporters of the 2003 invasion of Iraq, Kenneth Adelman, now laments that after the botched implementation of the subsequent occupation, "the idea of a tough foreign policy on behalf of morality, the idea of using our power for moral good in the world" is "not going to sell" for a generation.[12] If he means the particular kind of idealistic foreign policy that has been pursued in recent years—impervious to demonstrable facts, naïve in its assumptions, crude in its application of military power, and totally bungled in its general execution—then we should be grateful to be spared any more of the same.

But if idealism has its limits, the alternative is not a crude and one-dimensional brand of foreign policy realism either. We can, if we need to, always justify making R2P a reality on hard-headed, practical, national interest grounds. So-called rogue states, or evil states, or failed or failing states, that either perpetrate terrible crimes against their own people or are powerless to stop them, are now—we know much better than we used to—a risk to all of us in this globalized interdependent age. We know what they can do in harboring or supporting terrorism, weapons proliferation, and drug and people trafficking, and failing to curb health pandemics and all the rest.

But a foreign policy that is founded only on hard-headed realism is a policy that can all too readily descend into cynical indifference: the kind that enabled successive previous U.S. administrations (whose foreign policy performance in many other ways was much to be admired) to shrug their shoulders about Saddam Hussein's genocidal assaults on the Kurds in the north in the late 1980s and the Shiites in the south of Iraq in the early 1990s, or to find reasons for ignoring the rapidly unfolding Rwandan genocide in 1994.

What the United States needs, and what all the polling evidence suggests its public will support, is a foreign policy based on a principled and judicious mixture of both idealism *and* realism. And that's a foreign policy, for the United States, as everywhere else, in which the new international norm of R2P can sit both comfortably and proudly.

At the end of the day, the case for R2P rests simply on our common humanity: the impossibility of ignoring the cries of pain and distress of our fellow human beings. For any of us in the international community—from individuals to NGOs to national governments to international organizations—to yet again ignore that distress and agony, and to once again make "never again" a cry that rings totally emptily, is to diminish that common humanity to the point of despair. We should be united in our determination to not let that happen, and there is no greater or nobler cause on which any of us could be embarked.

Notes

* Gareth Evans is president and CEO of the International Crisis Group. In 2001, he was cochair of the International Commission on Intervention and State Sovereignty. This chapter draws on other speeches and published papers by the author, collected at http://www.crisisgroup.org, especially "From Humanitarian Intervention to the Responsibility to Protect," Wisconsin International Law Journal 24, no. 3 (2006): 101–20, and "Crimes Against Humanity: Overcoming Indifference," Journal of Genocide Research 8, no. 3 (September 2006): 325–39.

1. UN Secretary-General, *Millennium Report of the Secretary-General of the United Nations*, 48, UN Doc. A/54/2000 (2000), available at http://www.un .org/millennium/sg/report/.

2. The full text of the commission report and its accompanying volume of research essays, bibliography, and descriptive material is available at http:// www.iciss.ca.

3. The commission owed this insight and formulation to Francis Deng. See Francis Deng et al., *Sovereignty as Responsibility: Conflict Management in Africa* (Washington, DC: Brookings Institution, 1966).

4. African Union Constitutive Act, Article 4(h): "the right of the Union to intervene in a Member State pursuant to a decision of the Assembly in respect of grave circumstances, namely: war crimes, genocide and crimes against humanity," available at http://www.africa-union.org.

5. High-Level Panel on Threats, Challenges, and Change, *A More Secure World: Our Shared Responsibility*, available at http://www.un.org/secureworld.

6. UN Secretary-General, *In Larger Freedom: Towards Development, Security and Human Rights for All*, available at http://www.un.org/largerfreedom.

7. UN SCOR, Sixty-first Session, 5,430th mtg., UN Doc. S/RES/1674 (April 28, 2006): The Security Council "*reaffirms* the provisions of paragraphs 138 and 139 of the 2005 World Summit Outcome Document regarding the responsibility to protect populations from genocide, war crimes, ethnic cleansing and crimes against humanity."

8. UN SCOR, Sixty-first Session. 5,519th mtg., UN Doc. S/RES/1706 (August 31, 2006): "Recalling also its previous resolutions . . . 1674 (2006) on the protection of civilians in armed conflict, which reaffirms inter alia the provisions of paragraphs 138 and 139 of the 2005 United Nations World Summit Outcome Document, as well as the report of its Mission to the Sudan and Chad from 4 to 10 June 2006."

9. See, for example, Kenneth Roth's chapter in this book.

10. UN Department of Peacekeeping Operations, *Background Note* (November 30, 2006).

11. International Institute for Strategic Studies, *The Military Balance 2006* (New York: Routledge, 2006), 403, table 44.

12. Quoted in David Rose, "Neo Culpa," *Vanity Fair*, November 3, 2006.

2

Advancing the Responsibility to Protect Through International Criminal Justice

*Cherif Bassiouni**

There is nothing more difficult to take in hand, more perilous to conduct, or more uncertain in its success, than to take the lead in the introduction of a new order of things.

—*Niccolo Machiavelli*

And so it is for the "responsibility to protect."

Introduction

The United Nations (UN) General Assembly at the UN 2005 World Summit adopted a resolution embodying the position of forty-six heads of state. The resolution, A/Res/60/1 (October 24, 2005), adopted by consensus of 174 states represented at the summit, states, in part, the following:

Responsibility to protect populations from genocide, war crimes, ethnic cleansing, and crimes against humanity

138. Each individual has the responsibility to protect its populations from genocide, war crimes, ethnic cleansing and crimes against humanity. This responsibility entails the prevention of such crimes, including their incitement, through appropriate and necessary means. We accept that responsibility and will act in accordance with it. The international community

should, as appropriate, encourage and help States to exercise this responsibility and support the United Nations in establishing an early warning capability.

139. The international community, through the United Nations, also has the responsibility to use appropriate diplomatic, humanitarian and other peaceful means, in accordance with Chapters VI and VIII of the Charter, to help to protect populations from genocide, war crimes, ethnic cleansing and crimes against humanity. In this context, we are prepared to take collective action, in a timely and decisive manner, through the Security Council, in accordance with the Charter, including Chapter VII, on a case-by-case basis and in cooperation with relevant regional organizations as appropriate, should peaceful means be inadequate and national authorities are manifestly failing to protect their populations from genocide, war crimes, ethnic cleansing and crimes against humanity and its implications, bearing in mind the principles of the Charter and international law. We also intend to commit ourselves, as necessary and appropriate, to helping States build capacity to protect their populations from genocide, war crimes, ethnic cleansing and crimes against humanity and to assisting those which are under stress before crises and conflicts break out.

The UN is a states' organization that seeks to forge commonly shared values and interests through the political will of its members. In turn, these values and interests are translated into policies, practices, and actions covering a variety of subjects. Some of these subjects are more likely to produce political consensus than others. Those involving peace and security, as well as human rights and humanitarian protection, are less so. While these issues involve *largo sensu*, the commonly shared values and interests of the international community, they are also subject to the state-interest constructs of the world's major military and economic powers that commonly prevail over individual and collective value considerations.

The system of international security reflects this weighing of states' interests, and in particular, those states who are permanent members of the Security Council. Thus the UN charter confers upon the Security Council the unbridled discretionary right to act in the pursuit of the preservation and maintenance of world peace and security, subject to the veto power of the permanent five. The Security Council is therefore not required to act in order to preserve or maintain peace and security. Surely, if a legally enforceable responsibility to protect existed, the Security Council would have the obligation to act whenever the conditions triggering such a duty existed. If this were the case, it would reflect the prevailing nature of commonly shared values and interests over unilaterally perceived state interests.

Since the 1990s there has been a gradual meshing of gross violations of internationally protected human rights and serious breaches/violations of international humanitarian law with breaches of international peace and security. The inclusion of these violations in the determination of what constitutes a threat to peace and security led to experimentation by the Security Council with its direct establishment of two international criminal justice mechanisms, the International Criminal Tribunal for the former Yugoslavia (ICTY) and the International Criminal Tribunal for Rwanda (ICTR). The UN then proceeded to experiment with mixed models of international criminal justice for crimes in Sierra Leone, East Timor, and Cambodia. The final step was the establishment by treaty of the International Criminal Court (ICC) with a provision allowing Security Council referrals under the Charter's Chapters VI and VII, as was the case of the 2005 referral of the Darfur situation.

What these social experiments reflect is that the Security Council is more prone to act after the fact than before. Thus it cannot be said that such *ex post facto* action is in the nature of a responsibility to protect, meaning a duty to act in order to prevent humanitarian disasters. Instead, it can be interpreted as a tentative way of leading into an eventual duty to preventively act by means of establishing deterrence through accountability.

International criminal justice is thus seen as advancing the goals of prevention on the assumption that the prosecution and punishment of decision-makers and senior perpetrators of *jus cogens* crimes will produce deterrence. If this result is obtained, even in part, then prevention of crimes such as genocide, crimes against humanity, and war crimes will be achieved and the goals of R2P will be achieved. In this respect, international criminal justice can be seen as a corollary of R2P—a modest step that needs to be perfected.

The expectation that an internationally binding legal obligation to protect populations from genocide, war crimes, ethnic cleansing, and crimes against humanity will become part of either conventional or customary international law in the foreseeable future is far from certain. At this point it is only a desideratum that reflects the values and the expectations of part of the "international community." How to enhance the future acceptance of such an international legal obligation requires concerted action by states and nonstate actors who support this proposition. In the meantime, proponents of the responsibility to protect can advance the pursuit of international criminal justice as a necessary element of prevention achievable by means of reducing the prospects of impunity.

Why Protect?

The answer to this question will vary in accordance with philosophical perspectives. The perspectives range from the views of naturalists to pragmatists.

Irrespective of the differences between these perspectives, they are either reinforced or challenged by the facts.

During the period 1948 to 1998, there were 250 conflicts that took place on almost every continent. Irrespective of how they have been legally characterized—namely, conflicts of an international character, conflicts of a noninternational character, and conflicts of a purely domestic character—the estimated number of casualties resulting therefrom ranges from 70 million to 170 million persons. The low end of the estimate represents twice the number of victims of World War I and World War II combined. Yet, with only a few exceptions during the course of this long strand of human tragedies, little has been done to advance the notion of an international duty to prevent and to put into effect a duty to provide for international accountability. Moreover, in very few instances has the collective security system of the Security Council been effectively invoked to protect people from large-scale killings, human suffering, and other human depredations. In nearly all of these cases, an injudicious political realism leading to a failure to act has prevailed, even in the face of ample early warnings, as well as in the face of unfolding startling realities revealed by ongoing conflicts. Yet, almost never in the course of the Security Council's debate of some of these humanitarian crises has the question of a legally binding international duty to protect been posited as a basis for action. For sure, many hortatory statements have found their way into preambles of Security Council resolutions, evidencing the links between the harm created by such conflicts and international peace and security, but no resolution posits the duty to act in order to protect or to prevent. Even in the face of overwhelming evidence of human depredations on so vast a scale, the Security Council and the General Assembly rhetoric has seldom ripened into meaningful action designed to prevent or protect.

Just as R2P was sidestepped by the realpoliticiens, so was the responsibility to bring the most senior perpetrators to justice except in a few selected instances. Instead, political realists sought to avoid engagement in most of the post–World War II conflicts to prevent, let alone stop or mitigate, the harm brought about by these conflicts. There has seldom been collective humanitarian intervention, except when significant economic and strategic interests were at stake—for example, the 1991 U.S.-led coalition in Kuwait to bring an end to the unlawful Iraqi occupation.

Political realists have also consistently compromised international justice through political negotiations to end conflicts, using amnesties, explicit or implicit, to secure political settlements. In the long run, by preventing postconflict justice, they have weakened the prospects of peace. For it is frequently the case that without justice for the victims, the prospects for genuine peace, as opposed to political settlements, are reduced. And where there is no genuine peace, the likelihood of renewed conflict is increased. Thus it is axiomatic that to prevent is to protect.

If a responsibility to protect existed and the international community had intervened to prevent or mitigate humanitarian harm, one can only speculate at the extent to which the harmful human results described above would have been reduced. In a comparative cost-benefit analysis, the economic and human costs incurred by implementing a responsibility to protect are likely to have been far less than those that were actually incurred in these conflicts. It would be revealing to perform an economic analysis of the costs of UN humanitarian intervention after the fact compared to the estimated costs of a similar intervention before the fact. One can speculate that the economic cost would not be much more in the latter case than the former, except in the potential human costs for the intervening force. Thus the real cost-benefit analysis is a companion of the intervening forces' casualties in contrast to those lives saved by the intervention. One can speculate, based on the facts known since 1993, that a humanitarian intervention in Rwanda with a force of 30,000 may have resulted in an estimated 300 casualties, but may have saved 300,000 lives, *ergo sum.*

To this straightforward comparison one has to add the prevention of other human harms, such as physical injuries, the destruction of property, the break-up of a state, the cost of reconstructing a failed state, and ultimately the cost of healing the wounds of that society. Surely even the most objective economic analysis, devoid of any moral consideration, would argue in favor of a duty to intervene, and thus of a responsibility to protect. Only the higher human and material costs of failing to act to prevent such tragedies as we have witnessed in less than sixty years can stimulate acceptance of the duty to act and eventually enhance its implementation.

Considering the facts mentioned above and ongoing situations like those in the Democratic Republic of the Congo (DRC), where in less than six years it is believed that three million persons have been killed, we have to wonder what would trigger a collective intervention based on the responsibility to protect. The same tragic conclusion is evident in the Darfur situation. If the responsibility to protect existed, the Security Council would have had a duty to send forces to the DRC and to Sudan long ago.

While there has never been empiric verification of the following argument, it can be argued that the human and economic costs incurred by the international community since the end of World War II, which heralded the UN Security Council system of collective security, have far outweighed the costs which would have been incurred had that system been transformed into one based on the responsibility to protect against widespread or systematic gross violations of human rights and humanitarian law. While this may sound anathema to political realists, it evidences that contemporary political realism is blindly intent on ignoring its own realism by failing to assess the costs of conflicts, including their human harm, destruction of material and natural resources, and the wasting of economic resources.

International Governance and the Rule of Law

Various models of international governance hypothesize an international community bound by international obligations that flow from commonly shared values and interests. One model more applicable to the contemporary international system—the *civitas maxima*—derives from Roman law. This is a concept that reflects the existence of a higher body politic; in the Roman legal system it included the different nations and tribes that comprised the Empire, but it was the collective belief in the existence of this intangible whole that is greater than its individual parts. The Roman *civitas maxima* engendered a collective social bond from which emanated duties that transcended the interests of the singular. The moral or ethical ligament and the pragmatic and experiential bonds thus coalesced in the moral precepts of the *civitas maxima*. From that whole, legal obligations arose that the community had to enforce individually and collectively for the benefit of all. This approach can be the foundation of the responsibility to protect.

Against this vision stands the Hobbesian state of nature in which each state pursues its own interests, defines its own goals, follows its own path, relies on its own means, and is limited only by its own considerations of expediency and whatever it deems to be prudent to achieve its goals. This includes the ability of a state to free itself from any moral/ethical limitations, even when these moral/ethical considerations represent its own society's commonly shared values. Thus no moral/ethical rules restrain states in their relations with one another except those rules to which they voluntarily wish to submit themselves, including self-restraining limitations arising out of countervailing deterring forces. More significantly, the state could opt out of its hitherto voluntarily accepted obligations without any other consequences than what countervailing forces could exercise. The Hobbesian state, subject to its own considerations of enlightenment, expediency, and prudence, is essentially self-controlling. To a large extent this characteristic is reflected in the Westphalian model of 1648 which has managed to survive even in the age of global interdependence.

Philosophers from Aristotle to Rousseau do not set aside the morality and responsibility of states as some contemporary political realists do. These philosophers, notwithstanding their different views, consider morality and responsibility as components of state decision making. The Kantian methodology of pure reason, which has influenced many modern philosophers and political scientists, coexists with the metaphysical elements of ethics. Both are part of the rules which control interpersonal and intersocial relations.

A modern *civitas maxima* model includes self-imposed and externally imposed limitations that are voluntarily accepted but collectively enforced when they are transgressed. However, a process must guide such a model, lest it turn into a form of a collective Hobbesian state of nature where the powerful and wealthy nations dominate the community's collective processes and arrogate to themselves the prerogative of exceptionalism. The modern *civitas maxima* must therefore be subject to an international rule of law that includes both binding legal norms that transcend domestic norms as well as international legal processes that are similar to national legal processes, but which also apply to state action. These legal processes should have the capacity for "direct enforcement" through international mechanisms, which are complemented by "indirect enforcement" modalities, which in turn are dependant upon the intermediation of state enforcement based on national legal systems.

More importantly, the modern *civitas maxima* must be founded on substantive legitimacy and its acts must also conform to the legitimacy of processes. These two forms of legal legitimacy must be based on that which is inspired by what Aristotle referred to as the "right of reason." Legal legitimacy is the right reason premised on existing positive norms, though not excluding the application of higher norms deriving in part from the commonly shared values of the times, and enduring values represented in "general principles of law." Such an approach regulating international relations is likely to better govern interstate relations and other international relations and likely to produce better outcomes. This is the ultimate utilitarian reward for compliance with the norms and processes of an international legal system based on the rule of law. Legitimacy reduces the latitude of relativism to avoid having the latter undermine the certainty of the law. The result is predictability and consistency of outcomes in state and nonstate actors' actions. Without legitimacy in state and collective state action, the international legal system will have no predictable and consistent outcomes—worse yet, it will have little chance of effective compliance. The responsibility to protect becomes a corollary of the international rule of law.

Admittedly, rules governing interstate and international relations must necessarily be flexible because they are open to interpretation by those who are subject to them. These rules are also likely to respond or give way to countervailing considerations of different state interests and to power relations. Without that flexibility, states would not "buy in" to a system that hamstrings them into compliance with collective rules without having the countervailing benefits of an international social contract à la Rousseau. The basic *quid pro quo* that may exist in a national community does not have the same counterpart in the international community, if for no other reason than the imbalance of power and wealth among the members of that community can hardly be entirely redressed. On the contrary, in the international community, the unilateral quest for power and accumulation of wealth continues to be one of the avowed goals of that community. Thus the international community has yet to accept what the French philosopher Pascal urged, that in times of peace, nations must do to each other the most good, and in times of war, the least harm. To achieve this lofty goal requires an international social contract that includes the responsibility to protect as well as some basis for wealth-sharing and transfer of technology and know-how from developed to developing countries.

Existing notions of collective security in the context of the Westphalian system of interstate relations must thus give way to a new international collective responsibility to protect. Similarly, an equitable system of sharing world resources and transfers of technology and know-how must be included in the international social contract. In short, protection, resource sharing, and international criminal justice must be part of the international social contract in this age of globalization.

Modern political realism reflects the disjunctive and contradictory forces that exist in international intercourse under which it is implausible to accept the existence of binding rules capable of restraining states in their conduct other than by power. They see the international system as essentially an arena in which a Hobbesian state of nature controls the behavior of states without externally imposed limitations. Accordingly, international law has been based on a concept of equal sovereignty of states and voluntary acceptance of international obligations with no external coercion or enforcement, and no intervention in the domestic affairs of any state, subject only to the United Nations collective security system as determined on an ad hoc basis by the Security Council. This paradigm implicitly accepts the inequities of power relations whereby the stronger can impose their will on the weaker. Such a model is a contradiction in terms with an international legal order based on the rule of law, which tolerates no double standards.

The assumptions of political realists and, more particularly, of the school of *realpolitik* are that the relations between nations are in a constant anarchic state of change because they reflect an ongoing power struggle restrained only by countervailing power. However, in this age of globalization where so much interdependence exists, multilateral interests have, by their own force, bound unilateral power. The analogy is to the giant Gulliver, who represents the unbridled power of political realism at its best, and the

Hobbesian state of nature. However, Gulliver in the age of globalization is tied down by many large and small strings which represent in part the commonly shared values and multiple interests of the international community. These strings cumulatively represent the multilateral, which has tamed the power of the giant unilateral. Admittedly the giant is not entirely tamed, and should he want to he could surely break away from all or many of his bonds, unless of course he finds it of greater interest to remain bound, or he is further restrained.

The age of globalization has increased the incentives for the giant of unilateralism to remain bound, just as it has increased the disincentives for that giant to break away from the multilateral system of norms and legal processes. Globalization is thus far seen as involving communications, commerce, and finance and only in part, collective security, but it still does not include the collective responsibility to protect, wealth sharing, and international criminal justice. So far, globalization has not ripened into an international social contract, and only represents a small portion of the commonly shared values and commonly shared interests of the international community. Indeed, there is only some partial evidence that it includes the duty of international criminal accountability.

Multilateral problem solving and collective decision making by international institutions with rule-making authority transcending the powers of member-states serve as examples of the changes that have occurred during these past decades. Many international organizations and the mechanisms of collective decision making they embody have brought about a new reality concerning international governance without the need for world government. Moreover, the web of multilateral and bilateral agreements containing cooperative obligations, coupled with enforcement mechanisms that include some sanctions or disincentives, have created a web of interlocking relationships between states. These in turn have enhanced the acceptance of external obligations, while at the same time nurturing confidence among states that the relinquishment of individual decision making is not without its concomitant benefits. Experience has demonstrated that multilateralism, notwithstanding its weaknesses and shortcomings, accomplishes more than unilateralism can and that what is lost in unilateral freedom of action is compensated for by what is gained through collective decision making and collective cooperative action.

Reduced to their basics, what motivates states in their relations is not enduring values as those that bind human beings but interests whose significance and timeliness are in constant flux. Thus the dominant feature of interstate relations is characterized by state interests. Nevertheless, the evolution of interstate and international relations since World War II based on the international rule of law—until now defined by the Westphalian concept of sovereignty and the Hegelian concept of state interest bridled only by prudence and good judgment—evidences a significant change. This is characterized by the impact of commonly shared values that transcend the unilateral pursuit and preservation of power and wealth. This is reflected in the many changes that have occurred in the international legal system as of the twentieth century, particularly with respect to multilateral decision making and limitations on state sovereignty.

International relations are framed by a web of constitutive processes of multilateral authoritative decision making. The pervasive effect of this process cannot be solely applied to matters of common economic interests because what brought about this elaborate process is an array of values and policies that include human values. As a result, the identification, application, and enforcement of commonly shared values and interests by an international legal system presuppose the existence of an international community that postulates certain universal objects and moral imperatives that require inter alia the prescription and the proscription of certain actions. It is therefore necessary to identify the limits of state action and to establish thresholds of cooperation in the common interest. This proposition is not only moralistic, but is based on the lessons of justified pragmatic considerations that enlightened self-interest and prudent judgment requires. Consequently, it places limits on unilateral state action and impels collective state cooperation and action in the common interest and for the common good.

The acceptance of this postulate is not dependent on the existence or even the desirability of a world government. But it cannot be achieved without the existence of an internationally binding legal obligation to act whenever gross violations of human rights and humanitarian law occur or are about to occur. The responsibility to protect therefore achieves the goals of peace and security, as well as those of human rights protections.

Although we are in an age of globalization, which evidences our interdependence as nations and peoples inhabiting planet Earth, our instinct for social survival has not reached a developed stage where an international legal system based on the rule of law effectively regulates collective and individual state action, nonstate actors, and individual conduct threatening or harming world peace and security.

Conclusions

What the international community is willing to profess is not necessarily what it is willing to act upon. These two concepts are separate and apart from the UN collective security system, which does not partake of the same values and interests that are part of the responsibility to protect and the duty to bring about international criminal justice.

As each of the 250 conflicts mentioned above emptied its horrors, the need for prevention and protection has increased. However, legal experience demonstrates that the enunciation of rights without concomitant remedies are pyrrhic pronouncements, and that remedies without enforcement are empty promises. However morally compelling arguments about collective human rights and their protection may be, it is still necessary to offer states an inducement to "buy in" to the recognition of such rights and their enforcement. The need for such an inducement arises because outcomes deriving from an international legal system that is not based on the rule of law are likely to be detrimental to state interests. The states' "buy-in" argument must necessarily include corresponding state interests. The argument supporting this proposition is that protecting collective human rights enhances peace and security, reduces domestic, regional, and world disruptions, and is ultimately more economical than having to engage in military humanitarian intervention and by having states embroiled in regional conflicts. In other words, the argument advances the utilitarian side of the responsibility to protect in its reflection on state interests.

The recognition of the individual as a subject of law and the establishment of treaty rights inuring to the benefit of the individual, who is also granted standing to seek the enforcement of these rights, particularly that which we call human rights, necessarily implies that the international community as a whole, states individually and collectively, and international organizations have the responsibility to protect these human rights. A responsibility to protect is thus binding upon states insofar as they have assumed specific treaty obligations. As states accept to be bound by nontreaty obligations arising out of the peremptory norms of international law referred to as *jus cogens* there is, by implication, a collective obligation by the international community to enforce human rights, and that includes international criminal justice:

> The world rests on three pillars: on truth, on justice, and on peace.
> —*Rabban Simeon Ben Gamaliel*

A Talmudic commentary adds to this, saying: if justice is realized, truth is vindicated, and peace results.

If you see a wrong you must right it; with your hand if you can, or, with your words, or, with your stare, or in your heart, and that is the weakest of faith.

—*Prophet Mohammed, Hadith*

If you want peace, work for justice.

—*Pope Paul VI*

Note

*   Cherif Bassiouni is a distinguished research professor of law and president emeritus of the International Human Rights Law Institute at DePaul University College of Law in Chicago, Illinois.

3

In Our Interest

The Responsibility to Protect

Susan E. Mayer*

Too often the world community stands by while nations commit or permit genocide, ethnic cleansing, mass murder, and other atrocities. When this happens it is tempting to believe that the world community and especially its most powerful members lack moral courage or political will. But the reluctance of nations to take any but the least coercive actions when atrocities occur is the result of a collective action problem. This problem ensures that even when every nation would be better off if no other nation engaged in atrocity crimes, nations will be unlikely to intervene on their own against another nation solely to stop such atrocities. To ensure action against atrocities in the future requires a solution to this collective action problem. The principles embodied in the "responsibility to protect" (R2P) provide the most promising foundation for creating such a solution. This is why it is in every nation's interest that all nations adopt these principles.

Introduction

The key tenants of R2P as outlined in the December 2001 report of the International Commission on Intervention and State Sovereignty (ICISS) titled *The Responsibility to Protect* are that sovereign nations have a responsibility to protect their population from suffering serious harm "as a result of internal war, insurgency, repression or state failure," but when they cannot or will not the state abrogates its right to sovereignty and the international community through the United Nations (UN) has the responsibility to intervene. The intervention should be the least intrusive possible, but it can include military intervention under specific circumstances. R2P includes the responsibility to prevent as well as stop violence and to help rebuild a nation after an intervention. It calls for specific procedures to be followed to determine the intervention that is proportional to the suffering.

In a 2005 meeting of heads of state at the UN, a consensus summit declaration (known as the UN Summit Outcome Document) included a commitment to the principles outlined in the ICISS report. Specifically omitted were a strong statement of the obligation to intervene and the criteria for military intervention.

The acts of violence referred to in the UN General Assembly Resolution include genocide, war crimes, ethnic cleansing, and crimes against humanity. These terms have specific meanings in international law and some require specific actions on the part of the UN. In this chapter I use the term "atrocity crimes" to summarize the forms of violence listed in the World Summit Outcome document (See David Scheffer, Chapter 5 in this volume.)[1]

I use the term "intervention" to mean any of the many possible "tools" for preventing or halting atrocity crimes. Prevention tools can include financial and nonfinancial aid, changes in trade policies, debt reduction, mediation, and many other things. Tools for stopping atrocity crimes that are already occurring may include some of the prevention tools, but may also include economic sanctions, arms embargoes, and as a last resort, military intervention. The use of military intervention is the most controversial, and focusing on it can be divisive. I include the option of military intervention because it is unlikely that R2P can be effective without this option.

This chapter describes why the United States and the world community should support not only the principles embodied in R2P but also its consistent implementation. I summarize my argument:

- The conditions leading to atrocity crimes are more prevalent, and spillovers from such crimes more likely than in the past.
- The principles embodied in R2P comport with the moral values of Americans and their belief about the appropriate actions for the United States to take to defend those values.
- Atrocity crimes are potentially costly to the world community, but preventing and stopping them are very costly for individual nations.
- R2P provides a theory of intervention and an institutional structure for intervention that can (a) protect the most vulnerable nations against the capricious use of "humanitarian intervention," (b) ensure appropriate intervention when it is needed, and (c) deter future atrocity crimes.

- Implementation of R2P will not be possible with the current structure of the UN.

In the next section I discuss why the principles of R2P are more important now than in the past. I then detail the three specific reasons why R2P is in the interest of every nation. I then briefly turn to issues relevant to the implementation of R2P.

Why Do We Need R2P Now?

The world has changed dramatically over the last century in ways that make the principles of R2P more necessary and more acceptable than in the past. After World War I the nations that had colonized most of Africa began to abandon the continent, leaving behind many newly independent nations whose borders crossed historical tribal, linguistic, and ethnic lines. A number of Africa's postcolonial political leaders were poorly educated military generals who became dictators with little knowledge or experience in matters of governance. The cold war helped maintain an uneasy balance of power. The Soviet Union provided financial, military, and state support to shore up many of the newly independent African nations and keep long-standing ethnic and political rivalries in check. The United States did the same for its smaller number of African allies. At the same time, the Soviet Union was also able to use its military and economic power to keep the political and ethnic rivalries of Eastern Europe, especially Yugoslavia and Czechoslovakia, from erupting.

When the Soviet Union fell and the cold war ended, the political geography of the world changed rapidly. Without the financial and state support of the superpowers and without the order imposed by their militaries, the weakness of many African nations became apparent and greed and competition for natural resources escalated. Africa was left with several nations—Nigeria, Chad, Sudan, and Congo to mention only a few—with little ability to provide infrastructure, services, or security to their citizens. Similarly many of the nations that emerged from the breakup of the former eastern bloc had little in the way of history or institutions that could aid their nation-building or quell their internal political and ethnic rivalries.

As the number of weak nations in the world has increased so has the influence of nonstate actors, including multinational corporations, international organizations such as the International Monetary Fund, the World Bank, and the European Union, and countless nongovernmental organizations (NGOs).[2] These nonstate actors are increasingly the locus of international interactions, agreements, and political influence. For example, to establish the Chad-Cameroon oil pipeline, the largest single investment in sub-Saharan Africa, Exxon-Mobile, not the nations involved, negotiated the financing with the World Bank. In many weak and poor nations, NGOs and other nonstate actors have stepped in to provide schooling, health care, security, and other functions traditionally provided by the state, and multinational corporations control natural resources and direct economic policy. While the citizens of weak nations benefit from the aid of nonstate actors, that aid can further weaken the state. In addition, other less-benevolent nonstate actors, including gangs and nonstate armies, have also grown in importance in some nations. They have been aided by the increase in the availability of arms on the world market after the fall of the Soviet Union.

The increase in the number of international organizations is the outcome of globalization and the resulting interrelatedness of the economic and political interests of nations. New technologies such as satellite television and radio, telephones, and the Internet easily cross national borders. New means of transportation get people from one point to another in a fraction for the time it took a century ago. Information, money, and people flow rapidly around the world and in a way that cannot be controlled by any one nation. Globalization has increased the chances that a disturbance in one nation will spill over to other nations. When weak nations commit or permit atrocity crimes, they often create a flow of refugees that can strain the resources of other nations and create conditions for the spread of disease even beyond the refugee population. Instability in a nation with important natural resources can cause serious economic problems for other nations, as the oil markets have repeatedly demonstrated.

A key part of the UN charter, following the Westphalian tradition, holds that states are sovereign and that there is no right "to intervene in matters which are essentially within the domestic jurisdiction of any state." R2P weakens sovereignty by giving an international organization, the UN, the right and responsibility to intervene in nations when atrocity crimes occur.[3] But R2P is a consequence and not a cause of the demise of sovereignty.

The increase in the number of weak states and in the influence of nonstate actors along with globalization has weakened claims to the absolute sovereignty of nations. Weak nations often do not provide basic state functions or serve the interests of their citizens. When this happens the principle of self-government has little meaning and the protection of the citizens assumes greater importance than the protection of state sovereignty. Nations now routinely voluntarily give up aspects of their sovereignty when they join multinational agreements on trade, the environment, and other issues. Finally, a nation whose economic interests are threatened by violence in another nation may argue that it is legitimate to use military force to restore its economic interests. In this respect, globalization increases the interest of the world community in the internal violence of weak nations and increases the chance of international intervention when atrocity crimes occur. The resulting unilateral and self-interested intervention can be uncoordinated and inefficient and can escalate the violence. Leaving the policing of atrocity crimes to powerful self-interested nations also ensures that citizens of the poorest and most disadvantaged nations can count on little help from the world community.

Why R2P Is in Everyone's Interest

The proliferation of weak states, the rise of nonstate political and economic actors, and globalization require the world community to make adjustments to protect the most vulnerable populations. Clearly the world would be better off if all nations protected their citizens from atrocity crimes. This section describes three reasons why Americans and others should care about affirming the principles of R2P.

R2P is consistent with what Americans already believe is morally right

Americans almost universally condemn atrocity crimes as immoral, and most say that they support even military interventions in nations that commit or permit such crimes. A July 2004 poll by the Chicago Council on Foreign Relations found that 72 percent of respondents supported using American troops to "deal with humanitarian crises," and 75 percent supported using troops "to stop a government from committing genocide and killing large numbers of its own people."[4] When asked, "In the future, do you think that the U.S. and other Western powers have a *moral* obligation to use military force in Africa, if necessary, to prevent one group of people from committing genocide against another," 55 percent said yes. When asked the same question about Europe 70 percent said yes.[5]

Using Darfur as an example, in a 2005 poll conducted in the United States by the Program on International Policy Attitudes (PIPA), 74 percent of respondents said that the UN should "step in with military force and stop the genocide in Darfur"; 60 percent said that if other countries contribute troops to a UN force the United States should also contribute troops. Support for UN military intervention was slightly greater among Republicans than among Democrats.

Among respondents polled in 2004, barely a year after the humanitarian crisis in Darfur began, 84 percent said that they had heard little or nothing about the crisis. Yet 69 percent said that if the UN were to determine that genocide was occurring in Darfur, then the UN, including the United States, should act to stop it, even if it required military force. More than 70 percent of respondents to a 2005 poll by Zogby International supported the United States imposing a "no-fly zone" over Darfur to prevent Sudanese planes from bombing civilians, and the support was bipartisan, with majorities of both Republicans and Democrats supporting such a measure.[6] If Americans are willing to support military intervention and no-fly zones, they are also presumably willing to support less costly measures, including preventive measures, although polls seldom ask about these less costly measures.

The majority of Americans support engagement with the UN on international issues and support steps to strengthen the UN's ability to investigate and stop violations of human rights. In a 2006 poll conducted for the Chicago Council on Global Affairs, 60 percent of Americans agreed that "when dealing with international problems, the United States should be more willing to make decisions within the UN even if it means that it will sometimes have to go along with a policy that is not its first choice."[7]

While the majority of Americans seem to believe that the United States should work with the UN and perhaps other international organizations to prevent and stop atrocity crimes, the American political leadership has often been reluctant to intervene when atrocity crimes occur and have not always supported UN efforts.[8] Nonetheless, R2P institutionalizes what most Americans already believe is right—that atrocity crimes are wrong—and they also support actions consistent with the principles of R2P to stop it.

Atrocity Crimes Are Costly to the World Community

From economic sanctions to military invasions, all incursions into sovereign nations are costly to both the target of the intervention and the intervening nations. Economic sanctions can hurt innocent civilians and military interventions, even when they are not deadly to civilians, can leave environmental and psychological scares. Intervening nations can incur large monetary costs as a result of sanctions, and the monetary cost of military interventions can be very high. Failure can mean the loss of both domestic and international political capital. The flawed intervention in Somalia was a serious political blow to the Clinton administration, and the North Atlantic Treaty Organization's (NATO's) bombing in Serbia, which was criticized as illegitimate, illegal, and ineffective, was very costly to the relationship between the United States and Russia.

But the monetary and nonmonetary costs of not intervening when a nation fails its responsibility to protect its citizens may be even greater. Nations where large-scale atrocity crimes occur face huge costs in foregone human capital and international investments, loss of infrastructure, and medical and other direct costs associated with the physical and psychological harm to its people. The costs are especially high when it comes to children. Children forced to participate in or witness violent atrocities inevitably have psychological damage that impedes their cognitive and social development. When children are orphaned by violence, the cost of their care falls to international organizations. Those who are unlucky enough to find themselves with no one to care for them lack education and are susceptible to disease and exploitation. The cost of the lost human capital from a generation of children exposed to violence and its aftermath is incalculable. Accompanying the human destruction in the countries where mass atrocity crimes have occurred is destruction of what little infrastructure there was. The fragile education, health care, transportation, and communications systems can quickly be destroyed in the violence and as talented and skilled individuals leave the country.

One might wonder why a nation would permit atrocity crimes if they are so costly. In some cases these crimes occur where leaders and institutions are weak and therefore where national interests may not prevail. In other cases, individual leaders benefit from violence. Furthermore, the nation that permits atrocity crimes is unlikely to bear the costs of recovery because these costs usually fall to the international community. Not only does the international community pay the direct costs to replace infrastructure and repair lives disrupted by the crimes, it also pays the costs of political and economic instability created by the crimes. The Tutsi military government that seized power in Rwanda in 1994 sparked conflict across central Africa that eventually included a large number of African governments and armies and prompted the organization of several armed rogue gangs that continue to cause havoc in the Great Lakes region of Africa. The atrocities in Darfur are now destabilizing Chad and the Central African Republic.

The cost of trials, reconciliation, and international aid can easily exceed the cost of prevention or intervention. For example, estimates suggest that the International Criminal Tribunals for Rwanda and the former Yugoslavia cost more than $100 million per year. The International Criminal Tribunal for Rwanda cost more than $1 million per year, with the 2006–7 allocation equal to $2.7 million.[9] The costs have greatly exceeded $1 billion already.

For a nation like the United States, which tends to couch its international policies in terms of moral imperatives, an important nonmonetary cost of doing nothing when obvious atrocity crimes occur is the risk of undermining its credibility. As the distance between what a nation says and what it does increases, its credibility and the trust and legitimacy accorded by its own citizens and by other nations decline. The United States has lost legitimacy on human rights issues through its selective efforts to stop atrocity crimes and its own recent use of torture, detention, and legal theories that are contrary to accepted traditions, agreements, and precedents to justify them.[10]The R2P doctrine provides a theory of intervention and an institutional structure for intervention that can (a) protect the most vulnerable nations against the capricious rationale of "humanitarian intervention," (b) share costs and therefore ensure appropriate intervention when it is needed, and (c) deter future egregious violence.

Contemporary circumstances compel R2P: most people believe that they have a personal moral obligation to respect and protect the lives of innocent civilians and that their governments also have such an obligation; the norm of national sovereignty has weakened; and spillovers from intra-national conflicts have increased. Broad agreement exists that all nations would benefit if no nation committed or permitted atrocity crimes. Nonetheless, given the current circumstance, no nation will use coercive means to intervene in another nation solely to prevent or stop atrocity crimes. The political and economic costs of coercive intervention are very high, so nations will only intervene if they have a compelling self-interest. Thus nations might publicly denounce atrocity crimes, use diplomatic means to raise concerns about atrocity crimes, and even engage in low-cost sanctions. These noncoercive measures have limited effectiveness, especially if they cannot be coupled with the threat of increasingly coercive interventions. On the other hand, nations can and do use coercive means to intervene in other nations when it is in their interest, often using humanitarian goals as a rationale. To adequately address the problem of atrocity crimes requires both a mechanism to ensure that a range of coercive and noncoercive interventions can occur when it is necessary and a mechanism to prevent nations from capriciously using of the "humanitarian rationale" to further their own interests through coercive interventions in another nation. These mechanisms can only function through an international organization that can provide rapid, legitimate, coordinated, and efficient responses to the threat of or actual atrocity crimes.

The R2P doctrine articulates the responsibility of the international community, through the UN, to intervene to prevent or stop atrocity crimes and it provides a theory of intervention, procedures to determine the need for intervention and the kind of intervention, and the means to intervene. By investing the UN with the authority to determine when inter-vention is necessary, R2P also reduces the legitimacy of individual nations or ad hoc coalitions of nations that try to use the premise of humanitarianism to intervene in a sovereign nation.

Because intervening in another nation carries both monetary and non-monetary costs, whether a nation is willing to act to stop atrocity crimes will depend on factors such as the strength of its economy, the current balance of domestic power, and whether it is involved on other international fronts. The payoff to any intervention will have to be proportional to the costs and risk involved. Low-impact, noncoercive, and diplomatic interventions are low cost and low risk and therefore may frequently be used to show displeasure with nations that commit atrocity crimes. But low-cost and low-risk interventions are also likely to be ineffective. Because more coercive interventions in another nation can be risky and costly, the expected payoff for such interventions would have to be high for a nation to act alone.

Internal political pressure can provide a government with an incentive to act. Advocacy organizations that use information campaigns, demonstrations, and other means to increase the knowledge and moral conviction of the population can raise the political pressure to act. But it can take a long time for political pressure to become strong enough to be relevant. The issue of political motivation is made more complex by the increase in the influence of nonstate actors who can alter the interests of a nation and undermine the political voice of its citizens. Large multinational corporations that depend on particular natural resources may lobby for or against intervention in another country to suit their own interests. The political and economic power of such organizations can bring the voice of noncitizens to internal political debates. This can encourage intervention when citizens would prefer no intervention or discourage intervention when citizens would prefer it.

When nations are unlikely to intervene except to protect their own interests and when the decision to intervene depends on complex domestic and international political and economic considerations and the influence of nonstate actors, it will be hard to predict when any particular nation will be willing to intervene. Even if a nation does eventually act alone, it will take a long time to mobilize the political and economic support needed for action. Under these circumstances, weak or disreputable heads of government have good reason to believe that they can get away with using violence to acquire or maintain power or accumulate wealth by gaining control of natural resources such as oil or diamonds. This of course raises the probability of atrocity crimes.

Sometimes a nation might be willing to expend some financial and political capital to prevent or stop atrocity crimes but be unwilling to assume all the costs. This is especially likely when other nations will benefit from an end to the violence. When it is in the interest of many nations to prevent or stop atrocity crimes, any one nation will be reluctant to act alone because it will incur all the costs of the intervention but only get some of the benefit. Under these circumstances nations might form ad hoc coalitions as a way to spread the risk and costs of intervening. Ad hoc coalitions of nations with shared interests are common, but assembling such coalitions can be time consuming and nations that consult with other nations can be regarded as using multilateralism as an excuse for inaction. Standing coalitions such as NATO can act more quickly but, like individual nations, both ad hoc and standing coalitions often lack legitimacy and their actions can sometimes be inefficient and uncoordinated.

International cooperation has become more important to nations. This is evident in the emphasis the United States placed on having a coalition in Iraq. While the growing emphasis on multilateralism is positive, nations still mainly cooperate when it is in their own interest. The key principle of R2P is that it asks nations to support and contribute to intervention when it is *not* in their narrow interest to do so.

Ensuring legitimate, timely, and effective action to prevent or stop atrocity crimes requires an international organization that can secure cooperation, confer legitimacy, and ensure cost sharing and efficiency. R2P makes the UN the international organization entrusted with defining atrocity crimes, determining when atrocity crimes are likely or are occurring and what intervention is necessary, monitoring the intervention, and leading the rebuilding effort after such crimes have occurred.[11] Below I discuss some potential problems with the UN implementing R2P, but first I describe why an international organization can achieve what an individual nation cannot, and therefore why it is important to support implementation of R2P through the UN.

When nations join the World Trade Organization (WTO), International Monetary Fund (IMF), or other international organizations they agree to certain rules and in return they get certain benefits. In most cases membership provides a sufficient incentive for states to adhere to the rules since nations would not join if they were not inclined to agree with the rules or if the benefits of membership were not sufficiently important to make them follow the membership terms. When nations break the rules, international organizations can withhold the benefits of membership, such as protection or economic aid. For example, the IMF can cut off funds to member states that do not uphold their financial commitments. The UN Security Council has authorized economic sanctions against UN member states on multiple occasions over the last twenty years. These sanctions have a legitimacy that sanctions by individual nations do not have, and an international organization can arrange side payments among sanctioning states and provide other incentives for member nations to adhere to the sanctions. But international organizations have additional enforcement tools available and some can be applied to nonmembers. For example, they can collect and distribute information on member nations and use the power of the organization to criticize undesirable state behavior—that is, they can use the power of shame.

Collective action problems cannot be overcome solely by incentives and sanctions. To secure something more than minimal behavioral cooperation, nations need a sense of collective identity. The United States has more often developed ties with Europe than with Asia, Latin America, and Africa at least in part because of shared cultural identity.[12] Collective identity is fostered by a shared mission, trust, a similarity of understandings (language, religion), political and economic interdependence, and a convergence of political and economic values. An international organization can foster collective identity by requiring repeated interactions among nations, which can lead members to trust the organization and its members. A collective identity develops over time and not solely in times of crisis or emergency, which is why a standing international organization is better than ad hoc coalitions for developing a shared identity. International organizations that foster repeated trusting interactions also may transform the meaning of self-interest for individual nations in such a way that self-interest includes satisfying the interests of other nations. This socialization can reduce the need for incentives and sanctions.[13]

International organizations can alter domestic political dynamics by providing legitimacy for international actions. For example, when the UN supports interventions in a country, that support can attract domestic political support for the action. Opinion polls show stronger support for American participation in multilateral rather than unilateral actions.[14] International organizations can also alter domestic political support for intervening in another country by providing a means for action. The political costs of doing nothing increase when obvious forms of action are available. It is one thing when American citizens cannot imagine a way to provide aid to victims of atrocity crimes, but when a prescription for aid is at hand, not providing the aid becomes more politically unpalatable. Wide acceptance of the principles of R2P can therefore increase the political costs of inaction, making action more likely. For a powerful nation like the United States, international cooperation can also reduce the inclination of other nations to try to reduce American influence and power.

To summarize, left to their own devices, nations will be reluctant to use coercive intervention to prevent or stop atrocity crimes unless they have another compelling interest because it is financially and politically risky to do so. The result is that when atrocity crimes occur, other nations sometimes intervene and sometimes they do not. This leaves nefarious or weak government leaders with a reasonable chance that they can get away with committing or permitting such crimes. The result is an increase in atrocity crimes and an uncoordinated and ad hoc approach to preventing or stopping them. An international organization can use incentives, sanctions, collective identity, and legitimacy to secure cooperation to prevent and stop atrocity crimes and therefore ensure that appropriate interventions occur when they are needed.

Many people believe that R2P could provide rich and powerful nations with a humanitarian pretext for military interventions in poor and vulnerable nations when it suits their interests. Yet under the right circumstances, the opposite is likely to be the case. A consensus on the principle of national sovereignty does not prevent nations from militarily intervening in other nations, and it does not prevent them from using a humanitarian rationale for doing so when it suits their purpose. Sometimes nations use a humanitarian rationale for intervening in another nation when there is no clear evidence that atrocity crimes are occurring or imminent. When weapons of mass destruction failed to materialize in Iraq, the Bush administration argued that Saddam Hussein was an evil tyrant and therefore the invasion of Iraq was justifiable on humanitarian grounds (see Kenneth Roth, this volume). It was easy for the international community to be cynical about this argument given the rich oil fields of Iraq and the many regimes in which atrocity crimes seem to be occurring with little attention from the United States or other "coalition" members. Other times nations intervene in another nation where atrocity crimes are actually happening, but these actions are inevitably a result of narrow self-interest.

Powerful nations will not join an organization that they cannot influence, so powerful nations will have disproportionate influence in international organizations. But if a powerful nation completely undermines the international organization's independence in performing its functions, it reduces the usefulness of the organization, for example, by reducing its ability to confer legitimacy and encourage cost sharing. This would then reduce the advantage of membership for the powerful nation. To make this point, Abbott and Snidal (1998) observe that shareholders in a large corporation must monitor managers to limit agency costs, but if major shareholders cause managers to favor only their interests, others will refuse to invest. If shareholders exert undue control they also lose the advantages of professional management. Thus major shareholders balance their own narrow interests against competing group interests in order to achieve the efficiency and legitimacy that comes with membership. While no international organization will be able to entirely capture the interests of the most powerful nations, an international organization that offers important benefits can restrain such nations from acting entirely and always in their own narrow self-interest. Thus membership in international organizations can reduce the likelihood that powerful nations will "go it alone," especially when it comes to using coercive measures against another country, although recent evidence suggests that membership is not a guarantee that powerful nations will follow international consensus.

A strong commitment to R2P and its implementation would not prevent nations from invading one another, but it would shine a light on the capricious use of "humanitarianism" as a rationale for coercive intervention by requiring UN action to legitimize humanitarian intervention. Vesting an international organization with the right and responsibility to determine when the use of coercion is needed is the only way to ensure that coercive interventions take place when they are needed, and it is also the only feasible possibility for stopping powerful nations from using coercive interventions when no clear humanitarian need exists.

Without R2P the victims of some atrocity crimes will be saved by individual nations or coalitions of nations that have an interest in their country. Victims in nations rich in natural resources, victims who are culturally and racially similar to the rich and powerful nations, or nations whose fleeing refugees are costly to neighboring countries will have a better chance of international intervention to prevent and stop atrocity crimes. Victims in the most remote and disadvantaged nations will be ignored and left to suffer the most. To ensure that the most vulnerable citizens of the world do not suffer the most, all nations must be willing to support an international organization that can compel cooperation and support, provide cost sharing and coordination, and confer legitimacy to achieve the moral ends that no nation alone would otherwise attempt to secure.

Implementation of R2P

Hopefulness about the nations of the world adopting and adhering to the principle of R2P depends in large part on hopefulness that it could be implemented fairly and effectively. Poor implementation could be worse than no implementation. Currently, formidable obstacles to its implementation exist.

To implement R2P requires an international organization that can provide benefits and sanctions to its members, is trusted to be fair and efficient, and that can create a shared identity at least in so far as R2P is concerned. The

UN currently does not meet these requirements. This chapter is not the place for a critique of the UN—many already exist. However, it is important to concede that it is not enough to inspire support for R2P. Among both civil organizations and national governments, support for all the principles of R2P except military intervention is strong. Even apprehension about reconciling R2P with existing international law, including issues of sovereignty, appears to be minimal. It is feasible to get widespread commitment to most of the tenets of R2P in the very near future, but without major changes in the UN, R2P will go the way of the Genocide Convention. In just four months, between 500,000 and 800,000 Rwandans—more than three-quarters of the Tutsi population—were murdered despite the UN Genocide Convention and widespread agreement among the UN Secretariat and the Security Council that genocide was imminent and then occurring. Most nations agree that genocide is occurring in the Darfur region of Sudan, yet no effective measures are being taken to curtail the violence. In both cases the world community represented by the UN had a strong case for intervention, but was unable to act. The fact that the Genocide Convention has not prevented or stopped genocide does not provide much optimism regarding the UN's ability to implement R2P.[15]

The major concerns about implementing R2P are the political influences on Security Council decisions and the UN's inadequate operational capacity. The UN has a history of weak and inconsistent applications of sanctions. It often appears afraid to act against a member nation. Nation after nation has violated UN agreements with little response. Sudan has steadfastly refused to follow Security Council demands that it stop attacks on civilians, stop encouraging or allowing paramilitary groups carrying out atrocities, and so on. But instead of implementing diplomatic, political, legal, financial, or economic sanctions, the Council has fixated on a peacekeeping mission.

The permanent members of the Security Council less and less reflect the political balance of the world, yet they guard their own interests with few checks and balances. So long as the Security Council must authorize coercive action, its members will feel safe from the scrutiny that other nations receive. Russia can feel secure that no matter what it does in Chechnya it will not be subject to sanctions, tribunals, or other incursions. China can feel the same about Tibet. There can be no doubt that the current structure of the Security Council must be changed before the UN can be an effective and respected governing body.

The international balance of power cannot be changed by R2P. Powerful nations already have disproportionate power and they will no doubt have disproportionate power in decisions about when to take action and what kind of action to take to prevent or alleviate atrocity crimes.[16] The right question is not whether the principles of R2P will guide us to a perfect outcome, but whether the outcome with R2P is better for the world community than the current situation, or to put it more strongly, whether every country might gain more from R2P than it has to give up.

Other concerns about R2P come from critics in rich nations who fear that R2P is the top of a slippery slope toward a view of humanitarian intervention that would require nations to redistribute income and provide aid to the poor in a way that is contrary to free-market principles. The UN has often approached humanitarian issues in terms of economic concerns. The ICISS report notes that, "There is a growing and widespread recognition that armed conflicts cannot be understood without reference to such 'root' causes as poverty, political repression, and uneven distribution of resources" (para. 3.19, p. 23). It is no surprise that such language raises concern among some Americans, partly because the empirical basis for the claim is shaky, but even more so because it raises concerns about a future in which an income distribution as unequal as that in the United States could trigger a UN-backed intervention to "prevent" armed conflict.[17] For R2P to be attractive to rich nations like the United States this language will have to be carefully considered.

In addition to casting crimes against humanity as resulting from economic inequalities, the UN tends to approach rights as outcomes—the right to prosperity, for example—while the United States approaches rights in terms of process—the right to equal opportunity. To the political leadership of the United States, human rights follow from a free and open market. Discrimination in employment and pay diminishes as employers find it costly to discriminate, and collective bargaining is unnecessary in an open market. Child labor will decline when investment in schooling has sufficient return, and so on. The United States has not signed on to many of the important International Labor Organization (ILO) conventions on economic and social rights because these are contrary to American open-market policies.

The United States and other rich countries have many options for intervening when it is in their interest. Because the United States can intervene on its own or form coalitions outside the UN with friendly nations who share a common identity and interests, it has little motivation to enter into or adhere to a constraining agreement for intervention, even in the case of atrocity crimes. Furthermore, the fact that the United States will sometimes intervene unilaterally or with ad hoc coalitions means that other nations also have less motivation to join a binding agreement.[18] When other nations are deciding whether to support R2P they will weigh the probability that they will usually agree with U.S. actions. If they think that they will almost always agree with the American view, they will be happy not to support

R2P and instead let the United States assume all the costs for interventions. If they think they often will oppose the United States, they will support a formal agreement that would commit the United States to help support interventions that it would not otherwise support.

In deciding whether to ratify an agreement that imposes a responsibility to protect the United States will face a trade-off. On the one hand, if it does not sign on to such an agreement it could have the benefit of independence in deciding how to respond to atrocity crimes, but it also incurs the costs of acting alone or building ad hoc coalitions when it wants to intervene to stop atrocity crimes and the political costs when it does not. On the other hand, if it does sign on to such an agreement it could have the benefits of multilateral support in the cases where it supports intervention to stop atrocity crimes, but it suffers a loss of policy control and incurs the costs associated with interventions that it does not support.

One option for the most powerful nations is to approve an agreement on R2P and then obstruct its implementation when it suits their interests. This would provide the appearance of international cooperation and a commitment to moral principles and actions that are widely supported. But given the current structure of the UN, such an agreement would hardly constrain the future actions of a powerful nation. The United States is not the only country for whom this is an attractive option. The U.S.'s ability to thwart international organizations—preventing Security Council action in Rwanda, refusing to adhere to the landmine ban agreed to in the Ottawa Convention on Landmines, refusing to ratify the International Criminal Court Statute, and refusing to pay its UN dues—is strong evidence that a small group of nations, and in this case one nation, can obstruct international cooperation and block extensions of global governance. On the other hand, both the International Criminal Court (ICC) and the Ottawa Convention are evidence that it is possible, under some circumstances, to circumvent even the most powerful nation to achieve international goals. The rest of the world can choose a "do it together but without the United States" strategy or it can try to bring pressure on the United States to join a serious international attempt to eliminate atrocity crimes.

The history of international relations includes contradictory principles that lead to confusion regarding the rights and responsibilities of the international community. The principles of national sovereignty and nonaggression agreements are in conflict with the principles of protecting innocents in other countries. The history of nations competing for power and resources conflicts with the need for cooperation to save lives. The UN was established to promote peace, but it needs to include military intervention in its tool kit for doing so. There is no entirely optimal solution for the problem of atrocity crimes, but R2P is the best chance we have.

Notes

* Susan E. Mayer is the dean of the Harris School of Public Policy Studies at the University of Chicago in Chicago, Illinois.

1. Some people would like to expand the list of circumstances that would call for international intervention under R2P to include nonviolent humanitarian crises such as starvation and epidemics that a nation will not or cannot contain. This is likely to be unacceptable to an international community that is not yet ready to move far from the principle of national sovereignty as it is currently accepted in international law. International agreement about what forms of violence are covered is essential to implementation of R2P. This issue is addressed in David Scheffer's essay in this book. However, I avoid that discussion in this chapter.

2. International organizations could be considered "collective state" rather than nonstate actors. If international organizations were all democratic organizations with equal representation, they might act as collective state actors. However, I consider them nonstate actors because many, if not most, international organizations do not have equal representation, and they can and often do act autonomously and in conflict with the views of member states.

3. While the concept of national sovereignty is widely accepted, the principle of a "just war" has regained support in recent years. A just war is one that is declared by a legitimate authority, is motivated by a "just" intention such as protecting the weak, is declared as a last resort, adheres to moderation and proportionality, and has a reasonable chance for success. To admit military intervention as one of the "tools" for enforcing R2P requires some adherence to the concept of a just war.

4. See http://www.thechicagocouncil.org/UserFiles/File/POS_Topline%20Reports/POS%202004/US%20Public%20Opinion%20Global_Views_2004US.pdf. See also http://www.americansworld.org/digest/regional_issues/africa/africa4.cfm.

5. Emphasis added. The greater number of respondents supporting military intervention in Europe does not seem to reflect racist feelings but rather a belief that intervention is more successful in Europe. See http://www.americans-world.org/digest/regional_issues/africa/africa4.cfm.

6. See http://www.crisisgroup.org/home/index.cfm.

7. Global Views 2006 Team, *The United States and the Rise of China and India: Results of a 2006 Multination Survey of Public Opinion* (Chicago: Chicago Council on Global Affairs, 2006), http://www.thechicagocouncil.org/dynamic_page.php?id=56.

8. Public opinion alone cannot be depended upon to influence the actions of the U.S. government. The same poll shows that 71 percent of Americans think

that the United States should participate in the agreement on the International Criminal Court and 70 percent believe the United States should participate in the Kyoto agreement to reduce global warming.

9. This figure was reported by the UN Office for the Coordination of Humanitarian Affairs and is available at http://www.irinnews.org/webspecials/RightsAndReconciliation/54233.asp.

10. In its 2007 *World Report,* Human Rights Watch called for Europe to assume the lead in human rights issues. See "Stop the Bleeding of American Legitimacy" by Patrick Cronin, June 2006, available at http://www.cceia.org/resources/ethics_online/5381.html. The *Christian Science Monitor* (http://www.csmonitor.com/2006/0615/dailyUpdate.html) and the *Guardian* are just two of the many newspapers that have decried the loss of U.S. credibility in human rights issues. Note that the U.S. violation of human rights at Guantanamo and Abu Ghrab exacerbated what was already a slide in U.S. credibility.

11. See Kenneth W. Abbott and Duncan Snidal, "Why States Act Through Formal International Organizations," *Journal of Conflict Resolution* 42, no. 1 (1998): 3–32 for a broad description of the benefits to nations of acting through international organizations.

12. See Christopher Hemmer and Peter Katzenstein, "Why Is There No NATO in Asia? Collective Identity, Regionalism, and the Origins of Multilateralism," *International Organization* 56, no. 3 (2002): 575–607.

13. See Alastair Johnston, "Treating International Institutions as Social Environments," *International Studies Quarterly* 45 (2001): 487–515; Alexander Wendt, "Anarchy Is What States Make of It," *International Organization* 46, no. 2 (1992): 391–426.

14. See Russell Sobel, "Exchange Rate Evidence on the Effectiveness of United Nations Policy," *Public Choice* 95, no. 1–2 (1998): 1–25.

15. For a discussion of current global governance issues, see Craig Murphy, "Global Governance: Poorly Done and Poorly Understood," *International Affairs* 76, no. 4 (2000): 789–803.

16. Ibid., for a discussion of the consequences of unequal power in global governance.

17. See William Felice, "The Viability of the United Nations Approach to Economic and Social Human Rights in a Globalized Economy," *International Affairs* 75, no. 3 (1999): 563–98.

18. See Erik Voeten, "Outside Options and the Logic of Security Council Action," *American Political Science Review* 95, no. 4 (2001): 845–58.

4

Toward a Jewish Argument for the Responsibility to Protect

*Aaron Dorfman and Ruth Messinger**

Articulating a definitive Jewish perspective on any issue, no matter how seemingly straightforward, is a fraught enterprise. While there are certain fundamental realms of agreement for most Jews, diversity of opinion is in many ways the *sine qua non* of Jewish communal identity. As the old Jewish joke goes, for every two Jews, there are three opinions. Given that tendency to disagree, it should come as no surprise that an issue as complicated and rooted in contemporary geopolitics as the "responsibility to protect" does not produce a consensus position from the entire Jewish community. Nonetheless, we believe that there is a compelling argument to be made in support of the responsibility to protect, grounded in a rigorous reading of Jewish text and supported by the particular arc of Jewish historical experience.

We believe that the Jewish roots of this commitment to actively protect others are twofold. First, Jewish text and tradition clearly express the imperative for bystanders to intervene to protect human life. From our earliest biblical tales, even before the giving of the Ten Commandments, there is a consistent narrative thread that asserts the primacy of human life. From that thread emerges the principle that Jews must not only refrain from committing crimes of violence against others or from being complicit in those crimes as passive bystanders but also that Jews must actively intervene when confronted with the knowledge that such crimes are being committed. While many of the laws and stories that constitute this literature of intervention are cast narrowly around protecting Jewish victims, we argue in this chapter that the overall ethic is a universal one and, certainly in our time, must be universally applied.

Second, Jewish national identity is grounded in a history of empathy and solidarity with the oppressed. The Jewish people emerged from Egyptian slavery into nationhood with a particular mandate to "befriend the stranger, for you were strangers in the land of Egypt."[1] This founding Jewish narrative is one of extrapolating from our own historical experience of oppression to a commitment to stand in solidarity with other victims of oppression. The particular experience of the Holocaust and its aftermath fits clearly inside this historical framework and is captured in the simplest and most straightforward terms by the slogan "Never again!"

The Obligation to Save Human Life in Jewish Text and Tradition

Establishing the Value of Human Life

The primacy of human life is one of the central themes of the Bible's story of creation. In the text itself, human beings are deliberately identified as being created in the image of God. Later rabbinic commentaries read great meaning into the creation of the first human being in the image of God. These rabbis write, "For this reason the first human being was created alone: to teach that anyone who destroys a single life, it is as though he has destroyed an entire world, and anyone who saves a single life, it is as if he has saved an entire world."[2] Each human being, therefore, has infinite and equal value—the value of an entire world.

The idea that each person is equivalent to an entire world stems in part from our capacity to procreate: to the extent that each human being sits at the apex of a potentially infinitely branching family tree, each of us is the potential progenitor of an entire world of people. Ultimately, however, the notion that human beings are infinitely valuable does not rely on our capacity or choice to procreate. Our infinite worth stems from our being created in the image of God. Each of us has a spark of the divine. By necessary logical extension, then, killing a human being is a crime that not only encompasses ending a particular person's life and eradicating the possible existence of all of his or her potential descendents but is also tantamount to the murder of a part of God. Murder, in Jewish tradition, has a markedly dimension of deicide.

"You shall not stand idly by the blood of your neighbor"

This effectively infinite valuation of human life has multiple legal implications. First and foremost among them is the prohibition of murder, stated most clearly in the Ten Commandments: "You shall not murder."[3]

Beyond that prohibition of murder, and more relevant for our purposes, there is a clearly defined positive obligation to intervene to protect human life. The source for this obligation is the Holiness Code in Leviticus, where the text reads, "Do not stand idly by your neighbor's blood."[4] The Bible itself does not provide a detailed explication of the extent of this obligation, but later commentaries do.

The Babylonian Talmud offers a series of specific cases as a way of exploring the extent of this obligation: "From where in Scripture do we learn that if a person sees his friend drowning in a river, or being dragged by a wild animal, or being attacked by bandits, that person is obligated to rescue him? This is the meaning of 'Do not stand idly by your neighbor's blood.'"[5]

This text is an inquiry into the principle that underlies a series of existing "good Samaritan" statutes. In each of these cases, the rabbis understood the bystander's positive obligation to intervene as an application of the biblical principle that you may "not stand idly by your neighbor's blood."

The great medieval Jewish thinker, Rabbi Moses ben Maimon (also known as Maimonides) codified the principle among his list of 613 commandments. Using the Leviticus text as a foundation, he states, "The 297th Commandment is that we are prohibited from being passive in saving the life of one who is in danger of dying or being lost if we are in a position to save him or her."[6]

Not only does Jewish law definitively establish this obligation to prevent the loss of human life, it places it above virtually every other Jewish responsibility. In one of the most famous passages of the Babylonian Talmud we read, "There is nothing that can preempt [the duty of] saving human life, with the exception of [the prohibitions of] idolatry, incest, and murder [which are prohibited in all situations]."[7] In other words, Jewish law demands that a person must not only save human life but may actively breach nearly every other Jewish precept in order to do so.

Rescuing the Pursued From the Pursuer,
"Even If It Is Necessary to Kill the Pursuer"

Once the positive obligation to protect human life is established, the question arises of what we are permitted or obliged to do to confront a perpetrator— one who intends to take human life. This brings us to the set of laws governing a *rodef*. Literally translated as "one who gives chase," a *rodef* is understood as a person who pursues another with the intent to do harm.[8] Maimonides defines the essence of the statute in his *Laws of Murderers and the Protection of Life*. He writes: "When, however, one person is pursuing another with the intention of killing him—even if the pursuer is a minor—every Jewish person is commanded to [attempt to] save the person being pursued, even if it is necessary to kill the pursuer."[9] Maimonides extends this responsibility to include other individuals acting on his or her behalf: "Similarly, [this commandment applies] when a person sees someone drowning at sea or being attacked by robbers or a wild animal, he himself can save the victim, or can hire others to save him."[10] With this, Maimonides expands the obligation to protect over and beyond just those people one can save directly. So long as one "sees" the person at risk, one is obliged to save him, even if the rescue demands the intervention of a third party.

In the same section of this code, Maimonides reiterates the 297th commandment: "Whenever a person can save another person's life, but fails to do so, that person transgresses a negative commandment, as [Lev. 19:16] states: 'Do not stand idly by the blood of your neighbor.'"[11] In other words, the responsibility to protect someone from death is both a positive commandment to save a life and a negative admonition not to refrain from saving a life where one sees a person at risk of death.

The Sefer HaChinukh, a medieval text that offers a detailed explication of the 613 commandments, rearticulates Maimonides' imperative, stating:

> We Jews have been commanded to rescue the pursued from the hands of any who pursue them with intent to kill, if necessary at the cost of the pursuer's life. . . . Among the roots of this commandment is that God, who is blessed, created the world and willed that it be settled, and the settlement of the world is upheld by the championing of the weak against those stronger. Furthermore, the pursued will always have eyes and heart turned toward God to champion him against his pursuer, as Scripture says, "The Lord will seek out the pursued," meaning that the pursued seeks God and prays to God. Therefore God who is blessed has commanded us to assist the pursued.[12]

This thirteenth century text frames the obligation to protect in radically theological terms: God prefers those who are pursued, and those who are pursued are more likely to turn to God. Beyond inserting the theological into this equation, the text also understands the responsibility to protect in a particularly communal context: as Jews, we are specifically obliged to champion the weak. Finally, this text offers a categorical preference for the pursued against the pursuer, an argument that will be echoed below in the section titled "'Never Again' in historical context."

Anticipating and Preventing Potential Threats

Beyond stating this clear responsibility to intervene in a "murder in progress," Jewish law also prescribes the obligation to anticipate and prevent potential threats to human life. This is of particular salience since the responsibility to protect (R2P) movement identifies prevention among its core principles as "the single most important dimension of the responsibility to protect."[13]

The key source for this obligation to anticipate and prevent dangers is found in a relatively minor Biblical building code that reads, "And you shall build a guardrail for your roof, so that you do not bring 'bloodguilt' on your house if anyone should fall from it."[14] Conceived in a time and place of houses with flat roofs, this statute suggests that a homeowner must take preventive action to mitigate the risk that someone might fall from his or her roof and die.

From this relatively narrow and innocuous stipulation, Maimonides derives a comprehensive ethic for the protection and preservation of human life. First, Maimonides broadens the guardrail requirement and states that "any object that might pose a mortal danger requires that the owner take action."[15] In so doing, Maimonides greatly expands the Bible's limited roof-building requirement to include the responsibility of the owner to ensure that his or her property does not pose *any* mortal danger. According to Maimonides' precept, a homeowner is responsible for ensuring the safety of those who are in his or her house. (In this broad assignment of liability, we hear antecedent echoes of the legal principle of "attractive nuisance," which, in American jurisprudence, requires homeowners to cover their swimming pools [lest children fall into them and drown] and remove the doors from abandoned refrigerators [lest children playing hide-and-go-seek become trapped inside and suffocate]).

Second, and much more ambitiously, Maimonides expands the guardrail principle to demand the *removal* of objects that might threaten death. He writes, "Similarly, it is a positive commandment to remove any obstacle that could pose a danger to life, and to be very careful regarding these matters, as [Deut. 4:9] states: 'Beware for yourself; and guard your soul.' If a person leaves a dangerous obstacle and does not remove it, he fails to observe a positive commandment, and violates [the negative commandment]: 'Do not cause blood [to be spilled].'"[16]

In this passage, Maimonides sums up a broader duty to protect those around us—not only to ensure that the spaces we own are safe from harm, but also to actively remove any sources of danger we may encounter in our comings and goings.

Bystander Intervention in Practice—The Roots of
Moses' Leadership and Moral Authority

In addition to the laws that reify this underlying commitment to the preservation of human life, the Bible records narratives, called *aggadah*, which tell stories of people intervening to prevent the loss of human life. Perhaps the most interesting of these for our purposes is a series of brief episodes that describe the arc of Moses' development as a leader qualified to free the Israelites from slavery in Egypt. The first lines in the Bible that deal with Moses as an adult recount a series of his encounters with violence and conflict:

> Some time after that, when Moses had grown up, he went out to his kinsfolk and witnessed their labors. He saw an Egyptian beating a Hebrew, one of his kinsmen. He turned this way and that and, seeing no one about, he struck down the Egyptian and hid him in the sand. When he went out the next day, he found two Hebrews fighting; so he said to the offender, "Why do you strike your fellow?" He retorted, "Who made you chief and ruler over us? Do you mean to kill me as you killed the Egyptian?" Moses was frightened, and thought: Then the matter is known! When Pharaoh learned of the matter, he sought to kill Moses; but Moses fled from Pharaoh. He arrived in the land of Midian, and sat down beside a well. Now the priest of Midian had seven daughters. They came to draw water, and filled the troughs to water their father's flock; but shepherds came and drove them off. Moses rose to their defense, and he watered their flock.[17]

An eighteenth century commentator, Haketav v'Hakabalah, offers a creative reading of the first episode, in which Moses slays the Egyptian. A literal translation of the Hebrew reads "Moses turned this way and that and saw that there wasn't a person, an *eesh*, and struck the Egyptian." Haketav v'Hakabalah argues that, when Moses looked about, what he saw was not an absence of people, but of a human being willing to take action to save the life of another human being. To be fully human, to be an *eesh*, therefore is to take action to defend the victim.

It is only after all three of these events that Moses is selected by God as a leader of sufficient moral authority to ensure the liberation of the Israelites from Pharaoh's genocidal oppression. Among the necessary qualifications for him to assume his role as the greatest leader in Jewish history is his capacity to expand his universe of obligation to encompass threatened people with whom he has no apparent relationship other than shared humanity.

Rabbi Jacob Emden (eighteenth century, Germany) draws a much broader lesson from this story. He writes, "A Jew with political responsibility (*adam chashuv*) has the obligation to rescue the oppressed from the hands of the oppressor by all means available to him, whether by direct action or through political effort, regardless of whether the oppressed is Jewish. So Job praised himself by saying, 'I have broken the teeth of evil,' and the Torah says of Moses that 'He rose to their defense,' referring to the daughters of Jethro, even though they were the daughters of an idolatrous priest."[18]

Emden's declaration is predicated on the Jewish responsibility to protect non-Jews. This all-inclusive notion of obligation to encompass all people is fundamental to establishing a broad Jewish mandate for R2P, particularly because Emden articulated it at a time when Jewish political power was far less than it is today.

Never Again—Embracing Empathic Justice

These ethical and legal traditions present a moral obligation to guide our actions toward those who are suffering, and specifically those who are at risk of needless death. They do not, however, entirely explain the Jewish community's particular responsibility to respond to atrocity crimes. The unique historical experience of the Jewish community and its relationship to persecution and, in particular, genocide, has had a profound effect on the Jewish view of the responsibility to protect.

"Never Again" in Historical Context

In building a particularly Jewish case for intervention to prevent genocide, we must refer to the legacy of the Holocaust. This section will explore the place that the Holocaust occupies in shaping Jewish antigenocide activism.

The simplest starting place for exploring this relationship is the phrase "Never Again." The phrase originated with Abba Kovner, a Jewish partisan leader during the Holocaust, who stated: "Never again would Jewish blood be spilled unavenged." In its original form, the phrase functioned as a particular rallying cry for Holocaust survivors, a repudiation of their characterization as passive victims of the Nazis. It still holds this narrow meaning when it is used in response to anti-Semitic incidents or to galvanize Jewish communal unity in the face of real and perceived threats.

Over time, however, the words have come to include a broader commitment among both Jews and non-Jews to respond to atrocity crimes committed against any people. In 1979, President Carter declared: "We must forge an unshakable oath with all civilized people that never again will the world stand silent, never again will the world fail to act in time to prevent this terrible crime of genocide."[19] In 1999, Elie Wiesel invoked the phrase to challenge the commitment of U.S. leadership to respond to genocide by saying, "Is today's justified intervention in Kosovo . . . a lasting warning that never again will the deportation, the terrorization of children and their parents be allowed anywhere in the world?"[20]

In this more universal form, "Never Again" can be understood as a continuation of a much older Jewish narrative that traces its roots to the experience of the liberation of the Israelites from Egypt. In this context, "Never Again" functions as a contemporary parallel to the Biblical mandate, "You shall not oppress a stranger, for you know the feelings of the stranger, having yourselves been strangers in the land of Egypt."[21] With this admonition, repeated more frequently than any other, the Torah codifies for Jews a notion of empathetic justice.

The profound meaning behind "Never Again" is essentially the same. Because the Jewish people experienced genocide firsthand and were abandoned by the international community in their time of greatest need, Jews have a particular moral obligation to ensure that genocide is prevented. This invocation of past Jewish suffering to motivate contemporary Jewish activism is evident in a Jewish response to the Armenian genocide, which took place in 1915–16. Avshalom Feinberg, a leader of the Nili Group, a Jewish spy network that helped the British during World War I by gathering information on the Turkish army in Palestine, wrote of the destruction befalling Armenians, "I also asked myself if I have the right to weep 'over the tragedy of the daughter of my people' only, and whether Jeremiah did not shed tears of blood for the Armenians as well?! . . . it is imperative that a son of that ancient race which has laughed at pain, overcome torture and refused to give in to death for the last two thousand years, should stand up."[22]

Feinberg lays out a pre-Holocaust mandate for Jewish opposition to the as-yet-unnamed genocide of the Armenians. This mandate is grounded not in the Holocaust experience (which it predates), but in the much more ancient experience of anti-Semitism and related violence that culminated in the Holocaust some thirty years later.

The overwhelming catastrophe of the Holocaust, however, infuses this ancient ethic with renewed urgency and immediacy. The survivor-witnesses invoke the moral authority of their own experiences in the concentration camps to condemn the perpetrators of other genocides and to stand in solidarity with the victims. Nesse Godin, a Holocaust survivor and educator, describes her experience during the Holocaust as an education in empathy that inspires, even demands, her activism on behalf of the victims of the genocide in Darfur. She writes, "as the world is commemorating the 60th anniversary of the . . . liberation of the concentration camps, my thoughts are not only about the horrors of Europe's past but also about Africa's present . . . about the people of Darfur, Sudan . . . who need our help. My heart goes out to these human beings who are being attacked because of who they are . . . As someone who lived through the horrors of the Holocaust, and as a human being who believes we must never forget, I cannot remain silent."[23]

Elie Wiesel, the foremost spokesman of the survivor generation, repeatedly invokes the Holocaust to demand the involvement of his fellow Jews as well as that of world leaders who vacillate when faced with contemporary genocides. On May 5, 1993, Wiesel spoke at the dedication of the U.S. Holocaust Museum and delivered a thunderous moral rebuke to then-President Bill Clinton. Samantha Power writes of the dramatic public demand for military intervention in the genocide in Bosnia in the early 1990s put forth by a unified American Jewish establishment: "The American Jewish Committee, the American Jewish Congress, and the Anti-Defamation League published a joint advertisement in the *New York Times* headlined, "Stop the Death Camps."[24]

These repeated references to the Holocaust serve as a reminder of the consequences of failing to act to prevent genocide. In effect, calling up images of the Holocaust in the context of other atrocity crimes is an effort to declare, "Look what happened last time we remained bystanders—let's not allow that to happen again."

Bringing These Teachings Home:
Judaism's View on R2P

Taken together, this collection of laws and stories, the two threads of *halakhah* and *aggadah*, and the particular Jewish historical experience provide us with a fairly comprehensive Jewish perspective on the responsibility to protect. To review:

By telling us that God created human beings in God's image, the Bible in Genesis establishes the infinite value and uniqueness of human life. The inverse of this is also implied: because every human being carries the essence of the divine, murder has an element of deicide.

Perhaps because of this sense of the infinite worth of every person, the Bible in Leviticus commands us not to stand idly by the blood of our neighbor. The rabbis of the Talmud take the basic precept of obligation and extrapolate from it the principle that we must rescue someone if we see him or her in a life-or-death situation.

When confronted with the question of whether one may break a commandment to save a human life, the Talmud answers with a resounding "Yes," declaring that we are not just permitted to breach laws but are in fact obligated to do so.

Having established a broad commitment to saving a life, Jewish law then stretches the bounds of the limitations of that principle. Based on the law of *rodef,* Maimonides narrows the "murder" exception by excluding situations in which one sees someone being chased and at risk of being killed. In that situation, Maimonides states, a pursuer must be killed in order to save the life of the pursued. The Bible, according to Maimonides, thus lays out a dual requirement to save a life and not to refrain from saving a life if a person is at risk of death. The Sefer HaChinukh imbues the conversation with a communal overtone, arguing that, as Jews, we have a unique obligation to protect the pursued.

Maimonides expands the idea of protection to include not just those who are pursued, but all those who cross one's path. The Bible's regulation in Deuteronomy regarding the building of a guardrail around one's roof to prevent "bloodguilt" on one's house should anyone should fall from it is transformed by Maimonides into a broader obligation to ensure the safety of those who are in or around one's home, both by protecting against latent dangers and removing possible risks.

Biblical stories of Moses becoming a leader illustrate these principles. These stories are read by commentators to teach profound lessons about our obligations to each other. Haketav v'Hakabalah teaches that being fully human requires taking action to defend the pursued. Rabbi Jacob Emden tells us that it does not matter whether the pursued is a Jew or not—all people are human beings created in God's image and we are obligated to protect their lives if they are in danger. These laws and traditions serve as the backdrop to a thousand-year-old history relating to persecution and genocide that has become encapsulated in a commitment to protecting the stranger and, more recently, to the universally applicable principle, "Never Again."

Together, these shape the Jewish view on the responsibility to protect: Once we become aware that human life is at risk, we become responsible for the defense of potential victims of atrocity crimes.

Challenges Related to Globalization

It is important to note two particular obstacles to applying these ancient laws to the contemporary challenges of atrocity crimes. First, almost all of the examples given are framed in terms of the individual—one is obligated to save *a single* human life. While it is not entirely obvious that one can extrapolate from the local obligation of rescuing a neighbor who is drowning in a lake to the global obligation to, for example, protect internally displaced persons (IDPs) in Darfur, we believe that the traditional Jewish understanding of this issue can make a uniquely valuable contribution to the discourse of protection. Furthermore, the Jewish focus on the intrinsic value of each individual human life can also serve as a corrective to one of the core challenges of responding to the enormity of genocide: the moral paralysis that often results from the overwhelming scale of atrocity crimes and the barrage of news related to suffering around the world.

The essayist Annie Dillard uses the term "compassion fatigue" to describe this particular form of moral and political paralysis in the face of overwhelming suffering. In an article on the phenomenon, Paul Slovic, a professor at the University of Oregon, writes, "This same incapacity [to feel the shared humanity of large numbers of people] is echoed by Nobel prize winning biochemist Albert Szent Gyorgi as he struggles to comprehend the possible consequences of nuclear war: 'I am deeply moved if I see one man suffering and would risk my life for him. Then I talk impersonally about the possible pulverization of our big cities, with a hundred million dead. I am unable to multiply one man's suffering by a hundred million.'"[25]

The Jewish emphasis on identifying personal suffering and focusing on the individual victim instead of on mass graves reminds us that action on behalf of millions will always be more difficult to inspire and sustain than action on behalf of unique individuals. Jewish law does the same by reminding us not to despair of making a difference when confronted with the world of suffering, but to focus instead on each human being, who is as valuable as a whole world, and to take action, one infinitely valuable person at a time.

The second intertwined, but distinct, challenge to the applicability of these ancient laws is the impact of global interconnection, or as we at American Jewish World Service occasionally put it, "Am I my brother's keeper if my brother lives halfway 'round the world?" The Torah, the Talmudic rabbis, and the writers of the medieval codes of Jewish law delineated rules and ethical principles for a narrowly circumscribed world; they could never have anticipated the Internet or the 747. The world we live in has been made exponentially more accessible through international travel and instantaneous media exposure, making it hard to know how to apply what were once very local ethical prescriptions on a global scale.

Rabbi Jonathan Sacks, writing in *The Dignity of Difference*, clearly captures this challenge:

David Hume noted that our sense of empathy diminishes as we move outward from the members of our family to our neighbors, our society and the world. Traditionally, our sense of involvement with the fate of others has been in inverse proportion to the distance separating us and them. What has changed is that television and the Internet have effectively abolished distance. They have brought images of suffering in far-off lands into our immediate experience. Our sense of compassion for the victims of poverty, war and famine, runs ahead of our capacity to act. Our moral sense is simultaneously activated and frustrated. We feel that something should be done, but what, how, and by whom?[26]

Hume confronts one of the great dilemmas posed by modern life—the ethical consequences of an infinitely expanding universe of obligation. How do we maintain a sense of compassion, balanced by a sense of ourselves as capable of taking effective action, given the global challenges inherent in the need to respond to atrocity crimes all over the planet?

A First Attempt at a Solution

Jewish tradition offers a compelling, if extremely demanding answer. In Deuteronomy we find a set of laws governing the *met mitzvah*, a term for a murder victim whose body is found in the wilderness. According to the text, the elders of the town nearest the body should come to the site, sacrifice a heifer, and "make this declaration: 'Our hands did not shed this blood, nor did our eyes see it done. Absolve, God, Your people Israel whom You redeemed, and do not let guilt for the blood of the innocent remain among Your people Israel.'"[27]

In reflecting on this statement, rabbinic commentators noted a troubling element in the statement—the elders' declaration seems to be a profession of innocence, as if the community might suspect that they themselves committed the crime. It would be as though every time a dead body was found in a nearby unincorporated suburb, we would make the mayor of the city publicly declare his or her blamelessness. But of course we would not suspect our town elders or mayors of having committed every random crime that happens near the city limits. What, therefore, does the elders' statement mean?

Responding to this challenge, the rabbis interpret the declaration with a slight variation in meaning. Instead of reading it as, "We didn't do it," they teach that it should be read as, "He came not into our hands that we should have dismissed him without sustenance, and we did not see him and leave him without escort!"[28] In other words, the elders indicate that they had no knowledge that the victim was nearby and vulnerable, for if they had known and had still failed to protect him, they would have been culpable for his death because of their failure to act.

The story suggests two related parameters for the extent of our responsibility: (1) when we know someone is in danger, we must ensure his or her safety, and (2) our obligation is proportional to our capacity to affect the outcome. As the Babylonian Talmud explains, "Whoever can prevent his household from committing a sin but does not, is responsible for the sins of his household; if he can prevent his fellow citizens, he is responsible for the sins of his fellow citizens; if the whole world, he is responsible for the sins of the whole world."[29]

But where does this leave us? Even in the face of proportionate obligation, given the weight of our political and economic influence, we should be, in some sense, infinitely obligated to act. Yet the challenges of globalization, compassion fatigue, and distance from those in need are real, and our capacity, let alone our will, is not infinite. How can we take these texts and translate them into a powerful, but realistic call to action?

Mustering the Will to Act

The nations of the world have always found excuses for their failures to intervene in genocide. With the Armenians and the Jews, the prosecution of world wars served as sufficient justification for inaction. In Cambodia, cold war geopolitics and Vietnam fatigue weakened the international response. The Somalia debacle and its aftermath left the Clinton administration unwilling to intervene in Rwanda, and without U.S. leadership the rest of the world effectively ignored the slaughter of 800,000 Tutsi. Only in the Balkans—where the specter of concentration camps on European soil eventually proved too much to bear—and only after several years of dithering and the killing of several hundred thousand Bosnian Muslims did the international community finally rouse itself and apply its authority and resources to intervene in a genocide in progress.

So how do we "muster" the will and keep the discussion from being cloistered in books and academic debates? We offer one final story from Jewish tradition. The holidays of Purim and Passover fall close to one another in the Jewish calendar and there is a notable parallel in the two stories that speaks to our challenge. In the Purim story, the Jewish Queen Esther is reluctant to accept her role as the savior of her people. Her husband, the king, has been duped into authorizing the murder of all the Jews of Persia. Esther's uncle warns her of the plan and informs her that she is the only person in a position to prevent the impending genocide. She demurs, but he encourages her by saying, "And who knows if it is not for just this moment that you became Queen."[30]

Likewise in the Passover story, when God attempts to call Moses to lead the Israelites to freedom, Moses replies, "Who am I that I should go to Pharaoh and free the Israelites from Egypt?"[31] He protests that the people will not believe him and that he is not a man of words. God tries to reassure him with arguments and miracles until Moses finally implores, "Please, God, make someone else your agent."[32]

Moses' reluctance is referred to powerfully in a later rabbinic story that recounts how both before the parting of the Red Sea and again at Mount Sinai, Moses stood by passively until God intervened and said, "If you will not act, no one will act." Finally, after the Tabernacle was completed, as Moses once again stood to the side, God finally lost patience and demanded, "Until when will you keep yourself low? The hour waits only for you!"

Our ancestors Esther and Moses were reluctant to take up their historical responsibility. What distinguishes them, and what must inspire us, is that they overcame their reluctance. Even as we debate the finer ethical points of international law, atrocity crimes continue. And the hour waits only for us.

Notes

* Aaron Dorfman is the director of education at the American Jewish World Service (AJWS) in New York. Ruth Messinger is the president of AJWS.
1. Deut. 10:19.
2. Gen. 1:27.
3. Exod. 20:13.
4. Lev. 19:16.
5. Babylonian Talmud Sanhedrin 73a, translation from Edah, "The Jewish Obligation to Prevent Genocide in Darfur." http://www.edah.org/darfur sources.pdf.
6. Maimonides, *Book of Commandments*, Negative Commandment 297, trans. Aaron Dorfman.
7. Babylonian Talmud Yoma 82a.
8. The laws of the *rodef* are derived from Biblical verses that absolve a homeowner of "bloodguilt" if he kills an intruder he reasonably expects intends to do him harm. Exod. 22:1–3.
9. Maimonides, *Mishneh Torah*, Laws of the Murderer and Protecting Life, 1:6.
10. Ibid., 1:14.
11. Ibid.
12. Sefer HaChinukh (thirteenth-century Barcelona), Commandment 600: Promoting Peace in the World—Yishuv HaOlam, Edah. See note 6.

13. International Commission on Intervention and State Sovereignty (ICISS), *The Responsibility to Protect* (Ottawa: International Development Research Center, 2001), http://www.iciss.ca/pdf/commission-report.pdf.
14. Deut. 22:8.
15. *Mishneh Torah*, Laws of the Murderer and Protecting Life, 11:4.
16. Ibid.
17. Exod. 2:11–17.
18. Rabbi Jacob Emden, Responsa Sh'eilat Yaavetz 2:51, adapted from Edah. See note 6.
19. Jimmy Carter, *President's Commission on the Holocaust: Remarks on Receiving the Final Report of the Commission* (September 27, 1979), http://www .presidency.ucsb.edu/ws/index.php?pid=31430&st=&st1=, quoted in Samantha Power, *A Problem from Hell: America and the Age of Genocide* (New York: HarperCollins, 2002), xxi.
20. Elie Wiesel, "The Perils of Indifference" (speech, April 12, 1999), http:// www.historyplace.com/speeches/wiesel.htm.
21. Exod. 23:9.
22. Yair Auron, "Zionist and Israeli Attitudes Toward the Armenian Genocide," in *In God's Name: Genocide and Religion in the Twentieth Century*, ed. Omer Bartov and Phyllis Mack (New York: Berghahn Books, 2001), 273.
23. Nesse Godin, JTA News Service, "Act now in Darfur," Jewish News of Greater Phoenix, May 6, 2005.
24. Samantha Power. See note 19, p. 278, quoting "Stop the Death Camps: An Open Letter to World Leaders," *New York Times*, August 5, 1992, p. A14.
25. Paul Slovic, "'If I Look at the Mass I Will Never Act': Psychic Numbing and Genocide," *Judgment and Decision Making* 2, no. 2 (2007): 1–17, http:// journal.sjdm.org/7303a/jdm7303a.htm.
26. Rabbi Jonathan Sacks, *The Dignity of Difference How to Avoid the Clash of Civilizations* (London, New York: Continuum, 2002), 30.
27. Deut. 21:7–8.
28. Mishnah Sotah 9:6.
29. Babylonian Talmud Shabbat 54b.
30. Esther 4:14.
31. Exodus 3:11.
32. Exodus 4:13.

5

Atrocity Crimes
Framing the Responsibility
to Protect

*David Scheffer**

The principle of the "responsibility to protect" (R2P) has achieved, within a remarkably short span of time, a rhetorical presence in international politics and international law that has invited both praise and skepticism.[1] In its simplest and most widely accepted formulation, R2P represents the responsibility of governments and the international community to protect populations from genocide, war crimes, ethnic cleansing, and crimes against humanity—all of which are categories of significant crimes that should be designated as *atrocity crimes*, both for purposes of accuracy when describing the basket of relevant crimes and for simplicity as a means of communicating with the global populace. In this chapter I will examine what is meant by each of these categories of crimes and by the unifying term, atrocity crimes. An understanding of the legal basis for R2P must underpin efforts to activate the principles of R2P on the world stage. In reality, not all atrocity crimes, particularly some categories of crimes against humanity and war crimes, necessarily justify military intervention as the most extreme application of R2P. Drawing the line between atrocity crimes that would merit and those that would lack justification for military intervention when all else fails under R2P could become an extremely difficult task in world affairs. However, it should be possible to outline in this chapter a preliminary rationale for drawing that line and thus create a basis for the pragmatic and legally sound implementation of the many different measures (diplomatic, political, economic, and military) of R2P.

Contemporary Evolution of R2P

When, by consensus vote on September 16, 2005, the United Nations (UN) General Assembly confirmed the application of R2P in world affairs, it did so with a very sharp focus on atrocity crimes as the *sole* predicate for implementing R2P. The 2005 World Summit Outcome declaration states in paragraph 138: "Each individual State has the responsibility to protect its populations from genocide, war crimes, ethnic cleansing and crimes against humanity. This responsibility entails the prevention of such crimes, including their incitement, through appropriate and necessary means. We accept that responsibility and will act in accordance with it."[2] Then, in paragraph 139 of the 2005 World Summit Outcome, there are four references to "genocide, war crimes, ethnic cleansing and crimes against humanity" in describing the international community's responsibility to act collectively with respect to R2P.[3] Thus there is no ambiguity about what, in the collective view of the UN and its member-state governments, is the trigger for R2P: atrocity crimes. It is equally clear, at least in this rather narrow interpretation of R2P, what R2P is not designed to respond to, such as human rights abuses or acts of international terrorism falling short of atrocity crimes, the requirements of "human security" writ large, natural calamities, repressive or undemocratic governments, or threats to international peace and security absent atrocity crimes. The UN's focused application of R2P against atrocity crimes may prove controversial as sincere advocates of the evolving principle of R2P seek to argue a broader mandate as a matter of policy, customary law, or morality.

The alternative and broader formulation, advanced by the International Commission on Intervention and State Sovereignty (ICISS) in its December 2001 report, *The Responsibility to Protect*, which helped spur governments to take R2P seriously for purposes of a UN declaration, articulates the basic principles that "the primary responsibility for the protection of [a state's] people lies with the state itself. . . . Where a population is suffering serious harm, as a result of internal war, insurgency, repression or state failure, and the state in question is unwilling or unable to halt or avert it, the principle of non-intervention yields to the international responsibility to protect."[4] The "just cause threshold" for military intervention established by the ICISS requires that "there must be serious and irreparable harm occurring to human beings, or imminently likely to occur, of the following kind: A) large scale loss of life, actual or apprehended, with genocidal intent or not, which is the product either of deliberate state action, or state neglect or inability to act, or a failed state situation; or B) large scale 'ethnic cleansing', actual or apprehended, whether carried out by killing, forced expulsion, acts of terror or rape."[5]

Atrocity crimes, as further explained below, can easily fall within the ICISS formulation. But the ICISS principles range further and embrace circumstances for R2P that were not later adopted by the General Assembly in 2005. "Large scale loss of life," for example, can result from legitimate acts of self-defense or a state's failure to respond effectively to an epidemic or to warn its coastal population in a timely manner of a tsunami or to see its public officials govern so badly, divisively, or corruptly that the state "fails" and some type of anarchy results. All of these events can have devastating impacts on civilian populations, but they do not necessarily give rise to the responsibility to protect as that term is most broadly accepted by the international community at the start of the twenty-first century.

Later efforts at articulating R2P, prior to the 2005 World Summit Outcome, began to tighten the prism. For example, the *Report of the [UN] Secretary-General's High-Level Panel on Threats, Challenges, and Change* in 2004 explained that "the issue is not the 'right to intervene' of any State, but the 'responsibility to protect' of *every* State when it comes to people suffering from avoidable catastrophe—mass murder and rape, ethnic cleansing by forcible expulsion and terror, and deliberate starvation and exposure to disease."[6] However, while "deliberate starvation" might, although not always, qualify as a crime against humanity, "exposure to disease" is usually not regarded as criminal in purpose, including as an atrocity crime. These broader formulations did not survive in the High-Level Panel's narrower conclusion, which defined R2P as "the emerging norm that there is a collective international responsibility to protect, exercisable by the Security Council authorizing military intervention as a last resort, in the event of genocide and other large-scale killing, ethnic cleansing or serious violations of international humanitarian law which sovereign Governments have proved powerless or unwilling to prevent."[7]

In early 2005 UN Secretary-General Kofi Annan issued his report, *In Larger Freedom,* which was intended as the platform upon which the 2005 World Summit Outcome would be drafted later in the year and adopted by the UN General Assembly. On the one hand, Annan refers to R2P implicitly as a principle confined to atrocity crimes when he writes in his report that, "Much more, however, needs to be done to prevent atrocities and to ensure that the international community acts promptly when faced with massive violations."[8] On the other hand, he endorses the High-Level Panel's broader concept of R2P and explains "if national authorities are unable or unwilling to protect their citizens, then the responsibility shifts to the international community to use diplomatic, humanitarian and other methods to help protect the human rights and well-being of civilian populations."[9] These latter categories of protecting "the human rights and well-being of civilian populations" would not necessarily require the commission of atrocity crimes to trigger R2P under this formulation.

The 2005 World Summit Outcome sharpened the focus of R2P as an extremely significant, albeit narrow, principle of international relations and as an emerging, though neither codified nor fully enforceable, norm of international law. Doubtless there will be efforts in the years ahead to broaden the prism of R2P in an effort to protect civilian populations from a wider range of threats, and probably for good reason. But R2P remains a controversial principle among a large number of governments for varied reasons.[10] The narrow prism—responding to the threat or reality of atrocity crimes against civilian populations—may prove to be precisely the foundation upon which R2P must first demonstrate its strength of purpose and per-suasiveness as a binding principle of both world affairs and international law. Indeed, a broader mandate for R2P in the immediate years ahead may burden it with so much political controversy and dissent among international lawyers that it would collapse as a declared commitment, even with respect to atrocity crimes, before it has an opportunity to be fully tested.

The 2005 World Summit Outcome repeatedly identifies four categories of crimes as targeted for prevention and collective action under R2P: geno-cide, war crimes, ethnic cleansing, and crimes against humanity. Before examining each of these categories of crimes, we should understand what they mean as a group of crimes and how they can be described succinctly as *atrocity crimes* for both the public and the professional community.

The identification of genocide, war crimes, ethnic cleansing, and crimes against humanity as the premise for prevention or action under R2P derives much of its legitimacy from the jurisprudence of the international and hybrid criminal tribunals built during the 1990s, such as the International Criminal Tribunals for the former Yugoslavia (ICTY) and Rwanda (ICTR), the Special Court for Sierra Leone, and the permanent International Criminal Court (ICC). By 2005, scores of high-profile atrocity crime cases had been prosecuted and individual perpetrators convicted and sentenced before an assortment of tribunals and such crimes had been codified as the subject matter jurisdiction of the ICC, which became operational on July 1, 2002, and would carry forth the ever-expanding mission of individual criminal responsibility for such crimes into the future.[11] It thus became increasingly implausible to extend the basis for judicial intervention to enforce individual criminal responsibility for atrocity crimes and yet perpetuate a global system that tolerates, through inaction in prevention or response, the commission of such crimes against civilian populations. The disconnect in logic between the judicial activism of the 1990s and early twenty-first century to rein in atrocity crimes and the impotence of the international community in failing to respond effectively—be it politically, economically, diplomatically, or militarily—to atrocity crimes against civilian populations, finally revealed itself with the issuance of the ICISS report, *The Responsibility to Protect*. The logical next step was to connect atrocity crimes to R2P, and it was that logic that prevailed at the UN General Assembly in 2005 to craft the somewhat narrow basis in atrocity crimes for R2P.

When the International Court of Justice (ICJ) delivered its judgment on genocide in *Application of the Convention on the Prevention and Punishment of the Crime of Genocide (Bosnia and Herzegovina v. Serbia and Montenegro)* on February 26, 2007, it did not find direct participation by the government of Serbia in the commission of genocide at Srebrenica in July 1995.[12] But the ICJ found that the Serbian government had violated Article I of the Genocide Convention when it failed to prevent the genocide at Srebrenica by not using its influence with the Bosnian Serb forces and when it failed to punish the crime of genocide by not apprehending and transferring to the ICTY indicted fugitives such as Ratko Mladić and Radovan Karadžić. The ICJ's judgment was, without invoking its precise term, a clarion call for R2P. The Serbian government was held responsible for failing to protect the residents of Srebrenica and the result was genocide. The Serbian government was also held responsible for failing to assist with the punishment of the perpetrators of genocide, a state policy that only would encourage, indeed reward, those determined to further threaten civilian populations with genocide. The ICJ's judgment in *Bosnia v. Serbia* may well be the starting point for the modern enforcement of R2P.

Atrocity Crimes

What, then, is meant by atrocity crimes? The mandates and case law of the international and hybrid tribunals since the early 1990s have provided a very useful basis for answering that question.[13] For the purpose of understanding what justifies implementation of R2P, the four categories of crimes set forth in the 2005 World Summit Outcome have been extensively examined and defined by the tribunals in their constitutional statutes and jurisprudence. The Rome Statute of the ICC, in particular, offers the most sophisticated definitions for atrocity crimes drawn from treaty law and customary international law as existed in 1998 when the Rome Statute was finalized.[14] If one considers that to trigger R2P the commission of any one of these crimes must occur on a societal level involving a large number of potential or actual victims, then one can discover the starting point for a proper understanding of the relationship between R2P and atrocity crimes.

Five Characteristics of Atrocity Crimes

There are cumulative, definitional characteristics for genocide, crimes against humanity (including ethnic cleansing), and war crimes that, when they coexist in the perpetration of one of these acts, constitute an atrocity crime.[15] The international and hybrid criminal tribunals have focused on these characteristics in their prosecution of perpetrators of the crimes.[16] Although these factors have arisen in recent years in the realm of individual criminal responsibility, they are relevant as the defining characteristics for atrocity crimes meriting implementation of more robust (if necessary, military) measures of R2P. While there are some R2P responses that might be triggered with a minimalist act of genocide or a war crime or crime against humanity, it would be more likely that R2P assumes its larger importance and definitional character when an atrocity crime meeting the substantiality test occurs and compels a response.

The following five characteristics constitute an atrocity crime:

1. The crime must be of significant magnitude, meaning that its commission is widespread or systematic or occurs as part of a large-scale commission of such crimes. The crime must involve a relatively large number of victims (e.g., a fairly significant number of deaths and/or wounded casualties), impose other very severe injury upon noncombatant populations (e.g., massive destruction of private or cultural property), or subject a large number of combatants or prisoners of war to violations of the laws and customs of war. In short, the crime must meet the substantiality test developed by the international and hybrid criminal tribunals.
2. The crime may occur in time of war, or in time of peace, or in time of violent societal upheaval of some organized character, and may be either international or noninternational in character.
3. The crime must be identifiable in conventional international criminal law as the crime of genocide, a violation of the laws and customs of war (war crimes), a crime against humanity (the precise definition of which has evolved in the development of the international and hybrid criminal tribunals), or the emerging crime of ethnic cleansing. For purposes of R2P, additional crimes that may become identified in the future as atrocity crimes would be the crime of aggression (if and when it is defined so as to give rise to international individual criminal

culpability and is an assault on a civilian population, particularly as an operational crime before the ICC) and the crime of international terrorism (when it reaches a magnitude comparable to a crime against humanity).

4. The crime must have been led, in its execution, by a ruling or otherwise powerful elite in society (including rebel, insurgent, or terrorist leaders) who planned the commission of the crime or were the leading perpetrators of the crime.

5. The law applicable to such crime, while it may impose state responsibility and even remedies against states, is also regarded under customary international law as holding individuals criminally liable for the commission of such crime, thus enabling the prosecution of such individuals before a court duly constituted for such purpose.[17]

The third characteristic above suggests a broader list of crimes (aggression and international terrorism) than the four identified in the 2005 World Summit Outcome or, indeed, prosecuted before the international and hybrid criminal tribunals. This simply reflects the fact that the statutes of the tribunals do not include these crimes, except for the Rome Statute of the ICC, which endorses the crime of aggression for the jurisdiction of the ICC, but only when the crime is properly defined and its use triggered in accordance with the UN Charter through amendment to the Rome Statute.[18]

The Substantiality Test

The first above mentioned characteristic essentially requires that the "substantiality test" be met in connection with the crime before R2P would be a legitimate response (provided the other four criteria also exist). This is a logical requirement for R2P, as the concept only deals with the megacrimes that assault civilian populations wholesale and compel governments (and hopefully the host government of the crime) to act decisively and with timely effect to stop the commission of such crimes from creating massive civilian casualties and property destruction. Examples of where R2P would have served high moral purpose in the 1990s, based upon the substantiality test, occurred in Bosnia and Herzegovina, Rwanda, Sierra Leone, Kosovo, East Timor, and the Democratic Republic of the Congo, and into the twenty-first century, Darfur. Kosovo and East Timor were examples where early notions of R2P were used to justify international military intervention to protect civilian populations at risk.

There is a critical caveat to all that follows. R2P is as much a principle of prevention as it is of response. R2P cannot possibly be a viable concept if it is defined as a means of reacting to the most speculative suggestion of some relatively minor and isolated threat of genocide, crimes against humanity, ethnic cleansing, or war crimes. The threat has to have some meaningful content and the speculation about it must be centered on the plausible possibility of a crime of some magnitude. Therefore, even when considering R2P in its preventive capacity, the content of the threat to civilian populations remains important and it must demonstrate some meaningful magnitude.

Genocide

There has been no shortage of substantiality affirmations with respect to atrocity crimes in the judgments of the ICTY and ICTR. Even when interpreting the crime of genocide directed at destroying "in part" a national, ethnic, racial, or religious group, the tribunals have concluded that a "substantial part of the group" or "a considerable number of individuals who are part of the group" must be targeted.[19] For purposes of R2P, the substantiality requirement for genocide would be essential. It would be implausible to launch the more extreme methodologies of R2P—including military intervention—on the premise of either the intent or the act to exterminate one or a very small number of individuals on any of the grounds defining genocide. The latter may justify prosecution of an individual before a domestic court on the charge of genocide, but it would not rise to the level of gravity required by the tribunals or to what would engage the concern of governments or the UN as a basis for taking R2P action to protect either a part of or an entire national, ethnic, racial, or religious group of people.

Crimes Against Humanity

Crimes against humanity have long demanded substantiality as a prerequisite to criminal liability. All of the prosecutions for crimes against humanity before the Nuremberg Tribunal after World War II involved actions that involved large numbers of victims and were orchestrated in a systematic or widespread manner by high-level political, military, or business leaders. The ICTY, which in its statute does not stipulate any literal substantiality test for crimes against humanity, has established in its jurisprudence that an "attack" under this category of crimes must be "directed against a civilian 'population' rather than against a limited and randomly selected number of individuals."[20] The ICTY has found that a crime against humanity "may be widespread or committed on a large scale by 'cumulative effect of a series of inhumane acts or the singular effect of an inhumane act of extraordinary magnitude.'"[21] The second prong of a crime against humanity, namely, that it could be "systematic" rather than or in addition to being "widespread," has been explained by the ICTY in this manner:

> The systematic character refers to four elements which . . . may be expressed as follows: (1) the existence of a political objective, a plan pursuant to which the attack is perpetrated or an ideology, in the broad sense of the word, that is, to destroy, persecute or weaken a community; (2) the perpetration of a criminal act on a very large scale against a group of civilians or the repeated and continuous commission of inhumane acts linked to one another; (3) the preparation and use of significant public or private resources, whether military or other; (4) the implication of high-level political and/or military authorities in the definition and establishment of the methodical plan."[22]

In one judgment of the ICTY where the key requirement of crimes against humanity—that they be "widespread or systematic"—required the tribunal to consider what factors were involved, the judges looked to "the number of victims" and "the employment of considerable financial, military or other resources and the scale or the repeated, unchanging and continuous nature of the violence committed against a particular civilian population."[23] These requirements of high-level orchestration and magnitude for commission of crimes against humanity also frame, both in a logical and pragmatic sense, the requirements of R2P. They strengthen the argument for the importance of the R2P principle because the substantiality requirements create the self-evident and imperative need for an effective response, be it from the national government where the assault on the civilian population is occurring or, if that is implausible or unlikely, from the international community.

When one examines the constituent crimes of "crimes against humanity," the substantiality text pervades each one. The list of such crimes is relatively long and, at least in a technical sense, engages with R2P on many fronts that may not yet be fully appreciated, particularly if one assumes that the World Summit Outcome's invocation of crimes against humanity as a justification for R2P is to be taken seriously. Such crimes are codified in the Rome Statute of the ICC,[24] along with the definitions for many of them that are important to understand in the context of R2P.[25]

In the Elements of Crimes for the Rome Statute of the ICC, a clear marker is established for the magnitude of crime required to qualify as a crime against humanity.[26] These codified crimes against humanity in the Rome Statute, most (but not all) of which were also codified in the other tribunal statutes, stand or fall for purposes of R2P on the substantiality test. It would be implausible for R2P to be undertaken by a government or international organization for a single murder or single act of torture or single disappearance of a person—none of which would qualify as a crime against humanity because each would fail the substantiality test.

The jurisprudence of the ICTY and ICTR offer additional guidance on the substantiality test that triggers crimes against humanity. When examining these criteria, however, it remains important not to automatically translate the substantiality required for a criminal prosecution of a crime against humanity with the justification for R2P, particularly military action under R2P. The former concerns accountability for a particular individual and his or her perpetration of a crime that meets the threshold requirements of a crime against humanity. A far larger set of factors come into play when determining, as a matter of policy, whether to initiate R2P measures against a foreign government or other organized force on foreign territory in order to protect a civilian population at risk of crimes against humanity. The tribunals focus on crimes already committed and establish useful criteria for such crimes, but governments and international organizations confronted with the threat of atrocity crimes will consider additional factors when determining whether or not to take action under R2P.

Nonetheless, the tribunals' judgments offer some guidance for how to evaluate the commission, or likely commission, of crimes against humanity so as to determine the merits of an R2P action. The ICTY, for example, has ruled that, "It is sufficient to show that enough individuals were targeted in the course of the attack, or that they were targeted in such a way as to satisfy the Chamber that the attack was in fact directed against a civilian 'population,' rather than against a limited and randomly selected number of individuals."[27] The ICTY has further ruled that "a crime may be widespread or committed on a large scale by the 'cumulative effect of a series of inhumane acts or the singular effect of an inhumane act of extraordinary magnitude.'"[28] The "systematic" character of an attack on a civilian population, described above, is also a critical factor to consider. Thus, in determining the justification for an R2P action based upon crimes against humanity, several factors addressing magnitude, continuous commission, planning, and leadership need to be considered.

When one examines the individual crimes against humanity, the calculus for R2P can become quite challenging. Not all crimes against humanity would qualify easily for an R2P response if taken in isolation of any other crime against humanity or war crime or genocide. Indeed, when examining the list of crimes against humanity, one might roughly categorize a first basket of widespread or systematic murder, extermination, deportation or forcible transfer of population, persecution in the form of ethnic cleansing, and enforced disappearance of persons as the most realistic grounds for action under R2P. Other crimes against humanity, such as apartheid, sexual violence, torture, enslavement, imprisonment, or "other inhumane acts," may well rise to the level of inhumanity triggering the political will to take an R2P action. But this second basket of crimes against humanity can be deeply institutionalized within a society or be divorced from the kind of international or noninternational armed conflict that generates international interest. One is not necessarily experiencing violent conflicts or seriously disruptive internal conflicts in the context of these crimes against humanity. Deeply repressive or oppressive societies, which may be politically, socially, or economically stifling, may lead to the commission of such crimes against humanity. Even if the elements of the particular crime against humanity can be established, it would be more difficult to justify the kinds of governmental and institutional responses under R2P for this second basket of crimes against humanity than for the first basket described above. The best that might be accomplished in such "slow-motion" atrocities is using the R2P principle for diplomatic or economic pressure against the perpetrator government.

For example, the *enforced disappearance of persons* might involve a situation not unlike that which existed in Argentina and Chile in the 1970s, when an estimated 10,000 to 30,000 civilians and at least 3,000 civilians, respectively, disappeared by the action of state authorities.[29] While individual criminal responsibility can be and has been associated with such events, the crime is one that may evolve slowly and steadily and may not attract international attention so as to warrant an R2P action. However, if the enforced disappearance involves a very large number of civilians over a short period of time—such as occurred near Srebrenica in July 1995 and appeared possible in Kosovo during April and May 1999—then the significance of the crime is much more apparent in real or near-real time.

The disappeared at Srebrenica soon were confirmed as murdered men and boys numbering about 8,000.[30] The disappeared in Kosovo initially numbered about 100,000, but within a matter of weeks that number resolved itself as the situation on the ground clarified that most of the individuals survived.[31] Nonetheless, while it was a plausible estimate at the time given the lack of knowledge of the whereabouts of so many civilians during the armed conflict in Kosovo, the number of disappeared during a particular period of time should trigger justifiable concern of their fate and the consideration of effective action to clarify the situation. R2P action, including military intervention, would stand a better chance of being seriously considered if it is in response to such large-scale disappearances, particularly when they occur in the midst of an armed conflict that already has seized international attention and even if those believed to have disappeared later emerge alive. At the time of crisis, the outcome remains unknown, and that uncertainty could influence greatly how decisions are reached to respond under the R2P principle.

A second example is *sexual violence*, which is established as a crime against humanity in the Rome Statute constituting acts of "rape, sexual slavery, enforced prostitution, forced pregnancy, enforced sterilization, or any other form of sexual violence of comparable gravity."[32] Where such sexual violence is occurring with requisite magnitude in the context of other crimes against humanity, such as deportation, murder, extermination, or ethnic cleansing (as a form of persecution), it may prove easier to justify R2P action in order to prevent further sexual violence on such a large scale than if there were solely an orchestrated campaign of sexual violence sweeping across a country.

Apartheid not only is a "slow-motion" crime against humanity but it poses particularly challenging issues for R2P. The international community's experience with apartheid in South Africa never seriously contemplated military intervention to eliminate the state policy and practice of apartheid. Nonmilitary measures were used to pressure the South African government, including economic sanctions and extensive diplomatic efforts.[33] The same may be the case today and in the future if apartheid or apartheid-like practices emerge elsewhere on the globe. Although nonmilitary options would dominate most policymaking when confronted with apartheid as a crime against humanity, military options in some situations might be plausible options for some governments.

Imprisonment or other severe deprivation of physical liberty in violation of fundamental rules of international law and *torture* exist as matters of common practice in many countries.[34] They would qualify as crimes against humanity if all of the fundamental requirements—substantiality, breadth of application, planning, leadership engagement—are met. The R2P response in such cases can fairly easily be crafted in diplomatic and perhaps economic ways, but it would be extraordinary (though not impossible) to contemplate military action under R2P to "rescue" large numbers of individuals tortured or arbitrarily imprisoned as a crime against humanity. Nonetheless, when either one of these crimes is paired with other significant crimes against humanity, it can form part of the mosaic for an assertive R2P response.

Ethnic Cleansing

As a matter of law, the invocation of *ethnic cleansing* in the mandates of R2P is a nontechnical expression for what in fact is a subcategory of the crime against humanity of *persecution*. That being said, ethnic cleansing is a very powerful term, so much so that there is a growing basis for regarding it as a crime against humanity deserving of its own designation under the standard list of crimes against humanity. Ethnic cleansing is, by its very nature, an amalgamation of numerous crimes against humanity in any particular situation. In its simplest terms, ethnic cleansing is the discriminatory assault on an identifiable group within the civilian population for the purpose of removing that group permanently from territory sought by the perpetrators of the assault. The means used to achieve the aims of the assault can range across the entire spectrum of crimes against humanity, but must have at their core the crime of persecution.

The crime of persecution, as it is defined in the Rome Statute of the ICC, "means the intentional and severe deprivation of fundamental rights contrary to international law by reason of the identity of the group or collectivity." The ICTY Appeals Chamber has defined the crime of persecution as consisting of "an act or omission that (1) discriminates in fact and which denies or infringes upon a fundamental right laid down in international customary or treaty law (the *actus reas*); and (2) was carried out deliberately with the intention to discriminate on one of the listed grounds [of the ICTY Statute], specifically race, religion or politics (the *mens rea*)."[35] These attributes must be combined, of course, with the chapeau requirements of a crime against humanity, such as knowledge of a widespread or systematic attack against a civilian population. There are a large number of individual acts that, when taken in conjunction with other acts, may constitute the crime of persecution or that, when done individually, may qualify as persecution if the magnitude of the act is great enough or widespread enough to qualify as a crime against humanity.

In the Rome Statute of the ICC, the crime of persecution has a fairly narrow application, but one that works satisfactorily for the "crime" of ethnic cleansing. Persecution is described as a crime "against any identifiable group or collectivity on political, racial, national, ethnic, cultural, religious, gender as defined in paragraph 3 ["the two sexes, male and female, within the context of society"], or other grounds that are universally recognized as impermissible under international law, *in connection with any act referred to in this paragraph or any crime within the jurisdiction of the Court*."[36] The condition that the discriminatory attack take place in connection with another crime against humanity, genocide, or a war crime firmly associates persecution with other atrocity crimes. In effect, the crime of persecution adds discriminatory intent to the underlying crime or, in the case of genocide, supplements the more narrowly defined genocidal intent to destroy in whole or in part a racial, religious, national, or ethnical group.

Within the framework of the crime against humanity called persecution, then, can be found the many actions that can describe a campaign of *ethnic cleansing*. Since the mid-1980s the phenomenon of ethnic cleansing has swept over the Kurdish region of Iraq, Bosnia and Hertzegovina, Croatia, Kosovo, Darfur, and other atrocity zones. A useful example of how to identify ethnic cleansing within the framework of the crime of persecution can be seen in the ICTY Trial Chamber judgment of *Prosecutor v. Momcilo Krajisnik* (2006). Krajisnik was President of the Bosnian Serb Assembly and was charged with crimes against humanity that framed the ethnic cleansing campaign in Bosnia and Herzegovina from 1991 to 1992. While charging Krajisnik with and convicting him on the individual crimes against humanity of extermination (or murder in the alternative), deportation, and other inhumane acts (forced transfer)—all of which clearly contributed to the ethnic cleansing campaign—the ICTY also convicted him of the crime of persecution in a manner emblematic of the "crime" of ethnic cleansing.

The ICTY Trial Chamber 1 judges in *Krajisnik* first noted that "not every denial of a fundamental human right will be serious enough to constitute a crime against humanity. The underlying act committed on discriminatory grounds, considered in isolation or in conjunction with other acts, must be of the same gravity as other crimes listed under Article 5 of the [ICTY] Statute [namely, crimes against humanity]."[37] The judges found that, when taken together, various restrictive and discriminatory measures not even listed explicitly as crimes against humanity in the ICTY Statute nonetheless constituted the crime of persecution.[38] Then they examined acts that were charged in the indictment against Krajisnik, found a discriminatory intent associated with each such act, and thus established the crime of persecution within the context of ethnic cleansing.[39]

Discovering the emerging crime of ethnic cleansing within the statutes and jurisprudence of the international and hybrid criminal tribunals is important for the future of R2P as a principle upon which governments and international organizations can act with confidence in the legitimacy of their cause. Since ethnic cleansing became a popular term to describe what was occurring in Bosnia and Herzegovina, as well as parts of Croatia, in the early 1990s, its usage has only increased as similar patterns of discriminatory conduct have unfolded in other atrocity zones. Darfur would be the most obvious contemporary example of ethnic cleansing on a massive scale.[40]

Ethnic cleansing is a powerful justification for R2P. Since ethnic cleansing typically takes some amount of time to launch and press to its final conclusion, and since it can often meet armed resistance and delay in being fully achieved by the attacking force against a civilian population, there is some room for R2P to take hold. If the political will exists, governments, alliances, and international organizations can respond by whatever means may prove most effective in reversing the tide of ethnic cleansing. Ethnic cleansing has achieved a legal framework—premised so far on persecution as a crime against humanity—upon which to justify the entire range of R2P options for action, depending, of course, on the precise circumstances of the particular campaign of ethnic cleansing.

War Crimes

The fourth category of atrocity crimes underpinning the rationale for R2P is war crimes. For good reason, war crimes often are not subject to a substantiality test and when committed in isolated incidents normally would not merit action under R2P. The Geneva Conventions of 1949 and their 1997 Protocols I and II codify legal principles under which to hold individual soldiers, of whatever rank and responsibility on the field of battle, responsible for crimes against other soldiers who are *hors de combat* and against civilians.[41] Each soldier is well served knowing that he or she can be held responsible under the Geneva Conventions for either "grave breaches" or "violations" that have been rendered subject to criminal or military justice in domestic courts. Nonetheless, most of what is required in these instruments and others pertaining to the law of war and international humanitarian law invoke the responsibility of states and not the criminal responsibility of individuals. If the violations are serious and significant, then the state responsibility for such violations may indeed trigger an R2P response.

Nonetheless, the growing body of tribunal statutes and tribunal jurisprudence since 1993 focuses increasingly on individual criminal responsibility with respect to breaches of the Geneva Conventions and international customary law pertaining to the laws and customs of war. In that context there is a substantiality test for war crimes that normally applies before individual culpability is established. For example, for the noninternational armed conflict covered by the statute of the ICTR, there is a requirement that the war crimes violations be of a "serious" nature,[42] which the tribunal has interpreted to mean "grave consequences for the victim."[43] The ICTY has mirrored this principle in its judgments.[44] The Rome Statute of the ICC provides jurisdiction over "war crimes in particular when committed as part of a plan or policy or as part of a large-scale commission of such crimes."

The appendage of "in particular" was a negotiated compromise between those governments seeking an explicit substantiality test and those not wishing to completely undercut the utility of the Geneva Conventions' application to individual soldiers for individual and perhaps isolated actions. The "plan or policy" infers a multiplicity of criminal acts and the large-scale commission of such crimes explicitly invokes a scale of magnitude of some significance that normally would be recognized before the ICC would deem the war crime serious enough to exercise the court's jurisdiction.

There is an obvious reality when addressing the issue of R2P that if the principle were to be invoked in response to an armed conflict in which a civilian population is at risk (which appears increasingly to be the norm in modern warfare), then the threat or reality of war crimes would need to achieve a reasonably high threshold of magnitude and be sustained long enough to threaten or create a severe impact on the civilian population before R2P, particularly of a military nature, would be sustained as a viable justification for action. One would have to examine the degree to which forces engaged in the armed conflict are fighting in legitimate warfare as opposed to unjustified assaults on the civilian population or military personnel *hors de combat* (such as those being detained) before it would be possible to reach judgments on the degree to which war crimes exist and of what magnitude or whether they are likely to be committed on a scale warranting R2P responses. A credibly high substantiality test, one requiring a significant number of war crimes affecting a reasonably large number of victims or potential victims, would be central to whether the war crimes in question are indeed atrocity crimes and thus whether R2P is relevant to responding to the situation.

Joining Legal and Political Assessments of R2P

In the discussion above about crimes against humanity, the legal theory of R2P confronts the political reality that certain crimes against humanity may trigger a range of nonmilitary R2P measures (particularly diplomatic pressure or economic leverage) but not military intervention options. It remains vitally important for R2P to ground its source of legitimacy in the entire range of atrocity crimes set forth in the World Summit Outcome declaration. The *legal* justification for R2P as it may be established on any point along the spectrum from diplomacy to use of armed force remains firmly rooted in accurately identifying the atrocity crime and meeting its associated substantiality test in order to qualify for R2P action. That exercise may be frustrating to those who are seeking effective responses to a wide range of human rights abuses and political repression. But the task is essential to creating a manageable framework within which R2P, as a legal concept, can be justified. The *political* implementation of R2P necessarily will rely upon the legal definitions of atrocity crimes to establish the proper context for action.

The challenge arises where the particular atrocity crime (such as slavery or disappeared persons) is ill-suited to a robust (military) R2P response. The legal definition, then, can only take us so far. There also will be a political judgment that must be reached as to the nature of the atrocity crime, the societal context of how the particular atrocity crime is being committed, and the tools that governments and international organizations can realistically use to end such crime. The political reality is that atrocity crimes that might justify military intervention as an R2P measure, thus reaching beyond diplomacy or perhaps sanctions, clearly would have to meet the substantiality test.

How, then, does one activate R2P if a diverse range of genocide, crimes against humanity, ethnic cleansing, and war crimes are its legally defined targets? The most effective enforcement of R2P normally will precede an accurate legal description of the crime at issue, a task that may take years and several criminal trials or a judgment of the ICJ to establish. Policymakers must make the political decisions about whether and how to take action while gambling on the nature of the crime threatening a civilian population and how, if left unchallenged, that crime may unfold on the ground, including its likely severity. In some situations, the Security Council can cut through the complexities with adoption of an enforcement resolution under Chapter VII of the UN Charter, which mandates an R2P action long before the legal definitional exercise upon which R2P is predicated could be completed with certainty. In other situations, the caution required in determining whether certain actions meet the legal definition of an atrocity crime will prove to be a constructive brake on precipitous or overly ambitious R2P theorizing that otherwise might have launched unwise and unjustified military action.

The fusion of such legal and political assessments into a workable formula for R2P may prove too unwieldy for governments and international organizations to accomplish in the near future. But there is good reason to remain optimistic that in the long run a principled pragmatism will take hold—one that can distinguish between those atrocity crimes requiring "soft" R2P (diplomacy, judicial intervention, or sanctions) and those that may demand "hard" R2P (such as military action). In each case, the legal definitions will matter greatly, but the political judgments of policymakers will determine the fate of a civilian population whose survival is at risk.

"R2P Ends Atrocity Crimes"

There is an awkward structure in the UN's mandate for R2P. It invites one to repeat in every description of or justification for the principle that it stands to challenge the fate of civilian populations in the face of "genocide, war crimes, ethnic cleansing, and crimes against humanity." In the alternative, I plead for the unifying term of "atrocity crimes" to describe these four categories of crimes in accordance with the five fundamental characteristics for atrocity crimes described earlier in this chapter. The public and policymakers should be able to readily identify the purpose of R2P as a counterforce to *atrocity crimes*, a term that should evoke immediate, albeit general, understanding among the public and policymakers, but that itself is solidly grounded in legal criteria explained here and elsewhere. As I have written previously, atrocity crimes is "terminology that remains faithful to the requirements of international criminal law (particularly in the work of international and hybrid criminal tribunals and national criminal courts) and at the same time enables timely public discourse (by governments, activists, the media, scholars, and the general public) that actually stands some chance of leading to greater understanding of what is occurring and how effective responses might be facilitated."[45]

If we can reach the point where school children and their parents exclaim, "R2P Ends Atrocity Crimes," and policymakers ultimately comprehend this siren call of their peoples stamped on bumper stickers and broadcast through enlightened corporate sponsors, then we will know that the responsibility to protect has a fighting chance of diminishing, and perhaps even ending atrocity crimes in our own time, on our watch, and within our moral universe.

Notes

*   David Scheffer is the Mayer Brown/Robert A. Helman Professor of Law and the director of the Center for International Human Rights at Northwestern University School of Law.
1. Kofi Annan, former UN Secretary-General, "Final Address as Secretary-General to the Truman Museum and Library" (December 11, 2006), http://www.un.org/ News/ossg/sg/stories/statments_full.asp?statID=40; Ban Ki-moon, UN Secretary-General, "Acceptance Speech on Appointment as the 8th Secretary-General of the United Nations" (October 3, 2006), http://www.un.org/News/dh/infocus/sg _elect/ban_speech.htm; Gareth Evans, president of the International Crisis Group and cochair of the International Commission on Intervention and State Sovereignty, "From Principle to Practice—Implementing the Responsibility to

Protect" (April 26, 2007), http://www.crisisgroup.org/home/index.cfm?id =4802&l=1; Special Committee on Peacekeeping Operations, Security Council, "Responsibility to Protect Civilian Populations Paramount, Special Committee on Peacekeeping Told," press release, February 28, 2006, UN Doc. GA/PK/188, http://www.un.org/News/Press/docs/2006/gapk188.doc.htm (here inafter "Special Committee Press Release").

2. UN GAOR, Sixtieth Session, 8th plen. mtg., UN Doc. A/RES/60/1, para. 138 (October 24, 2005; hereinafter *2005 World Summit Outcome*). See also UN SCOR, Sixty-first Session, 5,430th mtg., UN Doc. S/RES/1674, para. 4 (April 28, 2006): The Security Council "*reaffirms* the provisions of paragraphs 138 and 139 of the *2005 World Summit Outcome* document regarding the responsibility to protect populations from genocide, war crimes, ethnic cleansing and crimes against humanity."

3. "The international community, through the United Nations, also has the responsibility to use appropriate diplomatic, humanitarian and other peaceful means, in accordance with Chapters VI and VIII of the Charter, to help to protect populations from genocide, war crimes, ethnic cleansing and crimes against humanity. In this context, we are prepared to take collective action, in a timely and decisive manner, through the Security Council, in accordance with the Charter, including Chapter VII, on a case-by-case basis and in cooperation with relevant regional organizations as appropriate, should peaceful means be inadequate and national authorities are manifestly failing to protect their populations from genocide, war crimes, ethnic cleansing and crimes against humanity. We stress the need for the General Assembly to continue consideration of the responsibility to protect populations from genocide, war crimes, ethnic cleansing and crimes against humanity and its implications, bearing in mind the principles of the Charter and international law. We also intend to commit ourselves, as necessary and appropriate, to helping States build capacity to protect their populations from genocide, war crimes, ethnic cleansing and crimes against humanity and to assisting those which are under stress before crises and conflicts break out." Ibid., para. 139.

4. International Commission on Intervention and State Sovereignty (ICISS), *The Responsibility to Protect*, XI (December 2001),http://www.iciss.ca/pdf/ Commission-Report.pdf.

5. Ibid., XII.

6. UN Secretary-General, *Report of the Secretary-General's High-Level Panel on Threats, Challenges, and Change*, delivered to the General Assembly, December 8, 2004, UN Doc. A/59/565 and A/59/565/Corr.1, para. 201, http://www .un.org/secureworld/.

7. Ibid., para. 203.

8. UN Secretary-General, *In Larger Freedom: Towards Development, Security and Human Rights for All*, delivered to the General Assembly, March 21, 2005, UN Doc. A/59/2005, para. 134, http://daccessdds.un.org/doc/UNDOC/GEN/ N05/270/78/PDF/N0527078.pdf?OpenElement.

9. Ibid., para. 135.

10. UN Security Council, Sixty-first Session, 5,577th mtg., UN Doc. S/PV.5577 (December 4, 2006), http://daccessdds.un.org/doc/UNDOC/PRO/N06/640/61/PDF/N0664061.pdf?OpenElement; UN Security Council, Sixty-first Session, 5,474th mtg., UN Doc. S/PV.5474 (June 22, 2006), http://daccessdds.un.org/doc/UNDOC/PRO/N06/401/01/PDF/N0640101.pdf?OpenElement; Special Committee Press Release, see note 1.

11. William A. Schabas, *The UN International Criminal Tribunals: The Former Yugoslavia, Rwanda, and Sierra Leone* (Cambridge: Cambridge University Press, 2006); William A. Schabas, *An Introduction to the International Criminal Court*, 2nd ed. (Cambridge: Cambridge University Press, 2004).

12. *Bosnia and Herzegovina v. Serbia and Montenegro*, "Case Concerning the Application of the Convention on the Prevention and Punishment of the Crime of Genocide," Judgment of the I.C.J., 26 February 2007, http://www.icj-cij.org/docket/files/91/13685.pdf; See David Scheffer, "The World Court's Fractured Ruling on Genocide," *Genocide Studies and Prevention* 2 (2007): 123–36.

13. David Scheffer, "Genocide and Atrocity Crimes," *Genocide Studies and Prevention* 1 (2006): 229–50 (hereinafter Scheffer, "Genocide and Atrocity Crimes"); David Scheffer, "The Future of Atrocity Law," *Suffolk Transnational Law Review* 25 (2002): 389–432.

14. *Rome Statute of the International Criminal Court*, July 17, 1998, UN Doc. A/CONF.183/9, http://www.un.org/icc, reprinted in ILM 999 (1998) (defining genocide in art. 6, war crimes in art. 8, and crimes against humanity in art. 7) [hereinafter "Rome Statute"]; *International Criminal Court, Elements of Crimes*, UN Doc. PCNICC/2000/1/Add.2 (2000) [hereinafter "Elements of Crimes"].

15. See Scheffer, "Genocide and Atrocity Crimes." See note 13.

16. Human Rights Watch, "Genocide, War Crimes, Crimes Against Humanity: Topical Digests of the International Criminal Tribunal for Rwanda and the International Criminal Tribunal for the Former Yugoslavia" (2004), http://hrw.org/reports/2004/ij/; Human Rights Watch, "Genocide, War Crimes, Crimes Against Humanity: A Topical Digest of the Case Law of the International Criminal Tribunal for the Former Yugoslavia" (2006), http://hrw.org/reports/2006/icty0706/; William A. Schabas, *The UN International Criminal Tribunals: The Former Yugoslavia, Rwanda, and Sierra Leone* (Cambridge: Cambridge University Press, 2006).

17. Scheffer, "Genocide and Atrocity Crimes." See note 13, p. 238–39.

18. Rome Statute. See note 14, article 5.

19. *Prosecutor v. Krstic*, Case No. IT-98-33-T, Judgment (August 2, 2001); *Prosecutor v. Bagilishema*, Case No. ICTR-95-1A-T, Judgment (June 7, 2001); *Prosecutor v. Jelisic*, Case No. IT-95-10-T, Judgment (December 14, 1999) [hereinafter "Jelisic Trial Judgment"]; *Prosecutor v. Kayishema and Ruzindana*, Case No. ITCT-95-1-T, Judgment (May 21, 1999).

20. *Prosecutor v. Kunarac, Kovac and Vokovic*, Case No. IT-96-23, Judgment (June 12, 2002) [hereinafter "Kunarac Judgment"]; *Prosecutor v. Kunarac, Kovac and*

Vokovic, Case No. IT-96-23/1-A, Appeals Judgment (June 12, 2002) [hereinafter "Kunarac Appeals Judgment"].

21. *Prosecutor v. Kordi and Cerkez*, Case No. IT-95-14/2-T, Judgment (February 26, 2001) [hereinafter "Kordi Judgment"].

22. *Prosecutor v. Naletilic and Martinovic*, Case No. IT-98-34-T, Judgment (March 31, 2003); *Prosecutor v. Blaskic*, Case No. IT-95-14-T, Judgment (March 3, 2000) [hereinafter "Blaskic Judgment"].

23. Jelisic Trial Judgment. See note 19.

24. Rome Statute. See note 14, article 7, section 1.

25. Ibid., article 7, section 2.

26. See the introduction to the section on "Crimes Against Humanity" in International Criminal Court, *Elements of Crimes*, reprinted in *Selected Basic Documents Related to the International Criminal Court* (ICC publication, The Hague, 2005) at 211.

27. Kunarac Judgment and Kunarac Appeals Judgment. See note 20.

28. Kordic Judgment. See note 21.

29. Amnesty International, *Argentina and Chile: The International Community's Responsibility Regarding Crimes Against Humanity* (1998), http://web.amnesty .org/library/Index/ENGAMR030011998?open&of=ENG-332. Amnesty cites for Argentina the statistics "Comision Nacional sobre la Desaparicion de Personas, Nunca Mas—Informe de la Comision Nacional sobre la Desaparicion de Personas" (Argentina's National Commission on Disappeared People), 1984, as well as "Nunca Más (Never Again), 1986. For Chile, Amnesty International cites "The Reparation and Reconciliation Corporation, established in 1992 as a successor to the Truth and Reconciliation Commission (Rettig Commission) set up by President Patricio Aylwin, that officially documented 3,197 cases of victims of human rights violations." See also Edy Kaufman and Patricia Weis Fagen, "Extrajudicial Executions: An Insight into the Global Dimensions of a Human Rights Violation," *Human Rights Quarterly*, November 1981, at 81.

30. UN Secretary-General, *The Fall of Srebrenica*, delivered to the General Assembly, November 15, 1999, UN Doc. A/54/549; Central and East European Law Initiative of the American Bar Association & the Science and Human Rights Program of the American Association for the Advancement of Science, "Political Killings in Kosova/Kosovo" (1999), http://shr.aaas.org/kosovo/ pk/p1_2.html, estimating that "approximately 10,500 [individuals were killed] and a 95 percent confidence interval with an approximate range between 7,500 and 13,750 individuals killed between March 20 and June 12, 1999."

31. U.S. State Department, "Ethnic Cleansing in Kosovo" (fact sheet, April 22, 1999), http://www.state.gov/www/regions/eur/rpt_990422_ksvo_ethnic.html. This fact sheet indicates that "150,000 to 500,000 military-age men remain missing in Kosovo." See also Human Rights Watch, *Under Orders: War Crimes in Kosovo* (2001), http://www.hrw.org/reports/2001/kosovo/.

32. Rome Statute. See note 14, article 7, section 1(g).

33. David Cortright and George Lopez, eds., *The Sanctions Decade: Assessing UN Strategies in the 1990s* (Boulder, CO: Lynne Rienner, 2000); Goler T. Butcher, "The Unique Nature of Sanctions Against South Africa, and Resulting Enforcement Issues," *New York University Journal of International Law and Policy* 19 (1987): 821.

34. Amnesty International, *Report 2006*, http://web.amnesty.org/report2006/index-eng (accessed May 17, 2007).

35. *Prosecutor v. Stakic*, Case No. IT-97-24-A, Judgment, para. 327 (March 22, 2006).

36. Rome Statute. See note 14, article 7, section 1(h); emphasis added.

37. *Prosecutor v. Krajisnik*, Case No. IT-00-39-T, Judgment, para. 735 (September 27, 2006).

38. Ibid.

39. Ibid., para. 741.

40. International Commission of Inquiry on Darfur, *Report to the Secretary General* (January 25, 2005), http://www.un.org/News/dh/sudan/com_inq_darfur.pdf; International Crisis Group, *Darfur: The Failure to Protect* (2005), http://www.crisisgroup.org/home/index.cfm?id=3314&l=1; See also, in the context of R2P, Lee Feinstein, *Darfur and Beyond: What Is Needed to Prevent Mass Atrocities*, Council Special Report No. 22 (New York: Council on Foreign Relations Press, January 2007), https://secure.www.cfr.org/publication/12444/darfur_and_beyond.html.

41. Geneva Convention relative to the Protection of Civilian Persons in Time of War, art. 3, August 12, 1949, 6 U.S.T. 3316, 75 U.N.T.S. 135; Protocol I Additional to the Geneva Conventions of 1949, and Relating to the Protection of Victims of International Armed Conflicts, December 7, 1979, 1125 U.N.T.S. 3 [hereinafter "Protocol I"]; Protocol II to the Geneva Conventions of 1949, and Relating to the Protection of Victims of Non-International Conflicts, December 7. 1978, 1125 U.N.T.S. 609 [hereinafter "Protocol II"].

42. See *Prosecutor v. Rutaganda*, Case No. ICTR-96-3-T, Judgment (December 6, 1999); see *Prosecutor v. Akayesu*, Case No. ICTR-96-4-T, Judgment (September 2, 1998).

43. Ibid.

44. See Kunarac Appeals Judgment. See note 20.

45. David Scheffer, "The Merits of Unifying Terms: 'Atrocity Crimes' and 'Atrocity Law,'" *Genocide Studies and Prevention* 2 (2007): 91.

Section II

Where the Rubber Hits the Road: The Responsibility to Protect in Northern Uganda, Darfur, and the Democratic Republic of the Congo. And Iraq?

6

Was the Iraq War a Humanitarian Intervention? And What Are Our Responsibilities Today?

Kenneth Roth*

The responsibility to protect people facing mass atrocities should not be reduced to military action. There are many nonmilitary steps, from sanctions to prosecutions, that the international community might productively pursue in such cases. But there is no escaping the fact that sometimes military action is necessary to uphold the responsibility to protect. Military steps might be consensual, as in the deployment of traditional peacekeepers, but in extreme cases the only feasible way to stop mass atrocities may be through nonconsensual military action, typically called humanitarian intervention.

Because of the assumed noble motives behind humanitarian intervention, governments that resort to nonconsensual military force are often eager to characterize their conduct in these terms. The Bush administration was no exception. It sought to invoke this justification for its March 2003 invasion of Iraq, at least after alternative justifications failed. It is thus necessary to ask, can the invasion of Iraq be justified as a humanitarian intervention?

This question received little serious attention before the war because the invasion was not mainly about saving the Iraqi people from oppression. Indeed, if Iraqis had overthrown Saddam Hussein and reliably dealt with the issue of weapons of mass destruction, there clearly would have been no war, even if the successor government had been just as repressive.

Over time, however, the Bush administration's principal-stated justifications for the war lost much of their force. No weapons of mass destruction were ever found. No significant prewar link with international terrorism was ever discovered. The postwar chaos and sectarian violence made Iraq an unlikely staging ground for democracy in the Middle East. More and more, the administration's sole conceivable justification for launching the war was that Saddam Hussein was a ruthless and dangerous tyrant—an argument of humanitarian intervention. The administration went on to cite that rationale not simply as a side benefit of the war, but as a prime justification.

Does that claim hold up to scrutiny? This is not a question about whether the war can be defended on other grounds; the mandate of my organization, Human Rights Watch, requires me to be explicitly neutral on that point. Rather, the question is whether a humanitarian rationale alone can justify the invasion. Despite the horrors of Saddam Hussein's rule, it cannot. Stating as much is important to preserve humanitarian intervention for when it is really needed to fulfill the responsibility to protect.

The Standard

War's human cost can be enormous, but the imperative of stopping or preventing genocide or other systematic slaughter can sometimes, in my view, justify the use of military force. In line with this view, Human Rights Watch has, on rare occasions, advocated humanitarian intervention—for example, to stop ongoing genocide in Rwanda and Bosnia.

Yet military action should never be taken lightly, even for humanitarian purposes. Death, destruction, and disorder are the predictable consequences of most wars. The Iraq War has been no exception. Given the very real risk that any war will lead to large-scale loss of life, humanitarian intervention should be reserved as a threshold matter for situations of ongoing or imminent mass slaughter. Other forms of tyranny are worth working intensively to end through other means, but only the most dire cases of large-scale killing can justify on humanitarian grounds the loss of life that so often results from war.

One might use military force more readily when a government facing serious abuses on its territory invites or at least consents to military assistance from others—as in the case of interventions in recent years in Liberia, Sierra Leone, the Ivory Coast, the Democratic Republic of the Congo, southern Sudan, and, to the extent that military deployment has been allowed, Darfur. Such consensual interventions are less likely to explode into all-out war, with its attendant humanitarian costs. But when it comes to military intervention without the consent of the government whose territory is being invaded—what most people mean by humanitarian intervention—only the imperative of stopping ongoing or imminent mass slaughter might justify the risk to life.

If this high threshold standard is met, one should then look to five other factors to determine whether the use of military force can be characterized as humanitarian. First, military action must be the last reasonable option. Second, the intervention must be guided primarily by a humanitarian purpose. Third, it should be conducted by forces that are committed to maximizing respect for international human rights and humanitarian law. Fourth, it must appear reasonably likely to do more good than harm. Finally, it should ideally, though not necessarily, be endorsed by the United Nations (UN) Security Council or another body with significant multilateral authority.

Mass Slaughter

The most important criterion is whether mass slaughter is under way or imminent. Brutal as Saddam Hussein's reign was, the killing by his security forces in March 2003 was not of the exceptional and dire magnitude that would justify humanitarian intervention. Granted, during the previous twenty-five years of Baath Party rule the government murdered some 250,000 Iraqis. Indeed, there were times in the past when the killing was so intense that humanitarian intervention could have been justified—for example, during the 1988 *Anfal* genocide, in which the Iraqi government slaughtered some 100,000 Kurds. However, by the time of the March 2003 invasion, the government's killing had ebbed. On the eve of war, no one contends that Baghdad was engaged in murder of anywhere near this magnitude, or had been for some time. "Better late than never" is not a justification for the bloodshed that so often is inherent in humanitarian intervention. Military action on humanitarian grounds should be countenanced only to stop mass murder, not to make up for past inaction, despicable as a regime may be.

But if Saddam Hussein committed mass atrocities in the past, was not his overthrow justified to prevent his resumption of such atrocities in the future? No. Humanitarian intervention may be undertaken preemptively, but only if slaughter is imminent—that is, if there is evidence that large-scale slaughter is in preparation and about to begin. No one seriously claimed before the war that Saddam Hussein's government was planning imminent mass killing, and no evidence has emerged that it was. There were claims that the government, with a history of gassing Iranian soldiers and Iraqi Kurds, was planning to deliver weapons of mass destruction through terrorist networks, but these allegations were entirely speculative; no supporting proof has ever emerged. There were also fears that the government might respond to an invasion with the use of chemical or biological weapons, perhaps even against its own people, but no one seriously suggested such use was an imminent possibility in the absence of an invasion.

The most that might have been said was that Saddam Hussein, having committed genocide and other mass atrocities in the past, might do so again. By that standard, once a leader commits such grave crimes, he becomes fair game for military overthrow at any time in the future because he might prove to be a recidivist. But that is too low a standard. Many tyrannical leaders pose some risk of mass slaughter, but that generalized risk cannot justify the deliberate bloodshed inherent in war. Some clearer evidence of imminent mass murder must be present to justify the loss of life that can accompany humanitarian intervention.

Moreover, in March 2003, Saddam Hussein faced anything but a clear path to resumed mass slaughter. Boxed in by sanctions and no-fly zones, he lacked the capacity to launch the kinds of major military operations that had characterized his past murderous outbursts without attracting the immediate attention of governments with substantial military assets in the region and, indeed, over Iraq. These constraining circumstances went a long way toward rebutting any presumption of recidivism that might have been drawn from his historical record.

In stating that the killing in Iraq did not rise to a level that justified humanitarian intervention, I am not insensitive to the awful plight of the Iraqi people. Summary executions occurred with disturbing frequency to the very end of Saddam Hussein's rule, as did torture and other brutality. But it is far from clear that this day-to-day repression added up to the kind of mass murder that, in my view, should alone justify the deaths inherent in military action. The tally of Saddam Hussein's victims tended to build in episodic bursts, and while the worst periods, as noted, could well have justified humanitarian intervention, there is no evidence that in early 2003 the scale of his repression was anywhere near attaining this magnitude.

Moreover, because military action is a finite resource, the cost of too low a threshold for humanitarian intervention may be borne by people more needy of rescue. For example, the pursuit of war in Iraq meant that American and British military resources were unavailable to meet large-scale ethnic cleansing that broke out at about the same time in Darfur. The pre-occupation with Iraq by two of the three Western militaries (along with the French) with the capacity to project their forces in substantial numbers meant that stopping the slaughter in Darfur was left to troops from the new, ill-equipped African Union. The people of Darfur, with more than two million displaced and tens of thousands dead, can in this sense be said to be indirect victims of the Iraq War.

The lack of an imminent threat of mass murder that would have justified humanitarian intervention in Iraq does not mean that Saddam Hussein's past atrocities should be ignored. On the contrary, those responsible for them should be prosecuted. But to urge criminal prosecution is not to justify humanitarian intervention. Indictments should be issued and suspects should be arrested if they dare to venture abroad, but the extraordinary remedy of humanitarian intervention, with the loss of life it so often entails, should not be used simply to secure justice for past crimes. This extreme step should be taken only to stop current or imminent slaughter.

The Last Reasonable Option

The lack of ongoing or imminent mass slaughter in March 2003 was itself sufficient to disqualify the invasion of Iraq as a humanitarian intervention. Nonetheless, particularly in light of Saddam Hussein's ruthless past, it is useful to examine the other criteria for humanitarian intervention. For the most part, they, too, were not met.

As noted, because of the substantial risks involved, an invasion qualifies as a humanitarian intervention only if it is the last reasonable option to stop mass killings. Since there were no ongoing mass killings in Iraq in early 2003, this issue technically did not arise. But it is useful to explore whether military intervention was the last reasonable option to stop what Iraqi abuses were ongoing.

It was not. At least one other option should have been tried long before resorting to the extreme step of military invasion—criminal prosecution. There is no guarantee that prosecution would have worked, and one would have been justified in skipping it had large-scale slaughter been under way. But in the context of the Iraqi government's more typical repression, this alternative to military action should have been tried.

To be sure, an indictment is not the same as arrest, trial, and punishment. A mere piece of paper will not stop mass slaughter. But as a long-term approach, an indictment held some promise. The experience of former Yugoslav President Slobodan Milosevic and former Liberian President Charles Taylor suggests that an international indictment profoundly discredits even a ruthless, dictatorial leader. That enormous stigma tends to undermine support for the leader, both at home and abroad, often in unexpected ways. By allowing Saddam Hussein to rule without the stigma of an indictment for genocide and crimes against humanity, the international community never tried a step that might have contributed to his removal and a parallel reduction in government abuses.

Humanitarian Purpose

A humanitarian intervention should be conducted with the aim of maximizing humanitarian results. I recognize that an intervention motivated by purely humanitarian concerns probably cannot be found. Governments that intervene to stop mass slaughter inevitably act for other reasons as well, but a dominant humanitarian purpose is important because it affects numerous decisions that can determine the intervention's success in rescuing people from violence and sparing them the hazards of military operations.

Humanitarianism, even understood broadly as concern for the welfare of the Iraqi people, was at best a subsidiary motive for the invasion of Iraq. The principal justifications offered in the prelude to the invasion were the Iraqi government's alleged possession of weapons of mass destruction, its alleged failure to account for them as prescribed by numerous UN Security Council resolutions, and its alleged connection with international terrorist networks. U.S. officials also spoke of their hope that a democratic Iraq would transform the Middle East. In this tangle of motives, Saddam Hussein's cruelty toward his own people was mentioned, sometimes prominently, but in the prewar period it was never articulated as anywhere near the dominant factor. This is not simply an academic point; it affected the way the invasion was carried out, to the detriment of the Iraqi people.

Most significant, if invading forces had been determined to maximize the humanitarian impact of an intervention, they would have been better prepared to fill the security vacuum that the toppling of the Iraqi government predictably created. It was entirely foreseeable that Saddam Hussein's downfall would lead to civil disorder. The 1991 uprisings in Iraq were marked by large-scale summary executions. The government's Arabization policy in Kirkuk raised the prospect of clashes between displaced Kurds seeking to reclaim their old homes and Arabs who had moved into them. Other sudden changes of regime, such as the Bosnian Serb withdrawal from the Sarajevo suburbs in 1996, have been marked by widespread violence, looting, and arson.

In part to prevent such disorder, the U.S. army chief of staff at the time, General Eric K. Shinseki, told Congress in February 2003—one month before the U.S. invasion—that "several" hundred thousand troops would be required after the invasion to maintain security and provide services. But the civilian leaders of the Pentagon, eager to transform the U.S. military into a leaner fighting machine, dismissed this assessment and launched the war on the cheap with considerably fewer combat troops—some 150,000. To make matters worse, the Bush administration soon disbanded the Iraqi army and announced a broad ban on government employment for former

Baath Party officials, regardless of their complicity in past atrocities. The result was a large pool of disgruntled, mostly Sunni Iraqis, many with military training, who laid the foundation for the deadly insurgency that soon emerged. The significantly understaffed coalition troops were quickly overwhelmed by the enormity of the task of maintaining public order in Iraq. Looting was pervasive. Arms caches were raided and emptied. Violence was rampant.

The problem of understaffing was only compounded by the failure to deploy an adequate number of troops trained in policing. Regular troops are trained to fight—to meet threats with lethal force. But that presumptive resort to lethal force is inappropriate and unlawful when it comes to policing an occupied nation. The consequence was a steady stream of civilians killed when coalition troops, on edge in the face of regular insurgent attacks, many perfidious, mistakenly fired on civilians. That only increased resentment among Iraqis and fueled further attacks. Troops trained in policing—that is, trained to use lethal force as a last resort—would have been better suited to conduct occupation duties humanely. But the Pentagon has not made a priority of developing policing skills among its troops nor did it build alliances with other governments that might have provided this policing capacity. As a result, relatively few police were deployed in Iraq, leaving a heightened toll among the Iraqi people.

Compliance with the Laws of Armed Conflict

To justify a humanitarian label, an invading country should do everything it can to ensure that its intervention is carried out in strict compliance with the international law of armed conflict. Compliance is required in all conflicts—all the more so for a humanitarian intervention. The U.S.-led force that carried out the three-week invasion of Iraq seemed largely determined to meet this requirement, but not entirely. Coalition doctrine required aircraft to take extraordinary care to avoid harming civilians when attacking fixed, preselected targets. But that doctrine proved deficient when it came to attacks on targets that arose unexpectedly in the course of the war, so-called emerging targets or targets of opportunity.

As described in a Human Rights Watch report of December 2003, U.S. rules for attacking leadership targets proved disturbingly lax. The 0-for-50 record reflected a targeting method that was not only an abysmal failure but was also dangerously indiscriminate, allowing bombs to be dropped on the basis of evidence suggesting little more than that a leader—or, to be more precise, his satellite phone—was somewhere in a community. The problem was not the accuracy of the bombs themselves, but the imprecision of the evidence allowed to suggest a leader's presence, with the result that bombs very accurately hit inappropriate targets. Substantial civilian casualties were the predictable result.

Coalition doctrine for the deployment of ground-launched cluster munitions also proved insufficiently attentive to civilian casualties, in that ground forces were permitted to use cluster munitions near populated areas despite the foreseeable loss of civilian life. After Human Rights Watch found that roughly one-quarter of the civilian deaths in the 1999 North Atlantic Treaty Organization (NATO) bombing of Yugoslavia had been caused by the use of cluster bombs in populated areas, the U.S. Air Force substantially curtailed this practice. But the U.S. Army apparently never absorbed this lesson. In responding to Iraqi attacks, Army troops regularly used rockets to scatter cluster munitions over populated areas, causing hundreds of casualties.

In the years after the fall of Baghdad and the rise of an insurgency in Iraq, U.S. forces continued to commit abuses, such as torturing and mistreating detainees and occasionally using excessive force in counterinsurgency operations. Courts-martial of soldiers responsible for these abuses have been few, focusing mainly on the bottom of the chain of command, and sentences have been light. This lack of rigorous commitment to upholding the laws of armed conflict is incompatible with a genuinely humanitarian intervention.

Better Rather than Worse

A humanitarian intervention should be reasonably calculated to make things better rather than worse for the people ostensibly being rescued. One is tempted to say that anything is better than living under the tyranny of Saddam Hussein, but unfortunately, at least in the years immediately following the invasion, life for most Iraqis was arguably worse. Vicious as his rule was, the subsequent chaos and sectarian strife were even deadlier. Car-bombings and assassinations became daily occurrences. At least for those unfortunate enough to live in those parts of the country such as Baghdad where civil war effectively raged, the death toll apparently surpassed most years of Saddam's rule and approached all but the most murderous ones.

Still, in March 2003 when the war was launched, the American and British governments clearly hoped that the Iraqi regime would topple quickly and that the Iraqi nation would soon be on the path to democracy. With the benefit of hindsight, those expectations were naïve, and America's and Britain's failure to equip themselves with the number of troops needed to stabilize postwar Iraq significantly diminished the likelihood of this rosy scenario coming to pass. However, in light of the sheer horror of Saddam Hussein's reign, even in its less murderous moments, I would tend to grant proponents of the war the reasonableness of their expectation that, on balance, Iraqis would be better off if his regime were militarily ended. But that one factor, in light of the failure to meet the other criteria, does not justify the intervention as humanitarian.

UN Approval

There is considerable value in receiving the endorsement of the UN Security Council or another major multilateral body before launching a humanitarian intervention. The need to convince others of the appropriateness of a proposed intervention helps to safeguard against pretextual or unjustified action. An international commitment also increases the likelihood that adequate personnel and resources will be devoted to the intervention and its aftermath. And approval by the Security Council, in particular, ends the debate about the legality of an intervention.

However, in situations of extreme humanitarian need, council approval should not be required. In its current form, the council is too imperfect to make it the sole mechanism for legitimizing humanitarian intervention. Its permanent membership is a relic of the post–World War II era, and its veto system allows those members to block the rescue of people facing mass slaughter for the most parochial of reasons. In light of these faults, one's patience with the council's approval process would understandably diminish if large-scale slaughter were under way. However, because there was no such urgency for Iraq in early 2003, failure to win council approval, let alone the endorsement of any other multilateral body, weighs more heavily in assessing the interveners' claim to humanitarianism.

Of course, the Security Council was never asked to opine on a purely humanitarian intervention in Iraq. The principal case presented to it was built on the Iraqi government's alleged position of and failure to account for weapons of mass destruction. Even so, approval might have ameliorated at least some of the factors that stood in the way of the invasion being genuinely humanitarian. Most significant, a council-approved invasion is likely to have seen more troops from other nations join the predominantly American and British forces, meaning that preparation for the postwar chaos might have been better. Invasion approved by the council would also have provided greater international legitimacy and thus a less compelling rallying cry for the Iraqi insurgency.

Summing Up

In sum, the invasion of Iraq fails the test for a humanitarian intervention. Most important, the killing in Iraq at the time was not of the dire and exceptional nature that would justify military action. In addition, intervention was not the last reasonable option to stop Iraqi atrocities. It was not motivated primarily by humanitarian concerns. It was not conducted in a way that maximized compliance with international humanitarian law. It was not approved by the Security Council. And while, at the time it was launched, it was reasonable to believe that the Iraqi people would be better off, it was not designed or carried out with the needs of Iraqis foremost in mind.

The prominence of the Iraq War—a result of the sheer size of the invasion, the central involvement of the world's superpower, and the enormous controversy surrounding the war—has given it great power to shape public perceptions. As a result, the effort to justify the Iraq War even in part in humanitarian terms risks giving humanitarian intervention a bad name. If that breeds cynicism about the use of military force for humanitarian purposes, it could undermine the concept of a responsibility to protect people facing mass atrocities and be devastating for people in need of future assistance.

Yes, Saddam Hussein was an awful tyrant. Few shed tears at his overthrow. But in the interest of preserving popular support for a rescue option on which future potential victims of mass slaughter will depend, proponents of the Iraq war should not try to justify it as a humanitarian intervention.

Five Years Into the War

Even if the invasion of Iraq cannot be justified as a humanitarian intervention, what meaning does the responsibility to protect have in the face of continuing sectarian strife in Iraq that has sometimes risen to the level of a civil war? That is, even if the responsibility to protect cannot justify the original war, writing in mid-2008 one might ask whether the killing since the invasion has been so intense as to justify, at the very least, ongoing military intervention?

There have been times since 2003 when the situation in Iraq has been dire enough to implicate the responsibility to protect. Iraqis at times were dying because of the conflict at a rate of tens of thousands if not hundreds of thousands a year. Although those killed were predominately males between the ages of fifteen and forty-four, the large number of execution victims regularly found on Iraqi streets indicates that many of the dead had not been killed in combat. Yet, as noted, it is wrong to equate the responsibility to protect with humanitarian intervention. To be justified on humanitarian terms, military action should meet the above-noted criteria, and in today's Iraq, it does not.

For these purposes, I will assume that two of the criteria for humanitarian intervention can be met. At times the level of slaughter has been and might continue to be sufficiently high to meet the first test of a humanitarian intervention outlined above—ongoing or imminent mass slaughter. In addition, while the UN Security Council did not approve the initial invasion of Iraq, it has sanctioned the continuing military presence.

However, the failure clearly to meet the other criteria leads me to conclude that current military operations should not be characterized as a humanitarian intervention. First, there is insufficient reason to believe that an ongoing foreign military presence will make things better rather than worse. The much-touted U.S.-led "surge" seemed to contribute to a reduction in the violence, although much of that reduction was also due to parallel U.S. efforts to buy off and co-opt Sunni tribal and militia leaders. On the other hand, there is evidence that the U.S. presence is fueling the conflict—by giving arms to the warring factions, providing a rallying cry to those who oppose a foreign occupation, and granting an excuse for Iraqi political leaders not to make the tough political compromises needed to stabilize the country. Under these circumstances, it is difficult to conclude with any certainty that the U.S. military presence is, all things considered, beneficial.

Second, this failure of Iraqi leadership suggests that military action is not the last feasible option for addressing ongoing violence. It is far from clear that serious efforts have been made to resolve the political disputes underlying many of the attacks by Sunni insurgents or Shiite militia, whether concerning the distribution of oil revenues, the extent of de-Baathification, the official role of Islam, or the relationship between the central and regional governments. The United States and other outsiders may have been reluctant to force through compromises on these issues out of deference to Iraqi sovereignty, but deference to national governments must give way when mass atrocities are under way.

Similarly, there has been no serious invocation of international justice mechanisms as a way of deterring the continued killing in Iraq. Although leaders of the Sunni insurgency can anticipate rough treatment should the Shiite-dominated government capture them, the leaders of the Shiite militia and other government allies have enjoyed effective impunity. The federal government has shown no willingness to crack down on them. Such circumstances, in which a national government is either unwilling or unable to prosecute war crimes and crimes against humanity, cry out for the involvement of the International Criminal Court (ICC). If militia or insurgency leaders faced the risk of prosecution by an international tribunal over which their intimidation and violence would hold no sway, they might think twice about leading brazen attacks on civilians. But the United States has opposed ICC involvement in Iraq, in part out of an ideological dislike for the institution and in part out of fear that the conduct of U.S. forces would be scrutinized. Since Iraq has not ratified the ICC treaty, the ICC could acquire jurisdiction only upon a vote of the UN Security Council, where the U.S. government has veto power. Given the lives at risk, Washington should transcend its squeamishness about the ICC (as it did for Darfur) and allow the council to confer jurisdiction on the court, at least before Washington can argue that humanitarian intervention is the last reasonable option.

Third, international military forces' compliance with international humanitarian law, at least in the past, has been spotty at best. That has been particularly true with respect to detention and interrogation practices, but also, at times, with respect to the imperative of avoiding civilian casualties during armed conflict. Because of security conditions, it is difficult to say whether these abuses continue and thus would be likely to plague ongoing military action in the name of humanitarian intervention. But the widespread failure to hold abusers accountable in any serious way means that a risk of recurrence exists and would tend to work against the humanitarian nature of the military endeavor. Such abuses, were they to occur, would not only be wrong and contrary to the humanitarian spirit in their own right, but would also fuel popular Iraqi resentment and thus add to the difficulty of the foreign military presence playing a constructive role.

Finally, current military efforts in Iraq are undoubtedly motivated in part by humanitarian motives, but geopolitical factors, such as containing Iran, also play a major role. That means that international troops may not be motivated foremost by the imperative of stopping the slaughter of civilians— a factor that undoubtedly contributes to the other failures outlined above.

None of this is to say that the world should stand complacently by as Iraqi armed groups murder each other and countless civilians. The responsibility to protect people facing mass atrocities requires active efforts to stop the killing, including the political and judicial efforts mentioned above. But in today's circumstances in which there is insufficient reason to believe that the continued presence of foreign troops in Iraq is stopping rather than perpetuating the killing, reasonable political and judicial options have not been tried, international forces have not been consistently held accountable for violations of international humanitarian law, and nonhumanitarian motives play a significant role in the conduct of international forces, the stringent standards for justifying humanitarian intervention have not been met.

Note

* Kenneth Roth is the executive director of Human Rights Watch. This chapter draws in part on an earlier and shorter version that was published in *Human Rights in the "War on Terror*," edited by Richard Ashby Wilson (Cambridge: Cambridge University Press, 2005), and *Human Rights Watch World Report 2004* (New York: Human Rights Watch, 2004).

7

The Democratic
Republic of the Congo

A Story of Lost Opportunities to
Prevent or Reduce Deadly Conflicts

Herbert F. Weiss*

In today's wars, civilian populations inevitably pay the greatest price in suffering, torture, and death. It is very difficult for responsible members of the international community to protect the victims of such deadly conflicts. Yet that is what is called for by the emerging norm of the "responsibility to protect." The need to protect is not only best served by prevention, often it cannot be served in any other way. The Democratic Republic of the Congo (DRC) is a case in point. The wars and local conflicts that have occurred there between 1996 and the present are said to have cost the lives of more than five million persons. It is estimated that these conflicts have also produced around two million internally displaced persons and several hundred thousand refugees in neighboring countries. To protect these millions would have taken an international force far beyond any number that is politically imaginable. Therefore, preventing or at least reducing violence is a more realistic and feasible goal than protection.

The different Congolese and African armed forces and militia that have been present and in conflict in the Congo have one common trait: they behave in an undisciplined and extremely abusive manner, especially when operating among people who are not their ethnic kin. They have caused many massacres, broken every "human right," recruited children, and raped women.

If the premise is accepted that prevention is sometimes the only effective means of protecting innocent civilian populations, and if this is indeed the case with regard to the history of the DRC, then it is more important to focus on the lost opportunities—when prevention or at least mitigation was possible but, for one reason or another, not acted upon—than it is to denounce the abuses or regret that so little protection was offered.

Some knowledge of the history of the DRC is necessary to understand how this country has become the theater of countless atrocities over the last fourteen years. It is difficult to know where to start because, as in every other country, past events are linked in chains of cause-and-effect relationships. For the purpose of this essay, this historical overview will begin with the Rwandan genocide. This event did not occur in the Congo, but it has had a catastrophic impact on it.

From the Genocide in Rwanda to the Rise of Kabila (1994–97)

Genocide in Rwanda (1994)

The first event that transformed the relatively nonviolent Congolese society into an arena of massacres and war is the genocide of the Tutsi people in Rwanda in 1994. It should be recalled that this involved Hutu leaders mobilizing almost the entire Hutu population in the mass murder of their Tutsi cocitizens and some moderate Hutus.

The Tutsi genocide completely changed the balance of power in the Kivu provinces in eastern Congo. When the Tutsi-dominated Rwanda Patriotic Army (RPA) defeated the Hutu government of Rwanda (which had perpetrated the genocide), about a million Hutu—some with French army cover—moved into eastern Congo. These Hutu border crossers were housed in United Nations High Commissioner for Refugees (UNHCR) camps close to the Rwanda border. In these camps the political and military personnel that had been responsible for the genocide reestablished themselves and launched attacks against the new Tutsi-dominated government of Rwanda. From the Congolese perspective, the ethnic balance in eastern Congo, in the Kivu provinces, was seriously upset. The Hutu became a dominant force in some parts of the Kivus and proceeded to isolate and attack Congolese Tutsi. These attacks gained political and eventually military support from the Congolese (then Zairian) army and some Kivu politicians.

The establishment of the UNHCR camps close to the border between the Congo and Rwanda, and their use as bases by the Rwandan Hutu militia (the Interahamwe) and former Hutu-dominated Rwandan army (the ex-FAR [Forces armées rwandaises]), was not only contrary to UNHCR principles, but constituted a danger to international peace. But with its limited resources, UNHCR was overwhelmed by the number of Hutu refugees. In a feeble and misguided attempt to gain some control over the camps, UNHCR hired members of Mobutu's presidential guard—allies of the Rwandan Hutu military—to police the camp populations.

With the changed balance of power in the Kivus, Congolese Tutsi society had to face the danger of an ethnic cleansing campaign organized against them. Some of them undertook a preemptive strike against the FAZ (*Forces armées zaïroises*) soldiers and the Hutu "refugee" camps in their neighborhood in September 1996. It is very probable that these attacks were coordinated with Rwanda. At any rate, Rwandan forces entered the fray and the war against the camps as well as the Mobutu regime had begun.

General Paul Kagame, at the time vice president of Rwanda, pleaded with the international community from 1994 to 1996 to separate the ex-FAR and the Interahamwe from civilian refugees and to make it impossible for the camps to be used to launch attacks against Rwanda. When nothing was done, he warned that in the end Rwanda would act on its own. His words were not taken seriously. The threat to expel some of the Congolese Tutsi from their homes in the DRC was, therefore, a gift from the heavens for Kagame, since Rwanda was able to defend its cross-border advances as preventing another genocidal attack against a Tutsi community.

In rapid succession, the Rwandan army attacked the Hutu camps and Mobutu's army with the result that the ex-FAR and the Interahamwe fled westward accompanied by many Hutu civilians. The vast majority of the Hutu civilians walked back into Rwanda where they were channeled to their home communities. In subsequent months, the retreating Hutu both fought for the Mobutu regime and were massacred—men, women, and children—by the advancing anti-Mobutu armies.

Could this invasion have been prevented? Possibly, if the international community had spent the funds necessary to distance the UNHCR camps from the Rwanda border and, even more importantly, brought in sufficient force to demilitarize them.

The First Congo War (1996–97)

It is obvious that it was very much in the interest of Rwanda—almost immediately joined by Uganda and somewhat later by Angola—to portray their actions as something other than an attack against a sovereign state. Finding Congolese allies against Mobutu was, therefore, a priority. But the problem facing them was that, although a broad and substantial Congolese opposition to Mobutu did exist, it had firmly opted for a nonviolent strategy.

Since the "nonviolent opposition" to Mobutu—as it was called—showed no inclination for joining the attacks on the camps and the FAZ, other allies had to be found. These were the circumstances that produced the Alliance des Forces Démocratiques pour la Libération du Congo (AFDL) made up of four Congolese revolutionary parties in exile, all of which had almost no following. One of the four initial leaders was Laurent Désiré Kabila, who had been a zone commander during the Congo Rebellion in the mid 1960s, and he appointed himself head of the movement. The AFDL, therefore, became the main Congolese partner of an invasion by Rwanda, Uganda, and Angola that was also given support by other African states determined to rid the Congo of the Mobutu regime.

Mobutu's army retreated on all fronts and in so doing looted, raped, and killed Congolese civilians. This was one reason why the Congolese welcomed the AFDL and allowed young men and boys to be recruited into its ranks. The motivation of Rwanda for undertaking this war has already been cited. For Uganda, a similar but less pressing motive existed. The DRC had for some time been used as a rear base by anti-Museveni forces such as the West Nile Bank Front and the Allied Democratic Forces, some of which were supported by the Sudanese government. By occupying the frontier region in the DRC, Uganda hoped to end this threat. Angola had very much the same motive. The National Union for the Total Independence of Angola (UNITA) had for years been supplied via the DRC, and there were UNITA bases in the country.

During the anti-Mobutu alliance's quick march to Kinshasa (September 1996 to May 1997), it soon became clear that Kabila planned to lead a veritable cultural revolution in the Congo with an authoritarian, leftist character, and he disdainfully rejected any participation by the substantial "nonviolent opposition."

During the short First Congo War, a substantial number of the Hutu who had been expelled from the UNHCR camps retreated westward. They were made up of former army, ex-FAR, and Hutu militia members, the Interahamwe, and thousands of civilians that had joined them in their retreat. Some observers have concluded that as many as 200,000 Hutu were involved. Some walked as far as western Congo, the Central African Republic, and the Republic of Congo (Brazzaville) to escape their pursuers. Reports began to appear in the media that they were being massacred. However, no serious effort was undertaken to protect them.

However, once the Kabila regime was installed in Kinshasa the international community did insist on investigating the alleged massacres that the retreating Hutu had suffered. For Kabila, relations with the UN and with Western states soon became dominated by this issue, and Kabila thwarted every attempt to undertake such an investigation. This resulted in a rapid change of attitude by Western powers as well as the UN—from one that placed great hope in and anticipated support for his regime to one of estrangement and virtual abandonment. Most projected foreign financial aid was held up because of this lack of cooperation.

The failure to investigate the massacres of the retreating Hutu military, militia, and civilians raises a number of questions pertinent to the issue of "responsibility to protect." First, it would have been virtually impossible to protect the retreating Hutu since these events occurred in the short span of seven months—hardly enough time to mount some sort of international force, even if there had been the will to do so. But since the Hutu were seen as the perpetrators of the Rwandan genocide, they had few sympathizers. The UN and the Western powers did exert a great deal of pressure on the Kabila regime to allow the investigation to go forward, but to no avail. Not only were these Hutu groups not protected, but their fate could not be investigated. This occurred despite the fact that the newly installed Kabila regime was weak and needed the financial support promised by the West.

A separate question is whether the focus of this Western pressure pointed in the right direction. There is substantial evidence that the massacres were committed by Rwandan troops, not the AFDL. Some Congolese have argued that Kabila would have been assassinated by the Rwandans had he permitted the investigation to go forward. So one may legitimately ask why the focus of the investigation was not on the Kagame regime in Rwanda instead of on Kabila, who at the time was literally surrounded by Rwandan bodyguards. Furthermore, if the reports of massacres had been taken seriously, pressure could have been put on Rwanda and Uganda to treat the retreating Hutu civilians in a manner consistent with international norms.

The Second Congo War (1998–99): The First "African Continental War"

The period between the First and Second Congo Wars amounted to a failed condominium between Kabila and his foreign sponsors. Kabila acted too independently and is reported again and again to have ignored advice given to him. Perhaps a conflict between them was inevitable, since any Congolese president would have sought to legitimize himself with the Congolese public and that would have necessitated distancing himself from foreign, especially militarily present, sponsors. But it must also be said that Kabila provoked both internal and external opposition that was not inevitable.

During June and July 1998 relations between Kabila and the Rwandans had reached a boiling point. Some of Kabila's collaborators were reported to have concluded that a Rwandan officer was about to assassinate him. In this atmosphere, Tutsi families in Kinshasa began to feel insecure and started to leave. On July 27, the Rwandan mission of cooperation was terminated by the DRC and the Rwandan military was asked to leave immediately. On July 29, they flew back to Kigali. A little over a year earlier they had been received as liberators; now public opinion in Kinshasa vehemently approved of their de facto expulsion.

It is not an exaggeration to say that the next twenty days profoundly changed the history of Africa and launched the continent into what some have called the First African World War. A few days after the expulsion of the Rwandan military, a "mutiny" or "rebellion" started in eastern Congo and Rwandan army units crossed the frontier in force to support it. On August 4, a spectacular cross-continent airlift was organized by Rwanda and Uganda in which a plane full of their troops landed at Kitona army base, located near the Atlantic Ocean coast close to Angola. Kitona held ten to fifteen thousand former FAZ soldiers who were being "reeducated" under very harsh conditions. The Rwandan/Ugandan force of approximately 150 soldiers managed to mobilize these troops in support of an uprising against Kabila. Within days, they captured a number of towns and most importantly the Inga hydroelectric dam, where they were able to cut off electricity supplies to Kinshasa as well as Katanga. In effect, the capital was threatened by a militarily advance from the west.

In the east, the alliance between the "mutinous" FAC units and the Rwandan and Ugandan armed forces soon controlled most of northeast DRC. Shortly thereafter, a group of Congolese politicians—for a wide variety of reasons and coming from very different political backgrounds—came together in Goma to form the RCD—Rassemblement Congolais pour la Démocratie—which rejected the legitimacy of Kabila's government in Kinshasa and sought to replace it.

A momentous decision by Angola changed what seemed to be the inevitable downfall of Kabila and much of subsequent Central African history. Unlike its policy in 1996–97, when it joined Rwanda and Uganda in their invasion of the DRC, this time Angola switched sides and attacked the Rwanda-Uganda positions in the lower Congo from its bases in Cabinda. The anti-Kabila forces were surrounded. Some of their troops had reached the outskirts of Kinshasa where they were attacked by the population and massacred. The cross-continent maneuver had failed, and the Kabila regime had been saved. Angola was soon joined by Zimbabwe, which also sent a military expedition to help Kabila.

In the Kinshasa-controlled areas, a pogrom against all Tutsi, whether of Rwandan or Congolese nationality, was organized by Kabila. No outside force was in a position to protect these Tutsi, nor was it contemplated. The Tutsi pogrom in 1998 has never been the subject of an official investigation.

In the period 1998–99, the Second Congo War created an expensive balance of power in Central Africa. In succeeding months, neither side was able to defeat the other. Much international pressure was exerted to end the fighting, especially by African governments. These conditions and pressures finally resulted in the signing of the Lusaka Cease-Fire Agreement in 1999. It established a complex road map for peace: the "genius" of the agreement is to be found in its acceptance by almost all the major actors involved in the war. It includes three principal pillars as the foundation for peace and reconciliation. First, obtaining the departure of foreign armies on both sides of the conflict. Second, realizing the disarming and reintegration of foreign insurgency militias operating on and from Congolese soil. Third, establishing an internal dialogue among all armed and nonarmed Congolese forces in order to create a transitional government leading to reunification, democratic elections, and legitimacy. The Lusaka Cease-Fire Agreement came about in large part because of extensive Western, especially U.S., and South African pressure. It is a moment when the terrible danger of a much wider war in Central Africa was avoided. This was a triumph of prevention even though it came after blood had been spilled and continued to be spilled in some parts of the Congo.

In order to accomplish these goals the agreement called for a Chapter VII UN Peacekeeping Mission that was expected to ensure implementation of the agreement. Once again, no one was there to protect the victims of the Second Congo War or of the Tutsi pogrom in the Kinshasa-controlled area or of the growing number of massacres committed by the Rwandan/Ugandan forces and their Congolese allies in the eastern Congo area they controlled. However, the Lusaka Agreement did promise to mitigate the harm already done, and the cease-fire did hold for the most part.

Although the Lusaka Agreement successfully contained a regional war, it failed to stabilize the east DRC where a guerrilla-type war developed in an area that the cease-fire defined as being ruled by the RCD and other "rebel" movements. This war pitted two alliances against each other. The first was composed of four forces: (1) the local Mai Mai militia groups; (2) the ex-FAR/Interahamwe now, called the *Forces Démocratiques de Libération du Rwanda* (FDLR); (3) the Burundian insurgency militia, the

Forces pour la Défense de la Démocratie (FDD); and (4) the Kinshasa regime. The second was composed of the RCD/Goma and the Rwandan/Ugandan armed forces, and to a lesser extent the Burundian armed forces.[1] The anti-RCD/Rwandan/Ugandan alliance had continual military, material, and moral support of Kinshasa long after the signing of the Lusaka Cease-Fire Agreement. In effect, a "Third Congo War" developed in eastern DRC. It is most important to note that in those RCD/Goma-controlled areas where no guerrilla activities had developed—mainly the part of Kasai Province under its control—little violence and far fewer casualties occurred.

The Third Congo War (1999–2007):
A Neglected, Lethal Conflict

The "Third Congo War" has produced by far the largest number of casualties and has continued for longer than either the First or the Second Congo War. It did not come to an end once the transition government came into existence in June 2003; neither did it end after the democratically elected government took office in 2007.

One of the biggest obstacles faced by the United Nations Mission in the Democratic Republic of Congo (MONUC) in dealing with the Third Congo War was the fact that politically, violence in the east—and this soon became the only place where there was serious violence—was the ace of spades in the hand of the Kinshasa authorities. The Kinshasa authorities had failed to unite the Congo militarily, the standard of living of the people under their authority was falling, and "little" Rwanda had humiliated them on more than one occasion, but in the Rwandan sphere of influence run by the RCD/Goma, conditions were far worse and violent confrontations occurred almost every day. For Kinshasa, the Mai Mai were patriots fighting the "Rwandan invaders" and their "stooges." Indeed, Kinshasa declared that the Mai Mai were part of its army.

The policies pursued by both the major Western embassies and MONUC supported the official "government" of the DRC and sought to get along with its leaders. That is probably the reason why, despite daily conflicts pitting the Kinshasa-supported Mai Mai against the RCD/Goma-Rwandan alliance, MONUC never declared a cease-fire violation. This head-in-the-sand reaction was compounded by the fact that MONUC failed to send any substantial military assets to the east until 2003.

In sum, from 1999 until 2003, when the transition government was established, Western powers and MONUC neglected the politics and the war in the eastern DRC. The emphasis of Western diplomatic efforts was constantly aimed at the establishment of a transitional government. A change in Western/UN policy occurred when the goal of establishing such a government—and thereby, at least formally, the reunification of the country—became a reality. Only at that late moment—roughly early 2003—did the various lethal conflicts in the east begin to receive real attention. In the meantime, the death rate skyrocketed—in 2001 the estimate of war-related deaths stood at about 3.5 million, in 2007 it had reached more than 5 million.

Did the international community lose an opportunity to mitigate violence in the east? At least in two respects the answer has to be yes. First, MONUC should have sent its military assets to the east where the violence was ongoing. Whereas it would be naïve to claim that the relatively small MONUC force could have ended this violence, subsequent events have shown that when a substantial portion of MONUC's military assets were sent to the east they did have a positive effect. And it should be noted that this deployment was preceded by a French military mission in Bunia in early 2003—the Artemis Mission—where a particularly lethal conflict between Lendu and Hema militia had taken place. Second, there were opportunities for negotiating and supporting local cease-fire agreements that were not pursued. An important example is the Butembo Agreement negotiated by Jean Pierre Bemba, at the time head of the Mouvement de Libération du Congo (MLC) in 2001. This agreement brought the major antagonists in north Kivu and Ituri together in a peace accord. They included the local Mai Mai groups, the Hema and Lendu leaders, the Catholic Church, the armed forces of the different rebel movements, and Ugandan military leaders. The agreement soon fell apart, probably because of Ugandan manipulations, but had the international community taken a serious interest in this attempt it might have born fruit. Why was such interest absent? Because it was not sanctioned by the Kinshasa authorities.

Western diplomats and MONUC appear to have assumed that once progress was made on establishing a transitional government in Kinshasa, such a government would be able to stop or sharply reduce the violence in the east. But this did not happen. The war in the east had gone on for too long and the establishment of the transition government in far off Kinshasa had not resolved the underlying tensions. In addition, the social fabric holding together some eastern ethnic groups had disintegrated under the impact of the war so that traditional leaders were often helpless when faced with militia groups largely made up of young men and child soldiers. Moreover, as time passed, armed militia groups increased in number and decreased in size. This multiplication of warring factions made it much more difficult to negotiate their disarming and disbanding.

Throughout the years 1999 to 2003 an alternative Western/MONUC policy could have been pursued. It would have involved extending the concern and energy shown in 1999 in favor of achieving a cease-fire between the main parties to the conflict, particularly the lethal, local conflicts in the east. But even when such an approach was attempted by elements of the UN it did not receive adequate support. For example, in 2001 the two most important opponents in the east, the Mai Mai and the RCD/Goma, indicated a willingness to negotiate. A high-level United Nations Development Programme (UNDP) mission report noted that the potential for local cease-fire negotiations between some Mai Mai groups and the RCD/Goma existed and could and should be pursued.[2] However, neither the UN nor the U.S. government nor the European Union (EU) adopted these recommendations. Some private and international nongovernmental organization (NGO) initiatives along these lines were undertaken, but without support from MONUC or key players such as the United States, progress was extremely slow. During 2003–4, some local cease-fire negotiations did succeed. The most important was the agreement between the Mai Mai leader General Padiri and the RCD/Goma, but the overall impact was quite limited as the carnage continued.

This complex history clearly suggests that until very recently the international community was only willing to seriously engage in peace initiatives in eastern DRC when they were supported by the Kinshasa authorities. In Ituri, that was the case after Kinshasa made an alliance with the RCD/ML—in whose zone Bunia fell—but not before. In the Kivus, that did not happen until the transition government—dominated by the Kinshasa authorities—came into being.

If one asks why so little was done in eastern Congo by the UN or the Western states with influence in Central Africa, there is no good answer. The best explanation one can come up with is that the UN, the European powers, and the United States put all their eggs in one basket, the move toward the transition government, and that government was largely dominated by the Kinshasa authorities led by Joseph Kabila. Proactively seeking to reduce violence in the east, where it was rampant, would have meant mediating between rebel movements like the RCD/Goma, the MLC, and the Mai Mai, and that would have offended the Kinshasa authorities. It is true that it would also quite possibly have strengthened the RCD/Goma or the MLC and therefore hindered progress in achieving the goal of forming the transition regime because Kinshasa was determined to bloc any compromise that undermined the future of the Kabila presidency. Indeed, in the few instances when mediation in the east was informally attempted, the Kinshasa authorities objected loudly. Once the goal of establishing a

Kinshasa-dominated transition government was in sight, MONUC moved its military assets to the east and began to have some impact on conflict reduction, but it was late, the impact was limited, and mediation was too infrequently attempted.

What was the price of the neglect, for several years, of the greatest arena of conflict, death, and torture? The International Rescue Committee sponsored several demographic studies to determine the mortality rate of the war. The study, covering the period August 1998 to April 2000, estimated that 2.5 million deaths had occurred because of the conflict. Most of the deaths resulted from the secondary effects of war. However, significantly for the present analysis, in the areas where conflict was intense (i.e., north and south Kivu and Ituri), there were ninety persons killed (versus "died") for every single person killed in nonconflict areas, even in eastern Congo (for instance, in the RCD/Goma-controlled area of Sankuru District in Kasai Oriental).[3]

The End of Transition:
Elections and Legitimacy

In June 2003, the long sought-after transition government was finally put in place. It involved a grand compromise among all internal parties to the conflict that had torn the Congo apart since 1996. The transition government tasked itself with a vast program: nationwide voter registration was organized, a new constitution was written and adopted, and presidential, legislative, and provincial elections were held.

International observers viewed the election itself as a great success. The international community supported this exercise in several ways: it paid the lion's share of the election costs, amounting to well over five hundred million dollars, and MONUC helped in numerous ways, including employing its fast fleet of planes to transport election materials. Yet large numbers of Congolese suspected that the election had been manipulated in order to give power to Kabila and his supporters. Kabila won the election by a margin of 58 percent to 42 percent.

Immediately after the election there was a precipitous decline in the power of the political opposition and a considerable degree of triumphalism on the part of the winners. Whether this expensive exercise will herald a new period of pluralism, checks and balances, decentralization, and respect for human rights—the ostensible goal—remains to be seen.

In the east, the elections and the installation of an elected government both in Kinshasa and in the provinces did not seriously impact the level of violence and conflict that had persisted there since 1996. By early 2008, militia groups in eastern Congo were still operating despite MONUC having transferred most of its military assets to that region and despite an effort to integrate militia members in the new DRC army, the Forces Armées de la République Démocratique du Congo (FARDC). Perhaps the most critical remaining issue is the continued presence of the Rwandan Hutu FDLR, the ex-FAR/Interahamwe militia that have refused to return to Rwanda and have resisted both MONUC and DRC government efforts to persuade them to accept repatriation. They are accused of gross human rights violations, especially aimed at women, and of attempting to chase villagers in south Kivu away from their homes so that they can establish themselves on their land in a quasi-permanent fashion. This has become one of the worst arenas of civilian abuse, and yet nothing effective is being done to protect the affected population. The problem is simply too large. On several occasions the FARDC has announced campaigns against the FDLR with MONUC logistical support. But these probes have not, up to the present, produced the desired result—the repatriation of FDLR members to Rwanda or their disarming.

A second major challenge is posed by a militia largely made up of Congolese Tutsi, the *Congrès National pour la Défense du Peuple* (CNDP), led by General Nkunda. This militia group has not only established a strong base in north Kivu, but dealt the FARDC a severe military defeat in late 2007.

These unresolved challenges have, however, resulted in a positive development. For the first time a peace conference has been called in eastern Congo with the specific goal of seeking peace and development for the Kivu Provinces. The Goma conference—*La conférence sur la paix, la sécurité et le développement du Kivu*—began in January 2008 and has had strong and very real support both from the international community, that is to say from the European Union, the United States, and the UN, and the DRC government. Just about every militia group active in eastern Congo has participated and has joined the follow-up process that was established by the conference. The only significant group that was not invited was the Rwandan Hutu FDLR.

It is too early to predict whether this effort will achieve the goal of peace and development, and above all an end to the bloodshed and the abuse of civilians, especially women. It is very late in the game and it is far from clear that the necessary compromises will be made. But at least all the major groups contending for power and fighting each other have participated in a process that seeks solutions to the long nightmare of violence in eastern Congo, and that effort has the strong support of the international community. If such conferences had been created and supported in the long period between 2000 and 2007, the incredible price in blood paid by the people of eastern Congo would probably have been greatly reduced and perhaps stopped altogether.

Conclusion

In accepting the request made in the Lusaka Cease-Fire Agreement that a peacekeeping mission be sent to the DRC, the Security Council placed itself in the position of being neutral between warring states and internal adversaries. One of these actors was the Kinshasa authority that, at the time, controlled less than half of the country. The Lusaka Agreement— signed by Kinshasa—explicitly stated that with regard to the "internal dialogue," all Congolese factions (i.e., including the Kinshasa authorities) would be negotiating as equals, but in the international arena, the Kinshasa authorities were viewed as the government of the DRC, and both vis-à-vis MONUC and the most important embassies in Kinshasa that made a world of difference. In an instance of what can be called "diplomacy as usual," the "government" was deferred to. As stated earlier, its record in the area it controlled was not that great. Militarily it had failed to win the Second Congo War despite massive foreign military support and intervention from Angola, Zimbabwe, Chad, Namibia, Sudan, and others. Social and economic conditions in the region it controlled declined steadily. Its human rights record was deplorable. Humiliated by the military success of Rwanda and Uganda and their Congolese allies, Kinshasa saw the Mai Mai uprising against the RCD/Goma and Rwanda as its trump card, for it weakened, day by day, its greatest enemies—the RCD/Goma and Rwanda. Understandably Kinshasa supported that uprising as much as it could. But what was the price of this policy? The ever-growing calamity that was the Third Congo War. It is less understandable why in the face of this calamity the international community, MONUC, the United States, and other major embassies stood by Kinshasa and neglected the east, never even calling the violence there a cease-fire violation, but that is what happened.

Of course, if the will had been there, if the responsibility to protect had meant something substantial, it might have been possible to reverse this horrific and deadly tide, but that would have required an international force many times the size of MONUC. Yet, not only was there no will to send an appropriate number of troops to a country the size of Western Europe with about sixty million inhabitants, but the major powers did not even use the real opportunities that existed from 1999 to 2003 to engage in mediation in order to reduce conflict and casualties where the blood flowed the most. The major lesson to be learned from this sad history is that the international community should engage itself in peacemaking, whether it is between states and major actors in a civil war—as it did in helping to give birth to the Lusaka Agreement—or between local militia. The effort should focus on the arena where the violence is the greatest.

Notes

* Herbert F. Weiss is emeritus professor of political science at the City University of New York and senior policy scholar at the Woodrow Wilson International Center for Scholars in Washington, DC. An earlier discussion of missed opportunities to prevent deadly conflict can be found in I. William Zartman, ed., *Cowardly Lions: Missed Opportunities to Prevent Deadly Conflict and State Collapse* (Boulder, CO: Lynne Rienner Publishers, 2005). The chapter on the Congo (Zaire) covers the period of 1991 to 1996.

1. In the north, in the Ugandan sphere of influence, violent confrontations continued in the area more or less controlled by the RCD/ML and others.

2. United Nations Development Program, *UNDP/Donor Mission to DRC/GLR, Defining UNDP's Role in Disarmament, Demobilization and Durable Solutions (D3), 6 August–13 September 2001*, p. 38, http://www.reliefweb.int/library/documents/2001/undp_glr_part2_28nov.pdf.

3. See International Rescue Committee, *Mortality in Eastern Democratic Republic of Congo: Results from Eleven Mortality Surveys, 2001*, http://www.theirc.org/media/www/mortality_study_eastern_dr_congo_februaryapril_2001.html. "Total death toll from the conflict (1998–2004) was estimated to be 3.9 million. Mortality rate was higher in unstable eastern provinces, showing the effect of insecurity. Most deaths were from easily preventable and treatable illnesses rather than violence. Regression analysis suggested that if the effects of violence were removed, all-cause mortality could fall to almost normal rates."; B. Coghlan et al., "Mortality in the Democratic Republic of Congo: A Nationwide Survey," *Lancet* 367, no. 9504 (2006): 44–51, http://www.thelancet.com.

8

Dealing with Atrocities in Northern Uganda

*Mary Page**

A prime case for considering the "responsibility to protect" involves northern Uganda, where, for the past twenty years, civilians have suffered from abductions, killings, and maimings by the Lord's Resistance Army (LRA), abuses by government military forces sent to fight the rebels, and disease and social disintegration in resettlement camps or "protected villages" set up in the northern districts. The long-term failure of the Ugandan government to provide security for the people in the north clearly raises questions about international action.

Atrocities and Loss of Life on a Large Scale

In 1986, after overthrowing the regimes of Milton Obote and Tito Okello and taking over the government, forces led by Yoweri Museveni marched north to subdue rebel groups associated with those leaders. As traditional stalwarts of the Ugandan military and generally loyal to Obote, members of the Acholi tribe in the north were particular targets. One Acholi rebel group, the Holy Spirit Movement (HSM), was led by a visionary, Alice Lakwena, who convinced her followers that rubbing shea butter oil on their skin would protect them from bullets and that rocks and bottles would turn to grenades when thrown at the enemy.[1] The HSM was surprisingly successful, winning several battles and reaching the outskirts of Kampala before it was defeated and Lakwena fled to Kenya in 1987. Lakwena's nephew, Joseph Kony, took up the cause, eventually rechristening it the Lord's Resistance Army (LRA). During the twenty years since that time, the

LRA has continued to be active against the government, with the level of fighting rising and falling, and alternating with thus far unsuccessful peace negotiations. At the time of this writing, a two-year-long peace effort centered around LRA-Government of Uganda talks in Juba, Sudan, has virtually collapsed.

Over the years the LRA has survived by seizing supplies, gaining recruits by force, and terrorizing the civilian population of northern Uganda, using mutilation and murder to frighten the population away from cooperating with government forces. Children have been the primary targets. In the course of the war, the LRA has abducted more than twenty thousand (perhaps as many as sixty thousand)[2] children to serve as soldiers, porters, slaves, and "wives" of commanders. Children have been required to transport heavy loads of arms and loot over long distances and endure other forms of forced labor under threat of beatings or death. They have often been forced to kill fellow captives or family members in their communities as a way of breaking connections with their past. They have been put on the front lines when the LRA confronts the Ugandan military. Some estimate that more than 85 percent of the LRA's combatants are children.

These crimes have been well documented by Human Rights Watch, Amnesty International, World Vision, and others. A few examples follow, given in the words of the victims.

Charles, fifteen:

> There had already been rumors that rebels were around, and we were very fearful. My grandmother was hiding in the bush. It was morning and I was practicing my music when I heard a shot. I started running into the bush, but there was a rebel hiding behind a tree. I thought he would shoot me. He said, "Stop, my friend, don't try to run away!" Then he beat me with the handle of the gun on my back. He ordered me to direct him, and told me that afterwards I would be released. But afterwards it was quite different. That afternoon we met with a very huge group of rebels, together with so many new captives. We marched and marched. In the bush we came across three young boys who had escaped from the rebels earlier, and they removed the boys' shirts and tied ropes around their throats so that when they killed them they would make no noise. Then they forced them down and started clubbing their heads, and other rebels came with bayonets and stabbed them. It was not a good sight.[3]

Edward T., eighteen:

> I was with the LRA for six months and during this time many abductees escaped. Not all were so lucky. One boy tried to escape and was caught, tied up, and marched back to camp. All the recruits from the various companies

were told that we were never going home, that we were fighting now with the LRA, so as a symbol of our pledge to fight on, this boy would be killed and we would help. Soldiers then laid the boy on the ground and stabbed him three times with a bayonet until the blood began seeping from the wounds. Then the new recruits approached the boy and beat him on the chest. Each one had a turn and could stop once the blood from the body splashed up on to you. This boy was sixteen years old. We were beating him with sticks, each recruit was given a stick.[4]

John, seventeen:

I did not kill anyone for the first four days of my captivity and then, on the fifth day, they said I had to prove I wasn't scared, they took me back to my village and ordered me to kill my father. At first, I said no, I can't kill my father, but then they started beating me with a panga [machete]. I took the panga and cut him up. I then saw them do it to my mother. The first night I was haunted by visions of my father as I tried to sleep. I could only cry silent tears as the rebels could not know that I regretted what I had done. They do it so you can't go back home.[5]

Stella, fifteen:

They came to our school in the middle of the night. We were hiding under the beds, but they pounded on the beds and told us to come out. They tied us and led us out, and they tried to set the school building on fire. We walked and walked and they made us carry their property that they had looted. At about six a.m. they made us stop and they lined up in two lines, and made us walk between them while they kicked us.

On the second day of marching our legs were swollen. They said, "Eh, now, what should we do about your legs? You must walk or do you want us to kill you? It's your choice." So we kept going.

On the third day a little girl tried to escape, and they made us kill her. They went to collect some big pieces of firewood. Then they kicked her and jumped on her, and they made us each beat her at least once with the big pieces of wood. They said, "You must beat and beat and beat her." She was bleeding from the mouth. Then she died. Then they made us lie down and they beat us with fifteen strokes each, because they said we had known she would try to escape.[6]

Raids on schools were common. The most famous of the school raids was the 1996 raid on Saint Mary's College boarding school in Aboke, from which 139 young girls were abducted. The deputy headmistress followed the LRA and convinced them to release 109.[7] Of the thirty that were left, five died while captive. The others were given as wives to commanders. All but two had returned by 2006.[8]

Government Response

The Ugandan government's military response to the LRA has been stronger sometimes than others, and peace initiatives have ebbed and flowed. The first major offensive, in 1991 (Operation North), was deemed a failure after attempts to arm local villagers with bows and arrows to fend off the rebels proved unsuccessful in the face of the LRA's modern weaponry and after Ugandan troop actions failed to dislodge the LRA from the bush. During this period the LRA moved its base into southern Sudan—with tacit endorsement of the Khartoum government—in response to Uganda's support of the Sudanese Popular Liberation Front (SPLA), which was engaged in a long civil war with the north. Following September 11, 2001, subsequent U.S. overtures to Khartoum in the war against terror, progress in the peace negotiations in southern Sudan, and waning Sudanese support for the LRA, the Ugandan government launched the Iron Fist offensive in 2002 on LRA bases in southern Sudan. This led to the return of the LRA in northern Uganda and a dramatic rise in violence, mutilation, and abductions.

Along with its military response to the LRA, the Ugandan government has offered incentives for surrender under the Amnesty Act. Enacted into law in 2000, the act promises amnesty for members of all rebel groups that surrender. A special commission was established to oversee amnesty applications and deliver resettlement packages (a blanket, mattress, seeds, and saucepans) and a small sum (about $150) to returnees. The LRA were at first slow to take advantage of the act, but beginning in 2003, spurred perhaps by the increasing pressure of the Iron Fist campaign and the gradual loss of a safe haven in southern Sudan, the number of applications by soldiers and abductees increased. By 2004 a total of more than five thousand people had applied, including some of the worst perpetrators, such as Brigadiers Kenneth Banya and Sam Kolo.[9] But it is not clear that the amnesty itself has been an inducement for persons to escape from Kony's army. According to recent U.S. Agency for International Development (USAID) interviews in centers set up to help reintegrate formerly abducted persons ("reception centers"), only 25 percent had received an amnesty card, applied for amnesty, or even heard about the Amnesty Commission, perhaps because information was hard to come by for rank and file in the bush or because Kony's commanders reportedly spread the word that the amnesty was a ruse and those who applied would be killed by the government.[10] After the initial surge of applicants, the numbers have slowed to just a few.

In addition to military action and amnesty, and in a further attempt to provide citizen protection and separate the populace from the rebels, the Ugandan government stepped up its program of "protected villages." These are camps for internally displaced people (IDP), collections of thatched mud huts thrown up around traditional roadside trading centers in outlying areas of the north. Begun in 1996, camps in the Acholi districts of Gulu, Pader, and Kitgum, and the Langi and Teso districts of Soroti and Lira mushroomed during the Iron Fist campaign, numbering more than two hundred and taking in nearly two million people—more than 90 percent of the population in some districts—in 2004.[11] The hastily planned and constructed government resettlement efforts were unequal to the task in many ways. People in the overcrowded camps—some of which housed as many as sixty thousand people—had limited access to food and water, minimal or no health facilities, few jobs, and minimal economic activity. The human immunodeficiency virus/acquired immunodeficiency syndrome (HIV/AIDS) rates in the camps skyrocketed, with an HIV prevalence of 9.1 percent in north-central Uganda in 2007.[12] The social fabric that had been built around kinship networks at the village level fell apart amid the poverty and violence in the camps. Traditional justice mechanisms that had helped to preserve social order no longer functioned.[13] And in the wake of the conflict, official justice institutions in the north collapsed.[14]

Uganda has been widely hailed as a model for the provision of education. Primary and, as of January 2007, secondary education has been free, although uniforms are required. But secondary schools in the IDP camps are rare and all camp schools function at a low level, with few basic materials and a high dropout rate, especially among girls. Added to this are the consequences of the high rate of abduction among young people, which has taken children away from organized schooling, leaving them not only with psychological scars, but behind their peers in formal education as well. Studies have shown that those who have undergone periods of abduction are more likely to have fewer years of education and to be illiterate.[15]

The camps failed to provide physical protection as well. Army detachments were often positioned in the center of the camps, making the perimeter a prime target for LRA incursions and abductions. Civilians have been subject to abuses by the Ugandan Army and during the conflict were under constant suspicion of collaborating with the rebels. In a region once known as "Uganda's breadbasket," men and women who attempted to cultivate small garden plots at the edges of the camps were in danger of being arrested or worse. A 2005 study by Human Rights Watch reported a number of

Ugandan Army (Uganda Peoples Defence Force [UPDF]) killings of civilians by troops sent to guard the IDP camps. The report documented arrests and killings of persons found outside the camp or out after curfew under the assumption that they were LRA members or collaborators, and found that more deliberate killings of civilians by soldiers had also taken place in many camps.[16] A number of rapes and cases of torture at the hands of the UPDF were reported with little or no consequence to the perpetrators.[17] A police presence was slim or nonexistent, even in the largest camps.[18]

"A population suffering serious harm as a result of internal insurgency with the state in question unwilling or unable to halt or avert it";[19] "the threat or occurrence of large-scale loss of life";[20] "the responsibility [of the state] to protect its populations from genocide, war crimes, and crimes against humanity":[21] by many interpretations, the government of Uganda failed in its responsibility to protect.

International Reactions

There were early warnings of disaster in Uganda. Many came from international human rights advocates who carefully documented the abuses, including abuses committed by the UPDF. Some of their findings are noted above. Amnesty International put out a press release in 1996 following the abduction of the Aboke girls; both Amnesty International and Human Rights Watch came out with reports on child abductions in 1997.[22] These were followed by reports in 1999,[23] in 2003,[24] and in 2005.[25]

These reports and the impending humanitarian crisis in the displacement camps spurred action from international aid agencies. The United Nations (UN) World Food Program (WFP) began to deliver food to the camps; "reception" centers were set up to deal with returning formerly abducted youth. The United Nations Children's Fund (UNICEF), the United Nations Office for the Coordination of Humanitarian Affairs (UNOCHA), and the United Nations Office of the High Commissioner for Human Rights (UNHCHR) all established a field presence. And in 2005 world attention was riveted by nongovernmental organizations' (NGOs') reports and videos of streams of children walking into towns to find safe places to sleep for the night. International donors stepped up to the plate and several films documenting the horrors of abduction were produced. In 2006 a coalition of more than fifty Ugandan and international NGOs working with victims of the conflict in the north[26] published a scathing report, citing the two-decade-long conflict that continued to spawn misery and death, calling on the government of Uganda and the international community to "uphold their legal obligations to secure the protection, security, and peace for the civilians of northern Uganda."[27]

Beyond humanitarian relief, NGOs were able to spur some international action on the political front. In 1999 the Carter Center negotiated a peace agreement between Sudan and Uganda that would ultimately weaken the LRA through the loss of Khartoum's support. Former Canadian Foreign Minister Lloyd Axworthy, at the Liu Institute for Global Issues, organized delegations of traditional and religious leaders and human rights advocates[28] to appear before policymakers at the African Union and in the United States, Canada, and the UN to bring attention to the crisis and to request that an international mediator be appointed. A subsequent mission to Uganda by the UN Undersecretary-General for Humanitarian Affairs, Jan Egeland, was the basis for increased international media coverage of the crisis—which he called "one of the last 'dark spots' for international attention in the world." In September 2006, Egeland spent a night in the Opit IDP camp to help bring media attention to the living conditions in the northern Uganda camps.

The UN Security Council was slow to take up the situation in Uganda, due in large part to objections by the Ugandan government and by some council members concerned about breaching nonintervention principles. In January 2006, a UN Security Council special session on the Great Lakes recast the LRA, then active in Sudan and the Democratic Republic of Congo (DRC) as well as Uganda, as a threat to regional stability and thus a focus of Security Council debate and possible action by UN peacekeeping missions. But in place of the special envoy for Uganda long promoted by diplomats such as Axworthy, Egeland, and others, an intergovernmental committee (Joint Monitoring Committee) was mandated to report on conditions in the north, including the IDP camps and efforts toward resettlement, as part of a larger regional effort. Ultimately, however, steady pressure by countries such as Canada (led by UN Ambassador Allan Rock), the United Kingdom, Norway, and The Netherlands led to the Security Council taking up the issue of Uganda in spring 2006—a decision that was likely influenced by the killing of United Nations Mission in the Democratic Republic of Congo (MONUC) peacekeepers by the LRA in eastern Congo early in the year. By late November the secretariat had reached an agreement with the Ugandan government, and Joachim Chissano, former president of Mozambique, was appointed special envoy for Uganda.[29]

Reports and actions by human rights advocates and humanitarian agencies also filled a gap in reporting by the Ugandan media, which have been closely monitored by the government, making it difficult for journalists to publish reports that contradict the government's public statements. A scan of *New Vision* and *The Guardian*—the two leading newspapers in Uganda—reveals a consistently upbeat view of the government's military successes against the LRA and a steady skepticism about chances for a negotiated peace. Newsletters and publications by internationally recognized humanitarian aid agencies such as Christian Action Research and Education (CARE), International Rescue Committee, Oxfam, Refugees International, and World Vision[30] complemented the reports of human rights monitors, highlighting the continued atrocities of the LRA despite the Ugandan military presence, and highlighting the abuses of civilians by the military itself and the appalling conditions of the IDP camps. Regular in-depth analyses by International Crisis Group analyst John Prendergast were a potent voice in the Western media and in policymaking circles.

Yet by far the most significant response from the international community was the 2004 decision by the International Criminal Court (ICC) to investigate the situation of the LRA following a referral to the court by President Museveni—the first in the ICC's short history—and the subsequent arrest warrants for Joseph Kony, head of the LRA, and four of his commanders.[31] Museveni may have hoped that international help against the LRA would not also entail close scrutiny of the abysmal living conditions of civilians in the north.

A potentially powerful mechanism in the "responsibility to protect" toolbox, the court was established in July 2002 to deal with circumstances in which governments cannot or will not provide effective protection or redress for victims. Uganda's failure to provide civilian protection was well documented. And while—for the most part—Uganda boasts a reasonably competent court system,[32] the conflict in the north has left empty or grossly understaffed court rooms and judicial mechanisms.[33]

Conducting an investigation in an ongoing conflict presented problems for the ICC. Witness protection and security were a principal concern; but attempts to pursue a "low-visibility" approach in this context were only partially successful. The lack of a public presence or a vigorous information campaign created initial local suspicion and distrust. Aid agencies and many northern Ugandans have supported the court in principle but have criticized the sequence of international efforts, arguing that justice should be sought only after peace has been achieved, and charging that ICC investigations have derailed peace negotiations.[34] There are signs that victims want both peace and justice. In a May 2005 survey of more than 2,500 residents of four northern districts, 65 percent of the respondents were in favor of punishing the LRA. Of those that had heard of the ICC, almost 90 percent believed it would contribute to both peace and justice.[35]

Recent events may support this view. After months of little progress on the peace front, in 2006 the LRA agreed to talks in Juba, Sudan, brokered by southern Sudan's vice president, Riek Machar.[36] Over a period of months, the LRA withdrew from northern Uganda and spirits rose, as people began to leave the camps and return to their villages or to smaller, less crowded encampments with better access to subsistence farming sites.[37]

At this writing, the LRA has not returned to northern Uganda, however, the Juba peace initiative seems doomed. A 2007 cease-fire agreement guaranteed security for the rebels in Congo's Garamba Park during negotiations. After months of wrangling, an accountability and reconciliation pact was signed on June 29, 2007, recommending traditional justice mechanisms for LRA leaders to be implemented through a legislated legal framework and suggesting the establishment of a special division of the Ugandan High Court to try midlevel perpetrators.[38] But the failure of Kony to appear for the signing of a peace agreement in April 2008 and then again in May was taken by many to signal the end of the talks. More ominous have been reports that the LRA, moving with relative freedom in eastern Congo, southern Sudan, and the Central African Republic, is terrorizing villages and has carried out more than one hundred abductions of boys and girls. Human rights advocates have called on the international community to both apprehend Kony and help the people of northern Uganda rebuild their lives.[39]

Lessons Learned

General lessons from the Uganda experience so far can be grouped according to the three major elements of the responsibility to protect: the responsibility to prevent, the responsibility to react, and the responsibility to rebuild.

Responsibility to Prevent

An early warning system is important. We have detailed how NGOs, governments, and UN officials and agencies put the world on notice that abuses were mounting in northern Uganda. But such early warnings need to be taken seriously. Individual governments, regional organizations, and the UN Security Council should be alert to such warnings and communicate with the government concerned. Perhaps a set of institutionalized procedures could be put in place to guide and raise the effectiveness of the response. Such guidelines could include closer oversight of military aid from foreign countries. (Critics have condemned the U.S. military assistance to Uganda, especially during the Iron Fist campaign, which was thought to spark a dramatic rise in LRA abductions and atrocities.[40])

Responsibility to React

Early actions by individuals, states, regional bodies, and the UN short of military action can be very helpful. In early interventions, it is especially important to choose the most effective instruments, whether private, governmental, or international; whether informal, diplomatic, or economic. The work by international and local NGOs has been outstanding. Often, however, offensive government policies can be turned around only through strong pressure by outside nations and international organizations.[41] In the case of Uganda, except for the ICC, such action has been scant.[42]

Enforcement capability is crucial. It is widely believed that the ICC indictments brought the LRA to the negotiating table in Juba, but the lack of an enforcement capability has hamstrung the court in its efforts to apprehend Kony and his commanders. Some type of mechanism should be considered for this purpose, perhaps a marshals service for the court. At some point, in cases like this one, the possibility of broader international military action also has to be considered. Another option would be to mandate the UN Mission in Sudan (UNMIS) to engage with the LRA, or to call on MONUC and UNMIS to cooperate with national forces in carrying out the ICC arrest warrants.[43]

Responsibility to Rebuild

It is essential to identify victims and assess damage. In northern Uganda, nearly everyone has suffered. According to one survey, 45 percent of the population has witnessed the killing of a family member and 23 percent have been mutilated.[44] HIV/AIDS rates in the IDP camps are about twice that of the rest of Uganda.[45] The primary victims have been children. Those abducted have undergone unspeakable horrors. Those left behind in the camps have endured lives of hunger, fear, and misery. One study estimates that more than 40 percent of the children living in camps in one northern district are physically stunted due to lack of food.[46] According to another IDP study, one-quarter of the children over the age of ten have lost one or both of their parents.[47] The education system has been largely destroyed. In June 2005, a UNICEF report noted that 60 percent of the schools in northern Uganda were nonfunctional.[48] With the social fabric tattered, a generation could be lost unless there are vigorous interventions.

Once the damage is assessed, it is important to provide needed resources. In the Uganda case, these include psychosocial counseling, community and foster care arrangements, life skills training and formal education, as well as the means to meet the basic requirements of medical care, housing, jobs, and economic recovery. This will not be inexpensive.

We must avoid distractions. It is important not to let Uganda's laudable achievements in the area of HIV/AIDS prevention and treatment[49] and poverty reduction,[50] or its official commitment to universal primary education—now extended to secondary education—eclipse the fact that the north of Uganda has suffered grievously. International NGOs and humanitarian agencies cannot be expected to fill the gap between needs and currently available services, particularly as the conflict wanes and more urgent calls come in from active conflict regions. Emergency assistance in Uganda must be followed up by programs with ensured support over a number of years to promote recovery and reconciliation.

Continued nonmilitary assistance focused on the north from countries with long-running programs in Uganda is a potential source of support. The United States, the United Kingdom, Norway, and The Netherlands constitute a "core group" of countries that have provided substantial aid to Uganda in the past. Ireland and Canada also have considerable programs. UN agencies such as UNOCHA, UNICEF, and WFP, which have been invaluable during the crisis, should also continue to play a role.

New approaches are also emerging. The nascent Trust Fund for Victims established under the Rome Statute of the ICC could consider long-range efforts on behalf of communities as it maps out reparations procedures and policies. And a promising model for postconflict support is exemplified by the Fund for War-Affected Children and Youth in Northern Uganda—a ten-year effort established by the MacArthur Foundation and focused on young people, with integrated programs for vulnerable children in education, economic opportunity, and justice and reconciliation.[51] With ensured funding over at least a decade and interventions that directly reach a population at great risk, the Uganda Fund and similar efforts can provide hope and a way forward for Uganda's next generation of leaders.

Notes

* Mary Page is director of the Human Rights and International Justice area in the Program on Global Security & Sustainability at the John D. and Catherine T. MacArthur Foundation in Chicago, Illinois.

1. Institute for War and Peace Reporting, *Africa Reports*, no. 40; http://atheism .about.com/library/world/KZ/bl_UgandaHolySpirit.htm.

2. See J. Annan et al., *The State of Youth and Youth Protection in Northern Uganda: Findings from the Survey for War-Affected Youth*, September 2006, p. 55, http://www.sway-uganda.org/SWAY.Phase1.FinalReport.pdf.

3. Human Rights Watch, *The Scars of Death: Children Abducted from the Lords Resistance Army in Uganda*, September 1997, p. 15, http://www.hrw.org/reports97/uganda/.

4. Human Rights Watch, Abduction and Abuses Against Children by the Lord's Resistance Army, in *Stolen Children: Abduction and Recruitment in Northern Uganda*, vol. 15, no. 7 (March 2003), available at http://www.hrw.org/reports/2003/uganda0303/uganda0403.pdf.

5. Amnesty International, *Uganda: Former Child Soldiers Excluded in their Adulthood*, October 14, 2005, available at http://www.amnesty.org/en/news-and-updates/feature-stories/uganda-former-child-soldiers-excluded-adulthood-20051014.

6. Human Rights Watch. See note 4, p. 19.

7. See Els De Temmerman, *Aboke Girls: Children Abducted in Northern Uganda* (Kampala, Uganda: Fountain Publishers, 2001).

8. Wikipedia, "Aboke Abductions," http://en.wikipedia.org/wiki/Aboke_abductions (accessed February 19, 2007).

9. Tim Allen, *Trial Justice: The International Criminal Court and the Lord's Resistance Army* (London: Zed Books, 2006), 74–75. Also, note photos of Banya and Kolo receiving blankets and seeds from a World Bank official, Alex Gromo, and saucepans from the Ugandan peace mediator, Betty Bigombe; *The Examiner: A Quarterly Publication of Human Rights Focus* 1 (2005).

10. Tim Allen and Mareike Schomerus, *A Hard Homecoming: Lessons Learned from the Reception Center Process in Northern Uganda: An Independent Study*, USAID and UNICEF, June 21, 2006.

11. OCHA, *Consolidated Appeal Process—Uganda, Mid-Year Review* (June 29, 2005), 1, http://ochaonline.un.org/cap2005/webpage.asp?ParentID=5994&MenuID=6019&Page=1213

12. See Norwegian Ministry of Foreign Affairs and UNDP, *Northern Uganda Displaced Peoples Profiling Study*, vol. 1, September 2005; "UNFPA Uganda Consolidated Appeals process 2007," http://www.unfpa.org/emergencies/appeals/uganda07.doc.

13. See *Roco Wat I Acoli: Restoring Relationships in Acholi-land: Traditional Approaches to Justice and Reintegration* (Vancouver, Canada: Liu Institute for Global Issues, September 2005), 28.

14. Human Rights Watch, *Uprooted and Forgotten: Impunity and Human Rights Abuses in Northern Uganda*, vol. 17, no. 12(A), September 2005, p. 50–51.

15. J. Annan et al., *The State of Youth and Youth Protection in Northern Uganda: Findings from the Survey for War-Affected Youth*, September 2006, pp. 24–25, http://www.sway-uganda.org/SWAY.Phase1.FinalReport.pdf.

16. Human Rights Watch. See note 14, p. 28.

17. Ibid., 32.

18. Ibid., 48.

19. International Commission on Intervention and State Sovereignty (ICISS), *The Responsibility to Protect*, at XI (December 2001), http://www.iciss.ca/pdf/Commission-Report.pdf.

20. Ibid., 33.

21. UN GAOR, Sixtieth Session, 8th plen. mtg., UN Doc. A/RES/60/1, para. 138 (October 24, 2005) [hereinafter *2005 World Summit Outcome*].

22. Amnesty International, "Uganda: 'Breaking God's Commands:' The Destruction of Childhood by the Lord's Resistance Army," September 18, 1997, http://www.amnesty.org/en/library/info/AFR59/001/1997; and Human Rights Watch. See note 4.

23. Amnesty International, "Uganda: Breaking the Circle: Protecting Human Rights in the Northern War Zone," March 17, 1999, http://www.amnesty.org/en/library/info/AFR59/001/1999/en.

24. Human Rights Watch, Abducted and Abused: Renewed Conflict in Northern Uganda 15, no. 12A (July 2003), http://www.hrw.org/reports/2003/uganda0703/.

25. Amnesty International, *Uganda: Violence Against Women in Northern Uganda*, July 15, 2005, http://www.amnesty.org/en/library/info/AFR59/001/2005; *Uganda: Child Night Commuters*, November 18, 2005, http://www.amnesty.org/en/library/info/AFR59/013/2005/en; Human Rights Watch. See note 14.

26. The Civil Society Organizations for Peace in Northern Uganda (CSOPNU) members included CARE, International Rescue Committee, Save the Children, Oxfam, Norwegian Refugee Council, and World Vision. UN agencies working on the ground in included UNICEF, World Food Program, United Nations Development Program (UNDP), and United Nations Office of Humanitarian Affairs. Donor agencies of the governments of the United States, Norway, the Netherlands, Ireland, and the United Kingdom were also active.

27. Civil Society Organizations for Peace in Northern Uganda, *Counting the Cost: Twenty Years of War in Northern Uganda* (March 2006), 2, http://www.careinternational.org.uk/6066/conflict-and-peace/counting-the-cost-twenty-years-of-war-in-northern-uganda.html.

28. The delegation included His Grace Archbishop John B. Odama from Acholi Religious Leaders Peace Initiatives (ARLPI); His Highness the Paramount Chief from Cultural and Traditional Leaders of Acholi; Sam Tindifa from Human Rights and Peace Center (HURIPEC), Makerere; Angelina Atyam from Concerned Parents Association (CPA); Geoffrey Oyat from Liu-Uganda; and James A. A. Otto from Gulu-based Human Rights Focus (HURIFO).

29. See UN Security Council, *Update Report No. 5: Uganda* (April 18, 2006), *Update Report No. 2: Uganda* (November 14, 2006), and *Update Report No. 2: Uganda* (March 20, 2007), available at http://www.securitycouncilreport.org/site/c.glKWLeMTIsG/b.2400719/.

30. See especially, World Vision, *Pawns of Politics: Children, Conflict and Peace in Northern Uganda* (2004), 56.

31. Only two of the commanders are still alive: one was killed by the UPDF in 2005, and one was reportedly killed by Kony in 2007.

32. H. Abigail Moy, "The International Criminal Court's Arrest Warrants and Uganda's Lord's Resistance Army: Renewing the Debate Over Amnesty and Complementarity," *Harvard Human Rights Journal* 19 (Spring 2006): 267–73.

33. Human Rights Watch. See note 14.

34. Humanitarian agencies initially came out strongly against the ICC investigations. See the 2004 CSOPNU statement: "We fear that the timing of the investigations may jeopardize any hope of further peace talks. We also believe that the actions and conduct of the ICC investigation may be putting at risk the very people to whom they aim to bring justice. . . . We urge the ICC to delay its investigation and issue a public statement to this effect," available at http://www.newvision.co.ug/downloads/13%20Oxfam%20peace%20in%20 northern.pdf. However, in a more recent CSOPNU study, the coalition includes in its recommendations to regional governments that peace efforts must include "full cooperation in relevant international processes, e.g., the International Criminal Court." Civil Society Organizations for Peace in Northern Uganda, "Counting the Cost: Twenty Years of War in Northern Uganda" (March 2006), http://www.careinternational.org.uk/6066/conflict-and-peace/counting-the cost-twenty-years-of-war-in-northern-uganda.html.

35. Phuong Pham et al., *Forgotten Voices: A Population-Based Survey on Attitudes about Peace and Justice in Northern Uganda* (International Center for Transitional Justice and the Human Rights Center, University of California, Berkeley, May 2005).

36. It should be noted that the March 2005 Security Council referral to the ICC of the situation in Darfur has further complicated the court's work in Uganda, given Sudan's links to the Uganda conflict.

37. According to aid agencies, an estimated 230,000 internally displaced people in the region returned to their villages in 2006, thanks to improved security following the start of talks between the Ugandan government and the rebel LRA. However, up to 1.2 million more remain in camps, while some have moved to satellite camps near their villages to gain access to their farms. See "Uganda: Thousands of IDPs go home, 1.2 million still in camps," http://www.irin news.org/report.asp?ReportID=56956 (accessed January 24, 2007).

38. See http://news.bbc.co.cuk/1/hi/world/africa/6257120.stm and http://www .sundayvision.co.uig/edetail.php?mainNewsCategoryId=7&newsCategoryID =123&newsID=573453.

39. See Julia Spiegel and John Prendergast, "A New Peace Strategy for Northern Uganda and the LRA," ENOUGH Strategy Paper 19, May 2008,http://www .americanprogress.org/issues/2008/05/pdf/enough28.pdf; Human Rights Watch, *Uganda: LRA Regional Atrocities Demand Action*, May 19, 2008, http://www .hrw.org/english/docs/2008/05/19/uganda18863.htm.

40. Joyce Neu, *Briefing on the Conflict in Uganda: Hope for a Negotiated Solution* (John B. Krock Institute for Peace and Justice, University of San Diego, June 1, 2005), 6, http://icar.gmu.edu/ICC/Briefing.pdf.

41. Antiapartheid policies toward South Africa are an example of effectively coordinated governmental, commercial, and nongovernmental action.

42. One important factor has been the Ugandan government's firm rejection of outside involvement within Uganda, for example, the situation in the north, which it sees as an internal matter, as opposed to its requests for assistance—both by the ICC and the UN—with the LRA problem that is couched in terms of a regional security threat.

43. Although this option has been discussed, resource constraints and concerns within the UN Department of Peacekeeping Operations (DPKO) about stretching the mission of peacekeeping forces have prevented much agreement along these lines. A significant factor may also be that at present, the relevant forces, MONUC and UNMIS, are closely involved in the peace process in Congo and southern Sudan.

44. See Berkeley and the International Center for Transitional Justice and the Human Rights Center, University of California, Berkeley. See note 35, p. 22.

45. M. Boas and A. Hatloy, *Northern Uganda Internally Displaced Persons Profiling Study*, vol. 2 (Fafo Institute for Applied International Studies, September 2005), http://www.fafo.no/ais/africa/uganda/IDP_uganda_2005.pdf.

46. Republic of Uganda, Ministry of Health/World Health Organization, *Health and Mortality Survey Among the Internally Displaced Persons in Gulu, Kitgum and Pader Districts*, July 2005, http://www.who.int/hac/crises/uga/sitreps/Ugandamortsurvey.pdf.

47. Boas and Hatloy, *Northern Uganda*.

48. UNICEF, *Humanitarian Action, Uganda, Donor Update*, June 2005.

49. The 1992 national average HIV/AIDS infection rate of 18 percent dropped to 6.4 percent in 2005. See figures in Uganda National Council for Children, *Equity and Vulnerability: A Situation Analysis of Women, Adolescents, and Children in Uganda, 1994* (Kampala: Government of Uganda, Uganda National Council for Children, 1994), 125; United Nations Office for the Coordination of Humanitarian Affairs, *Uganda CAP Midyear Review 2005*, June 22, 2005.

50. At the national level, the incidence of poverty declined from 56 percent in 1992 to 38 percent in 2003. Republic of Uganda, Ministry of Finance, "Poverty Eradication Action Plan" (2004), iii.

51. See Erin Baines, Eric Stover, and Marieke Wierda, *War-Affected Children and Youth in Northern Uganda: Toward a Brighter Future* (Chicago: John D. and Catherine T. MacArthur Foundation, May 2006).

9

Spread Wide the Word

Organizing the Grassroots
to End Atrocity Crimes

William F. Schulz*

In 1994 the genocide in Rwanda killed at least 800,000 people. Anthony Lake was national security adviser to President Bill Clinton at the time of the genocide. As the full dimensions of the catastrophe began to become clear, representatives of U.S. human rights organizations approached Lake to press for American intervention. Lake's response was chilling: the only way the U.S. government could be convinced to intervene was if the human rights community could mount massive popular protests demanding such action.[1] Despite its treaty obligations under the Convention against Genocide, and despite evidence of atrocities on a scale not seen since World War II, the United States would have to be pressured by its own citizens into doing the right thing. Lacking the capacity to generate such an outcry, the human rights movement could do little more than sound the alarm. Years later President Clinton apologized to the people of Rwanda for his government's deafness.

The failure of human rights leaders (of whom I was one at the time) to mobilize a sufficiently vocal segment of the population in 1994 to break through the government's willful hearing loss bespeaks of a far greater problem that plagues human rights: the lack of a broad-based identifiable constituency for its cause. More than fifteen million Americans belong to labor unions. If you count the number of people who join environmental organizations as indicative of how many Americans are moved to act on environmental issues, there are more than two million active supporters of environmentalism in the United States, and far more than that if we consider all those who recycle their newspapers or conserve on personal energy use. Similarly, the women's movement can claim more than a million formal adherents. The National Association for the Advancement of Colored People (NAACP) alone has 500,000 members. But human rights organizations focused on international issues would be hard-pressed to muster 350,000, and most of those belong to one group, Amnesty International.

This is not to say that only 350,000 people in the United States care about human rights. A February 2005 Gallup poll revealed that 86 percent of Americans believe that "promoting and defending human rights in other countries" is an important U.S. foreign policy goal.[2] Even fears generated by terrorism have not appreciably diminished Americans' support of fundamental human rights, 66 percent saying in 2004 that the United States should abide by international laws that prohibit the use of physical torture.[3] But holding an opinion about something and actually doing something about it are two very different things. Even among the some 300,000 members of Amnesty International USA, no more than 50,000 or so participate in activities other than donating money.

Of course when it comes to genocide or crimes against humanity, a responsible government should not need to wait until its populace demands action. Part of the role of leaders is to educate their citizens about their country's obligations. But the hard fact is that, with the exception of natural disasters, most governments are notoriously loathe to intervene simply to stop bad things from happening to suffering people if they perceive no direct ties to their economic or security interests. That is one reason President Clinton's decision to support North Atlantic Treaty Organization (NATO) intervention in Kosovo (taken in part, many have suggested, to expiate his guilt over Rwanda) was so unusual—because U.S. interests were only indirectly implicated there.[4] If mass atrocities are therefore to be met with more than rhetoric and if the "responsibility to protect (R2P)" is to become more than a slogan, popular outrage will need to outflank governmental reluctance. That makes the dearth of a significant grassroots constituency for human rights a major obstacle to the realization of a world free from genocide and massive crimes against humanity. What accounts for the human rights movement's relative lack of organizing heft?

The Limitations of Expertise

The slave trade was formally abolished in Great Britain in 1833 following fifty years of determined opposition to it, often led by Quakers. Similarly, in the early twentieth century Roger Casement and the Congo Reform Association brought international attention to the brutality of Belgian rule in the Congo, a story told admirably well in Adam Hochschild's best-selling book, *King Leopold's Ghost*.[5] And of course every American schoolchild is aware of the mass movement led by Dr. Martin Luther King, Jr. and many others in the 1950s and 1960s to secure the civil rights of all Americans.

In these cases and others like them—the birth of the American labor movement, the protests against the British Raj in India, the struggle to end apartheid in South Africa—efforts to ameliorate oppressive conditions and obtain recognition of rights were spurred by grassroots movements made up in good measure either of the oppressed themselves or, where that was impossible, as in the case of slavery, by their surrogates and sympathizers. It was, in fact, the existential urgency of the situations, the fact that the victims themselves or their emotional kin were making the appeals, that lent them much of their power.

But the modern international human rights movement was not founded in this fashion. To the extent that that movement can be dated from the passage in 1948 by the United Nations (UN) of the Universal Declaration of Human Rights (UDHR), efforts to guarantee international human rights originated not so much as a response to a particular ongoing outrage, but as a reflection upon the experience of the Holocaust and a desire to prevent similar tragedies in the future.[6] Moreover, the most instrumental proponents of a formal codification of human rights were not themselves victims of crimes, but world leaders, albeit leaders of great moral stature, principal among whom was Eleanor Roosevelt.[7]

That such was the origin of the modern international human rights movement is hardly surprising inasmuch as those world leaders were trying to articulate *universal* human rights, applicable to everyone merely because of their humanness, and not the rights of a particular group in a specific political context. But what it means is that the concept of "universal inter-national human rights" emerged not out of a groundswell of public sentiment, but out of what might be characterized as a more sterile environment than those that spawned various indigenous struggles. Then, too, for the early part of its life, the UDHR (which, upon its adoption, the U.S. State Department had proclaimed as no more than a "hortatory statement of aspirations") depended for its enforcement not upon any independent entity, but upon the very governments who were guilty of its violation. It was not until the founding of Amnesty International in 1961 that an independent agent emerged to monitor the human rights practices of miscreant governments.

Coupled with the subsequent passage of a series of treaties, covenants, and conventions elaborating upon the UDHR[8] and the corresponding growth of international human rights and humanitarian law, the result of this birth story is that human rights have often been seen as the province of the expert, the lawyer, and the academic rather than of the people whose lives are most directly affected by the abuse of rights. That most international human rights organizations (as opposed to indigenous rights groups) are made up of elites of one sort or another rather than "average citizens" and are largely dependent for their support upon well-endowed foundations or wealthy individuals simply reinforces that bias. This is not to say for a moment that there is not an important place for experts, lawyers, and academics, to say nothing of wealthy donors(!), in the human rights movement. It is only to explain one reason why that movement has been handicapped in generating mass appeal. The language of law, imperative as it is to the enforcement of rights, is rarely a rhetoric that moves people to action. And so as the human rights movement grew, it added the language of moral suasion to its lexicon in order to effect what has often been called the "mobilization of shame."

By telling the stories of individuals and their suffering, human rights workers managed to put compelling human faces on larger political dramas. Moral rhetoric quickly became the favorite lexicon of the human rights struggle in consonance with Camus's observation that "there is no evil that cannot be surmounted by scorn."

The problem is that only a certain number of people have enough energy to sustain that scorn for as long as it often takes to bring an end to human rights crimes. Moral rhetoric is a highly effective tool, but while moral arguments may appeal to a relatively small segment of a community for a very long time or to a fairly large segment of a community for a rather short time, they are unlikely, by themselves, to hold a large number of people's attention forever. Appeals to morality reach in a consistent fashion only that portion of the public in whose long-term understanding of the world morality trumps convenience.

What we need to make the human rights "sale," to build a broader constituency for human rights, to convince larger numbers of people that human rights matter, is a third form of rhetoric beyond the legal and the ethical, a third set of arguments, a third understanding of suffering's significance. What we need are compelling practical reasons why respect for human rights is in our own and our country's best interests. Perhaps because of its tendency toward elitism or because it suspected it could not make the case or because it regarded appeals to self-interest as lacking in the purity requisite to a moral struggle, human rights advocates have often neglected, if not shunned, the pragmatic argument, and that too has contributed to our relative political impotence.

Despite these deficits, however, human rights campaigns have been responsible for great victories over the past forty years. On a one-off basis, large numbers of people far beyond just those who formally join human rights organizations have been persuaded at one time or another to help bring down apartheid, to boycott companies that use child labor overseas, or to advocate for an end to globalization's excesses. During the years of George W. Bush's presidency, the evangelical movement, one of his key political constituencies, has been highly successful in lobbying the U.S. government to fight sex trafficking and religious persecution around the world and to take an active role in helping resolve the north–south conflict in Sudan, which threatened the lives of many Sudanese Christians.

But all these grassroots efforts have been focused on particular issues, and once they are resolved or addressed, rarely translate into added support for other human rights causes. Interestingly enough, mass atrocities—such as Rwanda, Congo, Bosnia, and Kosovo—have rarely been the focus of significant one-off organizing. The crisis in Darfur may well prove the exception, but added to the human rights movement's general ineptness at political organizing is a more specific reticence when it comes to the use of force, even in a noble cause—a reticence that simply must be overcome if R2P is ever to be more tooth than tonic.

Confusing the Left About What Is Right

The end of the cold war and the collapse of Communism were seen by most observers in the West as the apex of the twentieth century, the culminating triumph of democracy. But for a singular group of political theorists, it was cause for alarm, even a Pyrrhic victory.[9] Norman Podhoretz, influential editor often dubbed "the father of neoconservatism," worried about the "loss of a defining foreign demon."[10] Taking their cue from the political philosopher Leo Strauss, who wrote, "Because mankind is intrinsically wicked, he has to be governed. Such governance can only be established when men are united—and they can only be united against other people,"[11] Podhoretz and his neoconservative coterie were convinced that what they would come to call "national greatness" could only be achieved with the help of an adversary. Only in the face of a mortal enemy could a people sustain sufficient "moral clarity" to reject their own cultural demons and preserve their way of life.

The emergence of a truly threatening adversary on September 11, 2001, provided the perfect rationale for neoconservatives, now in political power, to revivify "national greatness," focus "moral clarity" on a demonstrably evil target (Al Qaeda), and link both projects to the ultimate removal of the "foreign demon" *par excellence*, Saddam Hussein. The rest, as they say, is woefully tragic history, and among the appalling consequences of that history is that it has further confused the progressive segment of the American population about the legitimacy of the use of American military force.

That confusion was born of course in Vietnam, nurtured by American misadventures in Central America in the 1980s, and sustained by deep-seated suspicion about the country's economic motives in its employment of military power. Such reticence on the part of those most inclined to take human rights seriously accounts in part for the silence about U.S. military intervention with which the Rwandan genocide was met in 1994. And when neoconservatives like Robert Kagan and William Kristol supported the Kosovo war at the same time that they were calling for "benevolent global hegemony" on the part of the United States, those suspicions turned to ice.[12] The Iraq War in turn has turned them to stone.[13] The result is that some, like the essayist David Rieff, who had previously supported humanitarian military interventions in places like Bosnia have become far more skeptical about the validity of such ventures—at least if they involve the United States.[14]

But if R2P is to become a viable principle in the twenty-first century, it will require human rights advocates of both Left and Right to rethink the use of force doctrine. The Left will need to give up its knee-jerk opposition to every manifestation of Western military power; the Right will need to acknowledge, as some like Francis Fukuyama now seem to be beginning to do,[15] that an international imprimatur on the use of that power has profound advantages. Nowhere today are both those needs better illustrated than in Darfur, Sudan.

R2P: Ground Zero

The Sudanese defense minister was not happy with the Amnesty International delegation of which I was a part in the fall of 2004. We had just returned from Darfur and were reporting directly to the minister on the atrocities there, but he was having none of it. Medals bouncing on his chest, he pounded the desk in fury. We were troublemakers, charlatans, tools of the imperialist United States (despite the fact that the leader of our six-member delegation, Amnesty's secretary-general, was Bangladeshi and I was the only American). And then, just as he was about to throw us out of his office, his cell phone rang. The tune was so familiar. "What was it?" I asked myself. And then it dawned on me: "Mary Had a Little Lamb." How perfect for one who was leading the lambs to slaughter.

At that point the war in Darfur had officially been raging for almost a year and a half, since April 25, 2003, when a combined force of the Sudan

Liberation Army (SLA) and the Justice and Equality Movement (JEM), two groups of guerilla fighters drawn from the so-called African tribes in the western region of Sudan, had attacked a government air base at al Fasher, destroying as many as seven Antonov bombers and helicopter gunships, killing at least seventy-five, and taking some thirty-two captive, including the commander of the base.

But the truth is that, whether the shooting war is dated to that April or to almost a year earlier when a police station in Golo was attacked in June 2002, or even to a year before that when fighters from the Fur and Zaghawa tribes—African tribes—met in Abu Gamra and swore on the Koran to oppose policies dictated from Khartoum that were designed to foster Arab supremacy, the roots of the conflict go far back before the twenty-first century.[16]

Darfur was until recently a land of some six million people divided into between forty and ninety different tribes, depending upon how a tribe is defined. All its residents are Muslim and the vast majority speak Arabic, in addition to their tribal tongues. The first Muslim state in Darfur was the Fur Sultanate ("Darfur" refers to the "homeland" of the Fur), which emerged in the mid-1600s, an African kingdom, but one in which Arabs, who arrived in the land between the fourteenth and eighteenth centuries, were treated as equals. Darfur was an independent state until January 1917, when the sultan, having miscalculated the winner of World War I by backing the Ottoman Empire, was defeated and killed by the British.

Over the next generations Darfur was subjected to systematic neglect, first by the British and later, after Sudan's independence in 1956, by the central government in Khartoum. Health care, roads, economic development—all of it was subpar, even by the standards of one of the world's poorest nations. With only a handful of Darfuris in positions of power in Khartoum and the central government preoccupied with conflict between Islamists and less ideologically driven politicians, Darfur languished. But far worse was yet to come.

By 1983 Khartoum had a full-blown rebellion on its hands, based not in the Islamic west, but in the Christian and animist south, led by John Garang of the Sudan People's Liberation Army (SPLA), a charismatic advocate of national power for minorities. At the same time a new racial ideology began to sweep through Darfur—that of Arab supremacy—fostered not by homegrown Sudanese Islamists, but by Libya's Muammar Gaddafi. With his dreams of a pan-Arab empire, Gaddafi sought to exploit tensions wherever he found them. Even more insidiously, he had his sights set on the annexation of Sudan's western neighbor, Chad. Desperate for arms with which to fight the SPLA, Khartoum made a pact with the devil. In exchange for weapons from Libya, Khartoum would turn a blind eye to

Gaddafi's use of Darfur as a military base from which to conduct his campaign against Chad. Little did the Sudanese government know that the influx of foreign troops would spark a major war between Arab tribes in Darfur and the Fur. By the time that war was brought to a close in 1989, thousands had been killed, hundreds of villages destroyed, and the seeds of the current disaster sown. It would take but an ecological development coupled with a strong tilt by the central government toward the Arabs to foster full-scale mass atrocities.

Before the 1980s the two sets of tribes had lived together in relative equanimity. African tribes were largely pastoralists and farmers; Arab tribes were nomads who followed their migratory routes every year, grazing their herds on the farmers' lands. But with increasing desertification through the 1990s, those lands began to contract and the farmers, under economic stress, began to throw up barriers to the herds, barring the nomads' way and threatening their way of life. At the same time, the conflict with the SPLA began spilling over into the southern reaches of Darfur. Stretched to their limits militarily and fearful that the SPLA would make common cause with the dispirited and marginalized African tribes, the central government began to align itself with Arab tribal militias—militias that had been bolstered by the ideology of Arab superiority and supplied with weapons, first by the Libyans and later by Khartoum.

By 1996 the stage was set for a showdown. That year the government and its Arab allies, who came to be known as *Janjawiid* ("bandits or riflemen on horseback"), initiated what would become an all-too-familiar pattern: first, the Sudanese army would search and disarm an African village, then a short time later the *Janjawiid* would swoop in, burning homes and crops, and slaughtering and raping the inhabitants. "Why us? We are not SPLA," the villagers would wail. The reply was straightforward: "Our orders come from the government." For the next five years these raids would go on virtually uncontested. But by 2001 the Fur and Zaghawa had had enough and began to form what would become the SLA.[17] Since then the conflict has spiraled further and further out of control, with the Sudanese Air Force having replaced the army as the agent of initial village destruction and the *Janjawiid* having grown only bolder and more systematic in their devastation of the innocent.

Given this history, it is easy to understand the difficulty in pinpointing the exact start of the war. But what cannot be contested are its consequences. As I write in the spring of 2008, at least 200,000 people have died and more than two million (or a third of the region's population) are displaced inside about two hundred refugee camps in Sudan and twelve in Chad.[18] Despite the presence of a small African Union (AU)/UN force charged with protecting the people; despite declarations in 2004 by the U.S. State Department and the Congress that genocide was under way in Darfur; despite a peace agreement between the government and one rebel force signed in 2006; despite the UN Commission of Inquiry on Darfur having referred fifty-one names of government, *Janjawiid*, and rebel leaders to the International Criminal Court (ICC) for possible prosecution; despite the withdrawal of more and more humanitarian agencies due to increased attacks upon aid workers; despite the crisis in Darfur threatening to derail the 2005 Comprehensive Peace Agreement that ended the north-south conflict in Sudan—a derailment that would throw the entire country, if not region, into chaos; and despite the conflict now threatening the stability of both neighboring Chad and the Central African Republic, the slaughter continues unabated.

Women are at particular risk in Darfur, even in the refugee camps, where, given the fact that so many men were killed in the initial raids on villages, they make up a majority of the population. Not only must they bear the burden of holding together decimated families, but when they venture outside the camps to collect firewood, for instance, they are frequently subjected to rape from *Janjawiid* or even from local police who are supposedly their guardians.

It is not hard to imagine how to stop the catastrophe in Darfur. The Sudanese Air Force is not one of the world's great fighting forces. The *Janjawiid* are largely what their name says they are, riflemen on horseback (or camel). The establishment by NATO, for example, of a "no-fly zone" over western Sudan, while not without logistical challenges, would quickly put an end to air raids on villages. The application of targeted sanctions, such as asset freezes and travel bans, against key Sudanese government officials and economic sanctions against those commercial entities, especially in the petroleum sector that provide revenue for the war would quickly get the attention of Sudan's leaders.[19]

But while the path to protection is clear, the political will to follow it has thus far been largely missing. China, which is one of Sudan's major trading partners, and hence principal defenders, has felt little heat from the West, other than protests related to the Beijing Olympics, about the role it has played in blocking effective international action and suborning mass atrocities. The AU/UN joint protection still lacks adequate personnel and equipment to do its job. The United States, while it has provided more than 65 percent of the World Food Program's food aid to Sudan and will provide more than $1 billion in humanitarian, development, and peacekeeping assistance in 2007,[20] has been distracted by Iraq and not made Darfur as high a foreign policy priority as a declaration of genocide would seem to entail. And hence, in the face of the major current challenge to the responsibility to protect, the international community allows as many as ten thousand people to continue to die needlessly each month. The simple question on the minds of every morally conscious individual is, "What can I do about it?"

The Dynamics of Organizing

In the absence of a broad-based constituency poised to fight genocide and crimes against humanity whenever they arise, the alternative—the only alternative, really—is the creation of ad hoc coalitions organized to stop particular atrocities one at a time. Darfur has provided a model of both the strengths and weaknesses of such an approach.

A significant number of individuals and groups have done all they can to focus the world's attention on Darfur. In the run-up to the 2004 U.S. presidential elections, the Congressional Black Caucus staged powerful demonstrations that forced both President Bush and Senator John Kerry to speak to the issue in the presidential debates. New York Times op-ed columnist Nicholas Kristoff has been relentless in his coverage of the tragedy. Many human rights and religious groups, both separately and under the umbrella of the Save Darfur Coalition, have organized communities and congregations, rallied student activists, and striven nobly to keep pressure on U.S. leaders. Drive through the community of Needham, Massachusetts, for example, and you will be amazed at the number of front lawns sporting signs calling for an end to the killing in Darfur.

These efforts illustrate key features of successful organizing: an identifiable enemy, for example. Few people can name Omar al-Bashir, the president of Sudan, but the *Janjawiid* militia, perched on horseback or camelback and swooping down on defenseless villages, have provided an easy target for (quite appropriate) demonization. Similarly, effective organizing requires a readily comprehensible "ask." The conflict in Darfur is extraordinarily complex—even more complex than we have described here—but average citizens do not need to understand all its permutations to absorb the simple fact that innocent people are dying in astounding numbers while the world watches. What is required is straightforward: *an end to genocide.*[21] But even these are not enough without an ability to generate publicity and get the message out, and that has not been easy, no doubt in part because Americans and their media have an almost constitutional indisposition to focus on matters African, be that a reflection of racism, frustration, a lack of perceived national interest, or a combination of all of the above. Media coverage of the Darfur crisis, which in all of 2004 totaled twenty-six minutes combined on the three major networks, has declined even further in the years since.[22]

Fortunately, that dearth has been addressed in part by a third feature of successful organizing, the need to provide effective, high-visibility spokespersons for the victims. If those spokespersons cannot be drawn from the suffering community itself, as in this instance they cannot, then others need to play that role for them, and among the most effective, in this case and in many others, have been celebrities such as the actress Mia Farrow and the actor Don Cheadle.[23]

There are risks associated with such star power (should, for example, a star's image become clouded, as was the case with Hertz's O. J. Simpson) and it is critical that the celebrities be truly knowledgeable and authentically moved by the cause they adopt, but on balance the benefits of celebrity involvement far outweigh the dangers. When he was asked by a congressional delegation to join a trip to Chad, Cheadle says he worried that too many cameras would be focused on him as opposed to the refugees. "But I know if [the journalists] can't feature me in some way, then they're going to [ask], 'Why do we need to go? Where's the "sexy" in the story for us?' So, it is always balancing celebrity interest with what you're trying to do. And it can come back and kick you in the teeth. But I don't think that's an argument for not trying. . . . If it is something that's close to your heart and it is something that's true, then your detractors are not going to deter you." More recently, the power of celebrity has reportedly even convinced the Chinese to exert pressure on Sudan's government to cooperate with the hybrid AU-UN force. Spurred by criticism from Mia Farrow that he could "go down in history as the Leni Riefenstahl of the [2008] Beijing [Olympic] games," the producer Steven Spielberg, an artistic advisor to the Chinese on the Olympics, prevailed upon President Hu Jintao to dispatch senior officials to Khartoum to encourage their ally to "show flexibility and accept" the peacekeepers.[24]

An identifiable villain, an easily articulated solution, spokespeople who can make the plight of the victims poignant and clear—not only for the media, but for the American people—these are all key components of building those ad hoc grassroots coalitions to stop mass atrocities. Moreover, genocide is often linked to causes not traditionally associated with human rights—the Darfur conflict was precipitated in part, as we have seen, by climate change and agricultural shortfalls, and it is hardly a coincidence that the Rwandan genocide occurred in the country with the highest population density at the time of any country in Africa—and these constellations offer thus far unrequited opportunities to leverage the power of two different advocacy communities for the benefit of both.

Such citizen movements will not by themselves put an end to genocide— only motivated public officials, a healthy international judicial system, and sometimes mobilized militaries can do that. Indeed, the downside of the ad hoc Darfur coalition is simply that, despite its best efforts, people in Darfur continue to die. But if anyone doubts that cultivation of grassroots opinion has an important part to play, not least in motivating those public officials to action, let him or her only contemplate where the struggle to stop the killing in Darfur would be today without the thousands of voices who have kept the plight of the victims alive in our minds. We would be with no media coverage at all, not even twenty-six minutes a year; with no wide-spread knowledge of the catastrophe, even among those inclined to act; with no congressional resolutions, not even largely rhetorical ones; with no pressure on national and international bodies to intervene; and with no answer to the question, "What can I do?"[25]

For the sad fact is, as we noted at the outset, even governments that care about human rights in the abstract are loathe to get their hands dirty if they see no direct tie to their strategic interests. Activists need to be prepared to argue to both governor and governed alike not just the moral points about Darfur, but the political ones as well. To allow Sudan, a country that once housed Osama bin Laden, to sink further into instability; to allow the scuttling of the Comprehensive Peace Agreement that ended twenty-three years of north-south war;[26] to allow the larger region (Chad, the Central African Republic) to be engulfed in debilitating conflict is to waste millions of taxpayers' dollars and to sow fertile ground for more anti-Western sentiment and, not incidentally, more terrorism. At a time when the U.S.'s favorability ratings, even among our allies, have plummeted and our prestige in the Muslim world is utterly precarious,[27] to play a leadership role in settling the crisis in Darfur could be an important step in the rehabilitation of our image as a justice-seeking, human rights-respecting country. Imagine how different our reputation would be today if, instead of invading Iraq in 2003, the United States had led an effective international effort to stop the slaughter in Darfur.

* * *

In her recent book Inventing Human Rights: A History, historian Lynn Hunt argues that human rights as a concept did not come into full effect until human beings gained the capacity to empathize with one another, to understand deep inside that when you are cut, you feel pain just as surely as I do.[28] This capacity is easily trumped by less noble urges, but if there is one thing we know about human beings it is that, for better or worse, we are remarkably susceptible to the influence of other people around us; that, contrary to the claims of southern segregationists, you *can* legislate morality; and that cultural norms change as people look to their neighbors even more than to their leaders for definition of what is and is not currently acceptable.

If in the long run R2P is to become an effective mechanism for ending mass crimes, it will be so because large numbers of people around the world insist upon it; because inaction in the face of genocide becomes so stigmatized that no reputable leader can afford such lethargy. R2P must therefore be implemented on all different levels of decision making at once, not just among the powerful and well-placed, but among the citizen and the commoner. For only then will there be a clear answer to a future national security adviser's query as to whether thousands of people could be importuned to take to the streets to demand an end to genocide, for only then would it never even occur to such an adviser to ask such a question in the first place.

Notes

* William Schulz is the former executive director of Amnesty International USA. He is currently a Senior Fellow at the Center for American Progress in Washington, DC, and adjunct professor of public administration at New York University's Wagner School of Public Service.

1. David Rieff, "The Precarious Triumph of Human Rights," *New York Times Magazine*, August 8, 1999, 41.

2. World Public Opinion, "Promoting International Human Rights," http://www .americansworld.org/digest/global_issues/human_rights/PromotingHR.cfm.

3. World Public Opinion, "U.S. Public Rejects Nearly All Forms of Torture or Coercion Even in Face of Possible Terrorist Attack, http://www.worldpublic opinion.org/pipa/articles/btjusticehuman_rightsra/111.php?nid=&id=&pnt =111&lb=bthr.

4. It has been argued that the United States was motivated by a desire to prop up the credibility of NATO, particularly after the disaster at Srebrenica. Interestingly enough, as the investigative reporter Seymour Hersh pointed out in a speech at Washington State University at Vancouver on February 4, 2007, of all the U.S. military interventions since World War II—Korea, Vietnam, the Dominican Republic, Grenada, Somalia, and so on—Kosovo was the first time the targets of U.S. hostilities had been white people.

5. Adam Hochschild, *King Leopold's Ghost* (London: Pan Macmillan, 1999).

6. The second whereas clause of the UDHR made this backward glance explicit: "Whereas disregard and contempt for human rights have resulted in barbarous acts which have outraged the conscience of mankind." Similarly, the Responsibility to Protect was adopted in part as a reaction to the failures to prevent mass atrocities in

Rwanda and Srebrenica and controversy over the legal basis for the intervention in Kosovo.

7. For a thorough description of the creation of the UDHR, see Johannes Morsink, *The Universal Declaration of Human Rights: Origins, Drafting and Intent* (Philadelphia: University of Pennsylvania Press, 1999).

8. I refer, for example, to the International Covenants on Civil and Political Rights and Economic, Social and Cultural Rights; the Convention Against Torture and Other Cruel, Inhumane and Degrading Treatment or Punishment, the Convention Against Genocide, and so on.

9. See, for example, Mark Gerson, *The Neoconservative Vision: From the Cold War to the Culture Wars* (London: Madison Books, 1996).

10. Gary Dorrien, *The Neoconservative Mind: Politics, Culture, and the War of Ideology* (Philadelphia: Temple University Press, 1993), 134.

11. Quoted in John G. Mason, "Leo Strauss and the Noble Lie: The Neo-Cons at War," *Logos* (Spring 2004): 7, http://www.logosjournal.com/issue_3.2/mason .htm.

12. Gary Dorrien, "'Benevolent Global Hegemony': William Kristol and the Politics of American Empire," *Logos* (Spring 2004), http://www.logosjournal .com/issue_3.2/dorrien.htm.

13. It is worth noting that the neoconservative project has been discombobulating to right and left alike. Regardless of the original mixed motives for the toppling of Saddam Hussein (alleged weapons of mass destruction [WMDs], alleged ties to Al Qaeda, real oil), the conviction that democracy can be spread by force around the world flies in the face of traditional conservative thought from political philosopher Michael Oakeshott's aversion to "adventurism," to the resistance of so-called foreign policy realists like Hans Morgenthau and Henry Kissinger, to the employment of military force for ideological purposes alone, and to absent corresponding strategic interests. It is of no little irony that those on the left who find neoconservatism's militant promotion of democracy abhorrent discover themselves to be sharing a bed with those like Kissinger who, in other contexts, they abjure.

14. See David Rieff, *At the Point of a Gun: Democratic Dreams and Armed Intervention* (New York: Simon & Schuster, 2005).

15. See Francis Fukuyama, *America at the Cross Road: Democracy, Power and the Neoconservative Legacy* (New Haven, CT: Yale University Press, 2006).

16. Much of the following history of the conflict is drawn from Julie Flint and Alex de Wall's *Darfur: A Short History of a Long War* (London: Zed Books, 2005).

17. The Justice and Equality Movement (JEM), dominated by Zaghawa, is a more Islamic-driven movement than the SLA, though with similar goals.

18. Exact numbers of victims are hard to come by. These figures are taken from the March 7, 2007 *Report of the High-Level Mission on Darfur of the UN Human Rights Council* (UN Doc. A/HRC/4/80). The Save Darfur Coalition posts far higher numbers on its Web site (see http://www.savedarfur.org/ pages/background).

19. Many other recommendations are contained in the report of the High-Level Mission as well as in Lee Feinstein, *Darfur and Beyond: What is Needed to Prevent Mass Atrocities*, Council Special Report No. 22 (New York: Council on Foreign Relations Press, 2007) and on Web sites of human rights organizations such as the International Crisis Group (see http://www.crisisgroup.org/home/index.cfm?id=3060&l=1).

20. "America: Helping the People of Sudan," Fact sheet, Bureau of Public Affairs, U.S. Department of State, Washington, DC, April 9, 2007, http://www.state.gov/r/pa/scp/76189.htm.

21. A debate has raged for months as to whether what is happening meets the legal definition of "genocide" as codified in the Convention against Genocide or whether it "merely" constitutes, as everyone agrees it surely does, war crimes and crimes against humanity. Major human rights organizations like Amnesty International and Human Rights Watch as well as the UN have resisted the genocide label, while the United States and many other advocates use it regularly. Most now agree that the debate is a distraction, but there is no question that the use of the word "genocide" in this context is helpful for the purposes of rallying public sympathy to the plight of Darfuris.

22. Jim Lobe, "Darfur Genocide Easily Trumped by Michael Jackson on Evening News," Inter Press Service, July 13, 2005, http://www.why-war.com/news/2005/07/13/darfurge.html.

23. One only has to think of the visibility stars like Bono have brought to the struggle to end poverty in the developing world, or Angelina Jolie to the cause of refugees.

24. Helene Cooper, "Darfur Collides With Olympics, And China Yields," *New York Times*, April 13, 2007, http://www.nytimes.com/2007/04/13/washington/13diplo.html?_r=1&oref=slogin#.

25. Seventy-four percent of Americans support UN military intervention in Darfur, and 60 percent support U.S. troops being included in that effort if other countries are unwilling to supply the necessary numbers. See PIPA/Knowledge Networks Poll, media release, http://www.pipa.org/OnlineReports/Africa/Darfur_Jan05/Darfur_Jan05_pr.pdf.

26. The dangers are described in the testimony that Andrew S. Natsios, the president's special envoy to Sudan, gave to the Senate Foreign Relations Committee on April 11, 2007. See U.S. Department of State, *Darfur: A Plan 'B' to Stop Genocide?*, http://www.state.gov/p/af/rls/rm/82941.htm.

27. Favorable opinion of the United States has dropped since 1999 to 2000 from 83 percent to 56 percent in the United Kingdom, from 78 percent to 37 percent in Germany, from 75 percent to 30 percent in Indonesia, and from 52 percent to 12 percent in Turkey, according to a June 13, 2006, survey by the Pew Global Attitudes Project, "America's Image Slips, But Allies Share U.S. Concerns Over Iran, Hamas," http://pewglobal.org/reports/display.php?ReportID=252.

28. Lynn Hunt, *Inventing Human Rights: A History* (New York: W. W. Norton & Co., 2007).

Moving the Responsibility to Protect from Rhetoric to Action: What it Means for Philanthropy, the United States, and the International Community

10

Reaching Across Borders

Philanthropy's Role in the Prevention of Atrocity Crimes

Adele Simmons and April Donnellan*

When the United Nations (UN) endorsed the "responsibility to protect (R2P)" framework at the 2005 World Summit, collective international responsibility to prevent atrocity crimes took precedence over the assumption of noninterference into the affairs of sovereign states. It was a sea change in international affairs achieved in five years, and it would not have come about without the support of philanthropy. The Carnegie Corporation, William and Flora Hewlett Foundation, MacArthur Foundation, Rockefeller Foundation, and Simons Foundation all supported the International Commission on Intervention and State Sovereignty (ICISS), launched by the government of Canada in 2000.[1] The ICISS report formulated the responsibility to protect, prevent, and rebuild doctrine that has now achieved worldwide acceptance.

That extraordinary achievement is all the more remarkable because it comes on the heels of two others, also engineered with considerable speed by a human rights lobby. In 1998 the Rome Statute created the International Criminal Court (ICC). In 1999, supported by foundations, individuals, and a core group of states, a coalition of six nongovernmental organizations (NGOs) achieved passage of the Mine Ban Treaty, seven years after the campaign to ban landmines began.

Yet the three accomplishments, remarkable and even stunning as they are, pale when compared to the atrocities and genocides perpetrated during the same time period. That war criminals can now be more easily prosecuted, that landmines may go the way of mustard gas, that despots can no longer trot out a sovereignty defense while thousands are massacred has not been enough, given the death toll in Darfur, Uganda, and the Democratic Republic of Congo.

On April 30, 2007, UN Secretary-General Ban Ki-moon opened an exhibition at the UN titled "Lessons From the Rwanda Genocide," stating, "Preventing genocide is a collective and individual responsibility. Everyone has a role to play: governments, the media, civil-society organizations, religious groups and each and every one of us. Let us build a global partnership against genocide. Let us protect populations from genocide when their own governments cannot or will not."[2]

To his list of actors, the secretary-general should have added private donors or philanthropists and the civil society groups they support. This chapter explores the ways in which philanthropy has and can engage in responding to the secretary-general.

Philanthropy's Comparative Advantage

Governments bear the primary responsibility and have the greatest resources to prevent atrocity crimes. But there are things that private donors can do when governments cannot or will not fulfill their responsibilities. There are some things that civil society groups do better than governments, and there are times when governments and civil society groups need to act together to accomplish a common goal.

In some cases, governments lack the political will to act. Focused on shorter term election cycles and faced with questions of how international engagements impact national security and other domestic priorities, governments hesitate to employ the kinds of prevention tools that often require significant investments of money and time. The most frequently cited case is of course Rwanda. The U.S. government, burned by Somalia, refused to get involved in any meaningful way. The only thing that would have made a difference might have been if civil society had been able to mobilize citizens to provide support for U.S. government action.

Reviewing the experience of foundations in preventing mass atrocities, the more limited ways they can engage once atrocities have begun, and the unique ways foundations can assist with peace-building suggests an agenda for philanthropy. To understand the comparative advantage of foundations one needs to understand what tools they have in their toolbox and how their role differs from government. These include resources and influence, the ability to act quickly, and their independence. The critical question is how to use the tools and take advantage of the unique characteristics of foundations.

In the case of the ICISS, the leadership was provided by the Canadian government. But it is far easier for a government to offer leadership than to provide extensive resources to support a commission. Moreover, any commission has greater flexibility if its funding comes from private sources, such as foundations.

The Canadians also provided leadership in establishing the Mine Ban Treaty, but foundations working closely with Canadian officials supported the civil society groups that mobilized a popular movement on behalf of the treaty. In the end, the United States did not sign the treaty, but it came close to signing, in spite of the opposition of the military who were concerned about what this would mean in the demilitarized zone in Korea. Without public pressure, it would not have been a close call. As is often the case, interagency government officials did not agree, and the strong voices of the advocacy community helped officials in the State Department make their case.

The establishment of the ICC provides another example of how foundations can support official organizations. Private foundations supported Professor Cherif Bassiouni in his work to develop the concept and create a plan that the UN could bring forward. When the ICC statute was adopted in Rome, there were nearly as many civil society groups, largely foundation funded, as there were governments represented. Among the many roles these organizations played in Rome was "staffing" of the governments of smaller member states, explaining changes or amendments, and providing sophisticated legal advice, thus ensuring that all the governments represented fully understood the issues.[3]

In each of these cases, the foundations contributed to the larger goal of establishing norms by supporting civil society groups whose work complemented and reinforced governments or official organizations.

Foundation funds also support groups that hold governments accountable, such as civil society groups that have people on the ground doing research on human rights abuses and then making practices and policies public. Because these civil society groups do not accept government funds they have no conflict of interest when investigating human rights violations. These same groups mobilize citizens to bring attention and pressure to bear on the local government, international organizations, "foreign" governments, and other civil society groups to act to reduce the chances of mass atrocities.

Using their convening power, foundations often bring people on all sides of a dispute together. Whether it is convening people on opposite sides of a conflict or people to sort through conflicting approaches to prevention of mass atrocities, foundations can get people to the table and ensure that the environment for any discussion is appropriate.

Foundations are flexible and can act quickly. Virtually all foundations and certainly individual donors can act outside of their regular funding cycles in cases of emergency, and respond within days or weeks.

Foundations can try out new ideas. Governments have a wide constituency—and usually multiple constituencies—and are happier when they support a project that already has a track record. Foundations can create that track record.

Finally, foundations support research and give visibility to findings that either challenge conventional wisdom or are critical of governments. They can look at past experience and document what worked and what did not work, and provide a place to explore contradictions or conflicts, such as the arguments between the "peace" and "justice" advocates around engaging perpetrators of war crimes or arresting them and bringing them before the ICC.

Increasingly foundations are working together, either informally, as the Ford and MacArthur Foundations did in their support for the Mine Ban Treaty, or more formally through funders' networks, including the International Human Rights Funders Group[4] and the Peace and Security Funders Group.[5] There is not yet a group that brings the two together to explore the different approaches to R2P of each group, a gap that needs to be addressed.

Philanthropy's Core Strength:
Preventing Atrocity Crimes

Where to Start

For the philanthropist who decides to invest in prevention, the first question may be location. A number of policymakers and academics have developed indicators to identify if and when mass atrocities could occur in a country, conditions that suggest a nation is "high risk," and other variables that suggest whether genocide is possible. None of these is perfect and this is clearly an area for further work. As academics such as Lawrence Woocher, program officer at the U.S. Institute of Peace, Center for Conflict Analysis and Prevention argued in a speech given in March 2007, "the field may be further than is commonly acknowledged from developing effective early warning methods and mechanisms for the prevention of genocide and mass atrocities."[6] For example, in Kenya, violence was not expected to break out in the wake of the 2007 elections, but had the international and local communities considered the possibility, they could have taken some preventative measures.

A growing group of NGOs are dedicated to early warning. Yet work needs to be done on prediction, on better articulating choices, and on setting norms for quick and effective action in case of high-risk situations. Academics, civil society, and government and official actors need to be involved in this work—something that philanthropy can support.

Strategies

Since the end of World War II, philanthropy has used three strategies in fighting atrocity crimes: defining norms, monitoring and exposing evolving situations, and building democratic institutions.

Defining Norms

The drive to create and secure acceptance of the R2P framework, the creation of the ICC, and the passing of the Mine Ban Treaty are examples of philanthropy supporting the establishment of human rights norms. The accomplishments of the foundation-backed NGOs that make up the Coalition to Stop the Use of Child Soldiers[7] also qualifies.

In early 2008, several groups working together, including International Crisis Group, Human Rights Watch, Institute for Global Policy, Oxfam International, and Refugees International, established the Global Center for the Responsibility to Protect near the UN headquarters in New York. The center, and its network of associated centers around the world, will work on practical R2P implementation issues alongside NGOs and governments. One key goal is to clarify the R2P concept and support strategies for norm consolidation.[8]

Monitoring Situations

Since the Rwandan genocide there has been a growing recognition that human rights is the canary in the coal mine of security, that mass atrocities in one nation are the harbinger of the destabilization of a whole region. What is not widely recognized is that the NGO sector, funded by foundations, is the canary doing the singing. The UN is not poised to prevent genocide. Many of the nations who most deserve watching are determined to keep their countries off the Security Council agenda. Secretary-General Kofi Annan appointed a special adviser on the prevention of genocide in 2004, and in 2007, Secretary-General Ban Ki-moon expanded the mandate of the advisor to cover mass atrocities. The adviser has a mandate for early warning, but in March 2007 the office had a professional staff of two.[9]

Human Rights Watch (HRW) and Amnesty International are the world's most prominent monitors. Amnesty International,[10] launched in 1961 as an international movement for "prisoners of conscience," works today for the rights of any prisoner. HRW,[11] now thirty years old, monitors seventy nations with a staff of 150 professionals, issuing reports, lobbying governments, attempting to shame bureaucrats into better behavior, and gathering evidence against war criminals. Neither of these two NGOs takes money from governments (both depend largely on philanthropy and a mass membership for their funds), a rule that allows both groups to speak without fear of losing crucial financial resources. Such a policy enabled HRW to lobby for the extradition to The Hague of former Liberian President Charles Taylor to stand trial for war crimes, as well as the arrest and indictment for torture of his son, Charles "Chuckie" Taylor Jr., in the United States.

The International Crisis Group (ICG) was founded in 1995 with a more refined focus—resolving violent conflict.[12] Its 130 specialists work in areas where deadly conflict is present or imminent, and they produce analytical reports containing practical recommendations for key decision-makers. ICG reaches out to governments and those who influence policymakers to prompt action. The ICG's work in Kosovo during the late 1990s and continuing through the present day is a solid example of this process. Beginning with an on-the-ground presence during the ethnic cleansing of the late 1990s, the ICG served as an authoritative voice to ensure engagement by the international community, including the North Atlantic Treaty Organization (NATO) military campaign. This set the stage for the return of refugees from Macedonia and Albania. Since that time, the continued in-country presence and outreach from the ICG, including at the UN and with key governments, has facilitated the relatively peaceful resolution of the question of independence for Kosovo.

The ICG does not rely on a mass membership for funding, but is supported by foundations, corporations, governments, and some individual donors. The quality and accuracy of their reports coupled with the "insider" experience of their leadership lends weight to ICG recommendations in complex environments.

Building Democratic Institutions

Philanthropists can strengthen democratic institutions and reinforce those who support them. Their investment is crucial in nations presided over by a repressive ruler who stays in power by force or threat of force and nations with weak or nonexistent democratic institutional checks in the parliament and the courts. The genocidal dynamics include squeezing of the press, academia, and civil society so that the space for dissent shrinks. The nation needs only a spark to enable the crime spree to begin—a political uprising, for example, or a perceived need to crack down on a scapegoat because of economic failure, or even a manufactured provocation. But foundations can also strengthen democratic institutions in countries that may have fragile but still viable democracies to prevent the downward spiral.

Some foundations take a governance-based approach—strengthening the electoral process, reinforcing institutional checks, training the judiciary and legislators, and expanding the space for dissent and association. The hoped-for result is that sparks and provocations do not arise, and if they do, that their power to ignite is diminished by political and legal discourse.

The Soros Foundation's Open Society Institute has been involved in hundreds of such projects.[13] A few recent examples include backing Radio Freedom FM's fight for a broadcasting license, denied by the government of Cameroon (the government confiscated the public affairs radio station's equipment, sealed its offices, and charged one of its founders with operating without a license); pushing for passage of a freedom of information bill in Nigeria; promoting greater police accountability in Peru, Nigeria, and South Africa; and publishing a handbook for NGOs monitoring election campaign financing.

Election monitoring is funded by government and private groups. The Carter Center,[14] which is privately funded, was early into the space of election monitoring and setting standards for how it should be done. Less thought has been given to what follows the management of the crisis brought on by a rigged election, particularly if it is perceived to impact the election outcome. Kenya's 2007 elections and their violent aftermath demonstrate this danger. Creating some understanding of shared power and responsibility and some mechanism for building trust in these situations is crucial. But norms need to be set before the crises happen. As we show in the peace-building section, a winner-take-all approach will not provide the healing required in these situations.

Another type of monitoring undertaken by groups such as Transparency International focuses on corruption in government, business, and throughout society.[15] Supported by foundations, governments, and individuals, Transparency International identifies corruption, raising awareness about related issues and recommending means to target various forms of corruption. Pervasive corruption can be an indicator of a society at risk of civil breakdown. Corruption also hampers economic development, undermines the rule of law, and intensifies political exclusion. These factors all contribute to creating a society ripe for atrocity crimes.

Philanthropists also can impact the quality of a society. Genocide often occurs in places where sharp economic differences exist between groups defined by nationality, ethnicity, race, or religion. A philanthropist wishing to reduce those differences can invest in efforts to address poverty and inequality, but those problems are resistant to short-term fixes and investors must take great care not to inadvertently exacerbate societal divisions. In his book *Aiding Violence*,[16] Peter Uvin describes development projects in Rwanda that shifted power from farmers and village leaders to corrupt bureaucrats and in turn created structures that furthered inequality, exclusion, and humiliation, which made privileged Tutsis more vulnerable to the rage of Hutus and ultimately contributed to the 1994 genocide. But there is no question that properly organized poverty reduction strategies, including education, health care, and income generation, are crucial prevention strategies.

Philanthropy's Tactics When Long-term Prevention Fails

In the last few decades, the human rights movement has had remarkable success, particularly in creating international conventions, protecting and freeing political prisoners, and building institutions to promote human rights. There is growing awareness that some human rights problems are not resolved by the tried-and-true methods. Torture is as popular today as it was thirty years ago, and genocides have been carried out despite the norms, the treaties, and the Herculean efforts of international monitors to expose societal collapse.

Direct Prevention:
When Mass Atrocities Threaten

In the months when mass atrocities seem likely or possible but no triggering event has yet taken place, democracy-building must take a back seat to efforts to forestall huge loss of life. Philanthropic organizations have funded, often very discreetly, "track-two" negotiations where citizen diplomacy can bridge differences that official government positions are unable to tolerate. "The truth is that many of the peace negotiations work more effectively when foreign governments and the UN aren't in the leadership role," remarks ICG vice president Don Steinberg.[17] Steinberg cites in particular the recent history of Burundi, which he calls "the unwritten story of where genocide prevention actually works."

During the Rwandan genocide in 1994, neighboring Burundi also seemed likely to explode in mass atrocities. Steinberg, then President Bill Clinton's advisor for Africa, recalls that "the international community—in large part because of NGOs—responded exactly right. They sent in a preventive force from South Africa. They convened an international donors conference to support peace-building efforts. They sent in mediators to work on the conflict. They sent relief to key players who might be tempted to take another route. They looked at strengthening the rule of law. And 13 years later, we haven't seen that genocide."

Steinberg credits groups funded by foundations, the Kroc Center at Notre Dame, the Carr Center at Harvard, and the Carter Center in Atlanta, but in particular Howard Wolpe, whose involvement began as Clinton's special envoy to the Burundi peace process but continued as he later worked with the World Bank and the Woodrow Wilson International Center. "Wolpe essentially went in, gained the confidence of all the different players on the ground, and then got negotiations going between all the warring parties, many times with government approval, many times without."

Steinberg does not argue that Burundi is now a model of democracy. Indeed the ICG's Web site notes that the nation's recent history is marked by the arrest of opposition leaders, torture, increasing government corruption, and a clampdown on the press and civil society.[18] But there has been no genocide, and Steinberg argues there would have been after the Rwandan episode "had the international community not said, 'Let's pay an awful lot of attention to this situation because we are all afraid it is going to deteriorate.'"

When the Atrocities Have Begun

When mass atrocities are under way, philanthropy has fewer options. The primary tool of foundation-funded NGOs has been to raise public awareness in an attempt to force governments or the UN to act. Those NGOs are now far better staffed and equipped than they were in 1994 when the Rwandan genocide began, and as a result, having information to present is no longer such a problem. The problem, ICG President Gareth Evans said in a speech in April 2006, "tends to be not so much what policymakers don't know, or can't know: it's what they don't *want* to know, or don't want to act upon."[19]

In a world where every news bulletin describes trouble somewhere and the market in human misery is unhappily, highly competitive, the task for those who want to overcome indifference is not just to get out the information that something bad is happening but to establish a general recognition that it is so bad and so wrong that it cannot be ignored. Private funding can get mediators on the ground quickly. The newly formed Elders, including

Nobel Peace Prize winners and respected former heads of state, has the capacity to deploy their members immediately to mediate between actors, and backed Kofi Annan in his mediation in Kenya.[20]

Military intervention is a last resort and faces multiple challenges, including lack of popular support in the countries asked to send their troops. Foundations can help civil society groups with other approaches to ending atrocity crimes. Shaming perpetrators works occasionally, though it had little effect in Sudan or Kosovo. Threatening perpetrators with legal consequences carries more weight and is much more real now than it was before the ICC was up and running. Among numerous projects in support of the ICC, the MacArthur Foundation has funded a training program to teach lawyers how to document war crimes in order to facilitate the indictment and prosecution of the perpetrators, and in June 2007, a group of Sudanese attorneys were the first graduates of the course.[21] But the threat is not as intimidating as one would like, particularly when the killings are carried out by rebels or unofficial death squads, or when whole populations are massacred in isolated areas. The intimidation factor is further diminished by the world's failure to arrest indicted war criminals more than a decade after their crimes (Bosnian Serbs Radovan Karadzic and Ratko Mladic, indicted in 1995 by the International Criminal Tribunal for the former Yugoslavia [ICTY], come immediately to mind). The threat of indictment might increase considerably, however, if the ICC had a marshal's service, advocated elsewhere in this collection.

Various NGOs working on Darfur have used economic threats in an attempt to goad the Khartoum government to stop the killing. The Sudan Divestment Task Force, a project of the Genocide Intervention Network, organized campaigns targeting a wide range of institutional and individual investors in a campaign to persuade them to sell their holdings in the most egregiously offending companies in Sudan.[22] Focusing on China's role as a supporter and friend of the Sudanese government, activists have lobbied an array of large investors, asking that they dump their holdings in the oil companies PetroChina and China Petroleum and Chemical.

Getting nations or the UN to establish embargoes or institute sanctions is another tool used by foundation-backed NGOs to deter atrocity crimes. On May 29, 2007, President George Bush announced U.S. sanctions against thirty-one Sudanese companies that have profited from genocide, forbidding them from doing business with U.S. companies or accessing the U.S. financial system. Bush also announced sanctions against three Sudanese officials, barring them from doing business with any American citizen or company.[23] It is unlikely that such action would have been taken without pressure from foundation-backed NGOs and Congress.

Protecting the Victims

Historically, donors have supported groups that protect victims. When vulnerable populations have been forced to flee their villages, they face a host of issues in refugee camps. They do not cease being victims of atrocity crimes because they no longer live on the site of the atrocity. While the best approaches to humanitarian relief are separate from the prevention of atrocities, preparing people in camps for their return home or another destination for permanent settlement can be important and impact the chances of a recurrence of mass atrocities.

Peace-building

As adopted during the 2005 World Summit—and contrary to the ICISS definition—the R2P doctrine does not specifically include rebuilding, either schools and water systems or, perhaps even more important, trust. Yet rebuilding after mass atrocity crimes is of critical importance, in no small part because one of the most reliable indicators of where violent conflict will occur is where it has occurred in the last fifteen years. According to the ICG's Steinberg, the rate of recidivism is greater than 50 percent.[24] Therefore, peace-building is essential to preventing the recurrence of atrocity crimes.

Wars have a tendency to destroy civil society, the glue that typically binds a citizenry. As a result, one of the key elements in peace-building is restoring that bond largely because it reminds people that they have the means to influence events and that governments should not be all-powerful, that differing interests and points of view should be accommodated. In the aftermath of bloody conflict, it is crucial to promote women's organizations, academic groups, labor unions, lawyers' associations, human rights groups, and other civil society organizations to hold government accountable and build trust across groups.

"I sometimes wonder if NGOs (or the international community more generally) have learned anything from Rwanda," notes Howard Wolpe.[25] Now serving as director of the Africa Program and of the Project on Leadership and Building State Capacity at the Woodrow Wilson International Center for Scholars, Wolpe is the man whom Steinberg credits with preventing a Burundian genocide. He laments that "too frequently assistance programs are insensitive to the manner in which the unequal distribution of aid can actually heighten political tensions and intergroup animosities;" that "the international community seldom shows much staying power once a peace agreement is signed, and seldom provides the resources it has promised to deliver a 'peace dividend' for the population." Leaders of wartime factions see each other no differently the day after the peace agreement than they did the day before, they are rarely prepared to address the issues that gave rise to the conflict, and the international community makes little effort to address existing mind-sets or to rebuild trust and relationships. Without that, Wolpe argues "there is little prospect of sustainable peace or even of transcending the dehumanization that is the precursor of all genocides." It is difficult for governments to support reconciliation and trust-building projects, but foundations can, and indeed have greater experience with various models of trust-building interventions.

Wolpe argues that strengthening the competitive dimension of already divided societies is the wrong approach, that what must be built is collaborative capacity—the recognition that the formerly belligerent parties are interdependent. To that end, he and his colleagues began the Burundi Leadership Training Program in 2002. Ninety-five leaders were selected from the political class (the political parties, army, and rebel groups) and civil society (churches, women's organizations, academia, business, the media, and youth) for an eighteen-month program.Wolpe argues that war had robbed the Burundian elites of their communication and negotiating skills: "Democracy and stability cannot thrive in a climate of constant accusations and demands." The goal was the building of an enlightened self-interest, a recognition that whatever conflicting interests the leaders brought to the table, they had more important interests in common, and that correcting the underlying social and political inequities would benefit all.[26] Wolpe argues that "much philanthropic support for institution building is absolutely a waste if this more fundamental transformative work is not accomplished." While the model Wolpe has developed will not work everywhere, it clearly provides a starting point, a way of working that foundations can bring to other countries and study carefully.

Establishment of a lasting peace in postconflict situations is further complicated by the demands of justice. Should peace come first and justice second? Or can peace only be achieved if justice is part of the deal? Views differ widely and can lead to strong disagreements over a course of action.

Whatever the view on how much justice considerations must be an integral part of peace negotiations, "it is critical," Wolpe says, "that the victims of atrocities, or their family members, believe there is an effective system to hold perpetrators accountable. Otherwise, the cycle of violence will be unending."

Future Investment

The atrocity crimes committed since the breakup of the Soviet bloc have been an unfortunate learning experience for the philanthropic and NGO community. Much of what has been learned is the depth of what we do not know about atrocity crime sprees. University of Wisconsin political science professor Scott Straus points out that we do not understand why some conflicts lead to relatively low levels of violence against civilians and others lead to very high levels, why some exclusivist ideologies lead to more compromise with their opponents than others, or what it is about some international actions that leads to increased radicalization of the parties while in other instances international action has a positive effect. Straus believes that most models of genocide overpredict when and where it will happen, in part because of a lack of understanding of what deescalating factors are present in situations when genocide is predicted but never develops.[27]

At the same time, the violence in Kenya is an example of the failure to fully anticipate the violence that a close or rigged election could generate. The voices of those who identified the need for preventative action did not resonate. There is no common understanding of what kind of mediation and advance planning could have prevented the violence. Elections can be very divisive. As Howard Wolpe has demonstrated in Burundi, the chances of postelection violence can be reduced if the parties involved in the election meet ahead of time and work out a clear code of conduct for the effective management of elections. The development of such an agreement needs to be accompanied by training and trust-building. Establishing norms for establishing agreements that the parties involved in the election agree to deserves priority attention from funders. Civil society groups such as the Woodrow Wilson Center and the Carter Center start this process far more easily than governments or international organizations.

Another area of research that would benefit from philanthropy's support is the need to address the contradiction between human rights funders and civil society groups that look to the ICC for deterrence and prevention, and peace and security funders and organizations that seek to bring all parties, however distasteful, to the table.

Another contradiction that needs better understanding focuses on democracy and democratic institutions. Winner-take-all electoral systems may not be best suited for countries that are deeply divided along religious or ethnic lines. As we saw in Kenya, the election exacerbated conflict. The complex election system in place in Mauritius that ensures that all minority groups are appropriately represented may be a better model to facilitate power-sharing.

Beyond this analytical work, there is also a need to better identify what tools work best to stop atrocities. HRW associate director Carroll Bogert believes that the Darfur genocide demonstrated "the paucity of tools in our toolbox. Darfur was a place where western intervention was not going to work, you weren't going to get U.S. military action. What we didn't have was a sophisticated array of other policy options to ratchet up the pressure on Khartoum, no series of policy ideas that we cranked through steadily."[28]

Within this toolbox, the role of the military remains the most controversial. It would be helpful if philanthropy could invest in clarifying when and how the military would have the most added value in ending atrocity crimes. One particular issue relates to the mandate of military forces that may be deployed in a crisis situation: how much coercion should they be entitled to use to protect civilians? Retired Australian Lieutenant General John Sanderson pointed out that many of those who cry for peacekeeping forces have failed to learn the lessons of history. "The media and the people always expect the military to do more than they are mandated and equipped to do, while the nations generally expect them to do much less than they need to do to be effective. . . . This confusion has led to sickening burdens on military forces who have to live with the sense of disgrace that comes from being witness to, and not being able to do anything about, horrific injustices to human beings. It is wrong to give coalition forces a peace-keeping role to salve the national conscience and then to blame them whenever they're unable to stop the violence."[29]

One way to close the gap between the expectations of what the military will achieve and what it actually can deliver is to improve the military expertise of the humanitarian actors that provide protection on the ground. Holly Burkhalter, now with the International Justice Mission after previous stints with HRW and Physicians for Human Rights, argues that human rights groups are in dire need of an accessible resource with military expertise, that presently NGOs clamoring for military intervention usually do so without precision and with minimal knowledge of what's needed or available militarily in a given situation. She pointed out that it was possible to come up with a list of the several dozen situations in Darfur in which civilians would be most vulnerable and work calculations from there. "Say, you've got a refugee camp of 10,000 people, you've got x number of marauders, what is the minimum security requirement?" If you know that, she said, you can have a conversation about military intervention that reflects reality. "You can make the case that it can be done, therefore it should be done. . . . If we rely on the U.S. military to be responsible for telling us how to do something they don't want to do, I don't think we are going to get the answers we want and need."[30]

At a time when the systems needed to more effectively prevent mass atrocities are lacking, foundations can play an important role. Expanding the toolbox, as Howard Wolpe did in Burundi is an area that lends itself to foundation support, as it involves new ideas that may not be supported by governments or international organizations right away. In addition, there are those who argue that foundations can do much to support moderate voices in at-risk societies and ensure that there is a space for civil society to operate.

Finally, it is critical that every country support the UN resolution on R2P. Some leaders have commented that the concept has not taken hold in some Asian and Latin American countries, which suggests that NGO groups based in those countries could help to strengthen the commitment to R2P.

In the face of these lessons and perceived failings, however, it is worth keeping in mind that philanthropy and the NGOs it has funded have had an enormous impact. Measuring the impact is difficult—in the field of human rights, you are often left pointing to something that did not happen—and pessimists point to Darfur.

And yet even in Darfur, while peace seems far off and the two million displaced may only dream of returning to their homes, as this chapter goes to press the killing has slowed considerably from what it was in 2004, the UN arms embargo has had some effect, and there are twelve thousand humanitarian aid workers on the ground. One shudders to think what the situation would be if philanthropists and NGOs had sat out the battle to save Darfur.

Notes

* Adele Simmons is the president of Global Philanthropy Partnership, and April Donnellan is the executive director of Global Philanthropy Partnership. John Conroy contributed to the research and writing of this chapter.
1. International Commission on Intervention and State Sovereignty, *The Responsibility to Protect*, cochaired by Gareth Evans and Mohamed Sahnoun (Canada: IRDC, 2001), 85.
2. UN Secretary-General, Department of Public Information, *United Nations has Moral Duty to Act on Lessons of Rwanda, Says Secretary General in Message to Mark Fourteenth Anniversary of 1994 Genocide*, SG/SM/11495, AFR/1674 (April 4, 2008).
3. Adele Simmons, *Global Giving in Just Money: A Critique of Contemporary American Philanthropy*, ed. H. Peter Karoff (Boston: Philanthropic Initiative, 2004), 220–23. See also the Coalition for the International Criminal Court, *History of the ICC*, http://www.iccnow.org/?mod=icchistory.
4. See International Human Rights Funders Group, http://ihrfg.org/.
5. See Peace and Security Funders Group, http://www.peaceandsecurity.org/.
6. Laurence Woocher, "Early Warning for the Prevention of Genocide and Mass Atrocities" (paper, prepared for the forty-eighth annual ISA convention, Chicago, March 1, 2007), 14.
7. See Coalition to Stop the Use of Child Soldiers, http://www.child-soldiers .org/home.

8. See Global Center for the Responsibility to Protect, "About the Global Center," http://www.globalcenter2p.org/about.html.

9. Woocher, 4, 18.

10. See Amnesty International, http://www.amnesty.org/.

11. See Human Rights Watch, http://www.hrw.org/.

12. See International Crisis Group, http://www.crisisgroup.org/home/index.cfm.

13. See Open Society Institute, http://www.soros.org/.

14. See the Carter Center, http://www.cartercenter.org/homepage.html.

15. See Transparency International, http://www.transparency.org/.

16. Peter Uvin, *Aiding Violence: The Development Enterprise in Rwanda* (West Hartford, CT: Kumarian Press, 1998).

17. Don Steinberg (vice-president, ICG), interview by John Conroy, June 2007.

18. See ICG's Burundi reports, http://www.crisisgroup.org/home/index.cfm?id =1172&l=1.

19. Gareth Evans, "Crimes Against Humanity: Overcoming Global Indifference," Gandel Oration for B'nai B'rith Anti-Defamation Commission, University of New South Wales, Sydney, New South Wales, Australia, April 30, 2006.

20. See the Elders, http://theelders.org/.

21. See the John D. and Catherine T. MacArthur Foundation, http://www .macfound.org.

22. See Genocide Intervention Network, http://www.genocideintervention.net/.

23. White House, Office of the Press Secretary, "President Bush Discusses Genocide in Darfur, Implements Sanctions" (May 29, 2007), http://www .whitehouse.gov/news/releases/2007/05/20070529.html.

24. Don Steinberg (vice-president, ICG), interview by John Conroy, June 2007.

25. Howard Wolpe, in correspondence with Adele Simmons, July 2007.

26. Howard Wolpe and Steve McDonald, "Burundi's Transition: Training Leaders for Peace," *Journal of Democracy* 17, no. 1 (January 2006): 126–32.

27. Scott Straus, interviewed by Jerry Fowler, U.S. Holocaust Museum program, "Naming Genocide," May 17, 2007, http://www.ushmm.org/conscience/ analysis/details.php?content=2007-05-17. See also Scott Straus, *The Order of Genocide: Race, Power and War in Rwanda* (Ithaca, NY: Cornell University Press, 2006).

28. Carroll Bogert (associate director, HRW), interview by John Conroy July 2007.

29. John Sanderson, "Genocide and Crimes Against Humanity: Early Warning and Prevention," (presentation at the U.S. Holocaust Memorial Museum conference, December 1998), http://www.ushmm.org/conscience/analysis/details.php? content=1998-12-09&page=3&menupage=History%20%26%20Concept.

30. Holly Burkhalter (International Justice Mission), interview by John Conroy, July 2007.

11

Beyond Words

U.S. Policy and the Responsibility to Protect

Lee Feinstein and Erica De Bruin*

The U.S. position on preventing mass atrocities and on the "responsibility to protect (R2P)" has developed over the course of nearly fifteen years. As a matter of policy, the United States has begun to articulate a policy and doctrine that supports a greater international role in preventing and stopping mass atrocities. As a practical matter, however, U.S. efforts have been sporadic. Concerns about how changing notions of sovereignty and international obligations affect U.S. freedom of action have remained a constant throughout the Democratic and Republican administrations of the past fifteen years. Surprisingly, formal support for an active U.S. role in preventing mass atrocities has weathered steadily declining public support for the war in Iraq. To understand the development of the U.S. position on the responsibility to protect, it is useful to go back to U.S. policy toward the genocides and mass atrocities in the years immediately following the end of the cold war, when the United States repeatedly grappled with the question of humanitarian intervention. Washington's response to crises in Bosnia, Somalia, Rwanda, and Kosovo shaped its response to the concept of the responsibility to protect years later.

The Clinton Administration

As a candidate in the first post–cold war presidential election, Bill Clinton was supportive of expanding international peacekeeping efforts and U.S. participation in them. In a 1992 statement, he criticized the U.S. response to the conflict in Bosnia. "United Nations demands," he argued, "should be backed up by collective action, including the use of force, if necessary. The United States should be prepared to lend appropriate support, including military, to such an operation. . . . If the horrors of the Holocaust taught us anything, it is the high cost of remaining silent and paralyzed in the face of genocide."[1]

On coming into office, however, the Clinton administration prioritized domestic policy, and found it difficult to build and sustain public support for humanitarian interventions. The administration initially declined to increase U.S. involvement in Bosnia, wary of doing so without the strong backing of U.S. military leaders, public opinion, and European allies. In October 1993 the death of eighteen American Rangers during a failed U.S.-led operation to seize the foreign minister and top political advisor of Somali warlord Mohamed Farrah Aidid precipitated both a withdrawal of the four thousand U.S. forces there and a broader political retrenchment on the jugular question of peacekeeping.

Presidential Decision Directive 25 (PDD-25) on reforming multilateral peace operations was the formal expression of the Clinton administration's reassessment.[2] Released in May 1994, it provided "factors for consideration" in making decisions about whether the United States would support or participate in peacekeeping operations, including humanitarian interventions. Although the directive was widely seen as limiting U.S. participation in future missions by providing an exhaustive list of factors to consider prior to committing, in truth, it outlined many factors that would later emerge among the "prudential considerations" offered by the International Commission on Intervention and State Sovereignty (ICISS), which would coin the phrase "responsibility to protect" a decade later.

Less than one month after the U.S. withdrawal from Somalia, the administration did not support U.S. military intervention as a possibility when signs of mass atrocities appeared in Rwanda in April 1994, and it did not press other members of the United Nations (UN) Security Council to increase the size of the small contingent of five thousand peacekeepers there.[3] The United States also downplayed the severity of the crisis, initially avoiding the word "genocide" in describing the killings, and limited its involvement to providing humanitarian relief to refugee camps in neighboring Burundi, Tanzania, and the Democratic Republic of Congo.[4] Clinton came to regret his administration's inaction in Rwanda. In 1998 he became the first world leader to publicly apologize for not intervening, telling Rwandans in Kigali: "We did not act quickly enough after the killing began. We should not have allowed the refugee camps to become safe havens for the killers. We did not immediately call these crimes by their rightful name: genocide."[5]

Over time, the administration took steps to better prepare the United States and the UN to respond to future atrocities. To support expanding peacekeeping capacity at the UN, Clinton agreed to pay about $400 million in U.S. peacekeeping arrears, resolving a long-standing source of dispute between the United States and the UN, and lent Defense Department personnel to provide advice on upgrades at the UN's Department of Peacekeeping Operations (DPKO). Under the direction of the Joint Chiefs of Staff, the Defense Department also worked to develop a manual to improve logistical operations and commissioned a study of the DPKO's communications and information needs. To increase the global reserves of peacekeepers available for UN missions, Clinton launched a State Department program to train and equip African troops for the task.[6] To improve early-warning capacity, the Central Intelligence Agency (CIA) commissioned a study on the preconditions for genocide and politically motivated mass killings. And to better coordinate the U.S. response, Clinton established an atrocities prevention interagency working group, which monitored and briefed administration officials on the potential for atrocities in a number of states.

These steps were intended to make working through the UN a more effective option. Even as it sought to improve UN capacity, however, the United States maintained that the UN could not be the only option. The case in point was the 1999 North Atlantic Treaty Organization (NATO) war to prevent mass killings of Kosovar Albanians by Serbian forces, which was waged without Security Council approval. Postcolonial states and others critical of the United States considered the action an illegal infringement into the "domestic jurisdiction" of a state.[7] So did the majority of international lawyers working for Western governments, who concluded that the response was illegal, even if justified, because it was not formally a war of self-defense and was not authorized by the UN Security Council.

In defending NATO's actions in Kosovo, the United States avoided stating a new doctrine of humanitarian intervention. Speaking to NATO troops in Macedonia, President Clinton announced: "We can say to the people of the world, whether you live in Africa, or Central Europe, or any other place, if somebody comes after innocent civilians and tries to kill them en masse because of their race, their ethnic background, or their religion, and its within our power to stop it, we will stop it."[8] Public support was behind Clinton's sentiment.[9] Yet Secretary of State Madeleine Albright and other administration officials quickly discouraged "sweeping conclusions" that "Kosovo will be a precedent for similar interventions around the globe."[10] Clinton's staff drafted a speech for him that outlined factors for humanitarian intervention, but he never delivered it.[11]

Instead, the administration offered an omelet-on-the-wall justification for the intervention. In a March 1999 radio address, Clinton argued that the action was needed to "save the lives of innocent civilians in Kosovo from a brutal military offensive."[12] The administration also appealed to traditional security concerns. A State Department fact sheet on the intervention highlighted the potential for the violence to spread, stating: "No one should forget that World War I began in this tinderbox. If actions are not taken to stop this conflict now, it will spread and both the cost and risk will be substantially greater."[13] In addition, the United States cited concern for maintaining NATO's credibility. The organization had repeatedly warned Serbian leader Slobodan Milosevic that it would respond to continued transgressions with force, and feared consequences to the organization's credibility if it did not follow through.

In the wake of the Kosovo intervention, the United States declined to take up calls from UN Secretary-General Kofi Annan and British Prime Minister Tony Blair to address more directly the conflict between deference to state sovereignty and the imperative to stop atrocities with or without the Security Council's approval.[14] Washington was wary of formalizing a set of guidelines that might limit future action and wanted to avoid creating an obligation to act in situations where it deemed that intervention would not be feasible or prudent. It also did not want to set a precedent that others might cite to justify international aggression. In a September 1999 speech to the UN General Assembly, Clinton emphasized that "our response in every case cannot or should not be the same."[15] When Blair's foreign secretary, Robin Cook, proposed talks among the five permanent members of the Security Council on factors for humanitarian intervention and circulated draft guidelines for review, the United States stalled, and ultimately rejected the idea.[16]

Thus by the end of his administration, Clinton had committed the United States to working with the rest of the international community to "prevent and, whenever possible, to stop outbreaks of mass killing and displacement," but did not have a cohesive or systematic policy to do so.[17]

The Bush Administration

When President Bush entered office in 2001, he was opposed to humanitarian intervention broadly speaking, and intervention to prevent mass atrocities in particular. As a presidential candidate, he told ABC's Sam Donaldson, "I don't like genocide and I don't like ethnic cleansing, but I would not send our troops."[18] Yet when a National Security Council memorandum describing Washington's failure to lead a global effort to staunch the 1994 Rwandan genocide and warning of the potential for ethnic violence in Burundi made its way onto his desk in the fall of 2001, Bush famously wrote "Not on my watch" in its margin.

This pledge, however, did not translate into support for the responsibility to protect. As conceived by the ICISS in its 2001 report, the responsibility to protect obligated the international community in general, and the Security Council in particular, to act in the event of mass killings or ethnic cleansing. In Washington, standard State Department concerns resurfaced. The administration was wary of specifying these two types of events as the threshold for intervention, fearing they might prove too difficult to establish and unduly limit its prerogative to determine when and where it would use force. The United States also did not want to appear to precommit its troops to interventions that it might decide were not in U.S. national interests.

The September 11, 2001, attacks cemented these concerns and overshadowed an earlier emphasis on humanitarian intervention. The administration's subsequent campaign against al-Qaeda and the Taliban government in Afghanistan exemplified a situation in which the United States feared new guidelines for the use of force might constrain its ability to act for legitimate national security reasons. When the Security Council hosted the ICISS cochairs at its annual retreat in May 2002, the United States was unenthusiastic about the report and rejected its proposed criteria for intervention.[19] This reception led observers to conclude: "The Bush administration does not and will not accept the substance of the report or support any formal declaration or resolution about it."[20]

So it was surprising that just a few years later the United States supported the inclusion of language on the responsibility to protect in the 2005 World Summit Outcome document. Part of the explanation for the evolution of the Bush administration's views on the responsibility to protect has to do with how it came to understand national security in the years following 9/11.

The Bush administration's views on the responsibility to protect evolved along with its perceptions of the security dangers facing the nation. In its 2002 National Security Strategy, the administration connected states' propensities to "brutalize their own people" with terrorism, proliferation of weapons of mass destruction, and state-to-state aggression. The Bush administration also adopted as its own the Clinton administration's concern about the danger posed by failing states, "Regional conflicts do not stay isolated for long and often spread or devolve into humanitarian tragedy or anarchy . . .

[they] can arise from a wide variety of causes . . . [but] lead to the same ends: failed states, humanitarian disasters, and ungoverned areas that can become safe havens for terrorists."[21]

The administration's 2006 National Security Strategy outlined a strategy to prioritize conflict prevention, intervention, and postconflict stabilization and reconstruction as part of an effort to shore up failed states. The 2006 Quadrennial Defense Review (QDR) also emphasized the importance of U.S. military efforts to "build partnership capacity" in the developing world to "inoculate societies against terrorism, insurgency, and non-state threats."[22]

The administration's newfound concern with atrocities and other problems of failed states was reinforced by growing interest in the issue of genocide prevention among politically mobilized religious communities, non-governmental organizations (NGOs), and congressional leaders prompted, in part, by the developing crisis in Darfur, Sudan, in 2003 and 2004.

Perceptions that the Darfur crisis was being ignored mobilized religious communities that were core supporters of the Bush administration. Evangelicals who had earlier lobbied the administration to assist Christians persecuted in southern Sudan soon turned their attention to Darfur. Washington was slow to recognize the carnage in Darfur, having focused its attention on the successful effort to resolve the longer and more brutal north–south civil war. The administration also believed pressure to stop the conflict in Darfur would jeopardize counterterrorism cooperation with Khartoum, which began after 9/11. Although the United States and Britain were the most vocal critics of the government of Sudan, neither government put sustained pressure on China, the main impediment to strong Security Council action. In August 2004, thirty-five evangelical leaders signed a letter to President Bush that called for "active exploration of all available intervention options—including sending troops to Darfur as has been proposed by the United Kingdom and Australia—in order to stop the killing."[23]

Congress also exerted pressure on the administration to get serious about Darfur. Senator Sam Brownback (R-KS) and Congressman Frank Wolf (R-VA) undertook a fact-finding trip to the region in June 2004, returning to the United States with recommendations to sanction those responsible for the atrocities. The next month, Congress determined that the atrocities constituted genocide; it urged the president to recognize the same, to pursue sanctions against Sudanese leadership, and to support the establishment of a multinational peacekeeping force for the region.[24]

In December 2004, amid growing frustration with the UN's progress in Sudan and the recently exposed "oil-for-food" scandal, Congress authorized former House Speaker Newt Gingrich and former Senate Majority Leader

George Mitchell to lead a task force on American interests and UN reform. The language calling for the task force stated: "The conferees are deeply troubled by the inaction of the United Nations on many fronts, especially in regard to the genocide in Darfur, Sudan."

In the meantime, the ground was beginning to shift on the specific issue of the responsibility to protect. The Gingrich-Mitchell task force on UN reform made the doctrine one of its principal recommendations, overcoming opposition within the task force from the political right and left. The report phrased its endorsement in a way that addressed U.S. concerns about restricting or obligating future action. The task force emphasized that the responsibility to protect was first and foremost a responsibility of states not to condone, acquiesce, or commit genocide. It affirmed that "every sovereign government has a 'responsibility to protect' its citizens and those within its jurisdiction from genocide, mass killing, and massive and sustained human rights violations." The secondary responsibility of the international community to act was phrased in a much less direct way: "In certain instances, a government's abnegation of its responsibilities to its own people is so severe that the collective responsibility of nations to take action cannot be denied." The report also underlined the importance of not giving the final word to the Security Council: "In the event the Security Council fails to act, its failure must not be used as an excuse by concerned members to avoid protective measures."[25]

The Gingrich-Mitchell report was well received within the administration, yet in the months following the report's release and leading up to the 2005 UN World Summit, the administration was silent on the responsibility to protect. In testimony before the Senate Foreign Relations Committee on July 21, 2005, under Secretary of State for Political Affairs R. Nicholas Burns supported several of the Gingrich-Mitchell report's findings, but did not mention the responsibility to protect.[26] Instead, the administration prioritized a standard set of reform issues.[27] The appointment of John Bolton as the new U.S. ambassador to the United Nations only a month before the summit contributed to public uncertainty about the U.S. position on the responsibility to protect.

Heading into World Summit negotiations, opinions on the responsibility to protect outside the United States were divided. Britain, France, Canada, Australia, and Japan were strong backers. The strongest opponents included China, India, Pakistan, and Malaysia. The nonaligned movement (NAM), which represented nearly two-thirds of the member states at the United Nations, initially said there was no basis in international law for the types of intervention envisaged by the ICISS report.[28] The Group of 77 raised cautionary notes about preserving the principles of sovereignty and territorial integrity.[29]

As the negotiations progressed, however, a broad consensus developed behind including a statement on the principle in the summit's outcome document. Early opponents of humanitarian intervention on sovereignty grounds—including, most notably, China—came to acknowledge that humanitarian crises were a "legitimate concern of the international community."[30] The spoiler potential of the NAM was undermined by its inability to maintain a cohesive position through the negotiations, as several NAM members, including South Africa, Rwanda, Tanzania, Chile, and Peru, emerged among the strongest proponents of the responsibility to protect at the United Nations.

Behind the scenes, the United States was also supportive of the push to adopt language on the responsibility to protect. The U.S. position had evolved to support a formal statement on humanitarian intervention, although concerns about retaining freedom of action that first arose in the aftermath of Kosovo resurfaced and were reflected in the revisions the United States proposed to the draft outcome document.

The United States had two priorities in framing the responsibility to protect at the World Summit negotiations. The first was to ensure that the responsibility of the international community to prevent atrocities discussed in the outcome document did not create a new legal obligation, but instead referred to a moral responsibility. Echoing the Gingrich-Mitchell report, the United States argued the responsibility of the international community was different from—and secondary to—that of individual states. In an August 30 letter to other UN members, the United States proposed revisions to the summit's outcome document that would stress the different nature of these responsibilities.[31]

The second U.S. priority was to retain the freedom to address each case that might warrant intervention as it comes up, including the possibility of action outside of the Security Council. The United Stated pointed to "cases that involve humanitarian catastrophes but for which there is also a legitimate basis for states to act in self-defense" as those in which it may be appropriate to take action without UN authorization.[32]

Britain and other long-time champions of the responsibility to protect criticized U.S. revisions as too limiting and complained that late changes threatened to undermine carefully negotiated agreements on the text.

The United States did not play a lead role in pushing for adoption of the responsibility to protect, but its support was critical nonetheless. U.S. recommendations that moderated the obligation on the international community helped to bring undecideds to the table. In the context of the Iraq War, the perception that Washington had concerns about the doctrine actually helped allay concerns in the developing world that the principle was simply a new basis for major powers to justify the use of force against them.[33]

As the summit negotiations wound down, disagreement remained in two areas. The first was whether the principle would provide for action to be taken outside of the Security Council. The second was over what, if any, criteria for the use of force should guide interventions. The ICISS, the High-Level Panel on Threats, Challenges, and Change, and Kofi Annan's 2005 report on reform, "In Larger Freedom," proposed the adoption of criteria governing a Security Council decision to authorize force.[34] Britain, Canada, and other early champions of the responsibility to protect supported the inclusion of criteria and had at various times proposed their own. The United States and many developing states were opposed, though for different reasons: Washington was concerned that any criteria that would garner the support of all 191 UN members would be too constraining, while developing states viewed the criteria as a potential source of abuse.

The outcome document's resulting language on the responsibility to protect describes this principle in two parts. The first element of R2P addresses the basic obligation of states toward those living within their borders: "Each individual State has the responsibility to protect its populations from genocide, war crimes, ethnic cleansing, and crimes against humanity. This responsibility entails the prevention of such crimes, including their incitement, through appropriate and necessary means. We accept that responsibility and will act in accordance with it."[35]

The second element of R2P addresses the responsibility of the rest of the world when a state fails to address the risk of mass atrocities within its own borders or is itself the source of the threat. The General Assembly described this duty comprehensively:

> The international community, through the United Nations, also has the responsibility to use appropriate diplomatic, humanitarian and other peaceful means, in accordance with Chapters VI and VIII of the Charter, to help to protect populations from genocide, war crimes, ethnic cleansing and crimes against humanity. In this context, we are prepared to take collective action, in a timely and decisive manner, through the Security Council, in accordance with the Charter, including Chapter VII, on a case-by-case basis and in cooperation with relevant regional organizations as appropriate, should peaceful means be inadequate and national authorities are manifestly failing to protect their populations from genocide, war crimes, ethnic cleansing and crimes against humanity.[36]

R2P redefines sovereignty. Its adoption is a watershed, marking the end of a 350-year period in which the inviolability of borders and the monopoly of force within one's own borders were sovereignty's formal hallmarks. Instead, the responsibility to protect says that sovereignty entails rights as well as responsibilities. The extent to which a state enjoys the full benefits of sovereignty is a condition of its behavior.[37]

The significance for preventing mass atrocities is clear. First, the United Nations has skirted Talmudic debates about whether an atrocity is genocide by concluding that international action is warranted for a range of actions even if they do not meet a formal definition of genocide.[38] Of importance for the United States, the outcome document states that each situation will be addressed "on a on a case-by-case basis," and does not specify criteria that may have constrained or appeared to precommit action in a given set of circumstances.

Second, endorsement of the responsibility to protect by the General Assembly places "genocide, war crimes, ethnic cleansing, and crimes against humanity" on par with other threats to international peace and security. The outcome document emphasizes the role of the Security Council in addressing them, but does not explicitly require its authorization or that of the General Assembly for action, leaving open the possibility of working through regional organizations, coalitions, or unilateral action.

Adoption of R2P also begins to resolve the historic tension between human rights and states' rights in favor of the individual. Where the state had been erected to protect the individual from outsiders, the responsibility to protect erects a fallback where individuals have a claim to seek assistance from outsiders in order to substitute for or protect them from the state. The responsibility to protect places individual citizens and their most basic human right—as the Declaration of Independence says, "the right to life"—at the center of the international system. In doing so, the responsibility to protect erodes the classic rational for inaction, namely that intervention to prevent mass atrocities constitutes illegal interference in the sovereign affairs of a UN member.[39]

The Responsibility to Protect and
Current U.S. Foreign Policy

Following the World Summit, the United States began to lend rhetorical support to the responsibility to protect. Testifying before Congress in October 2005, Ambassador Bolton gave the first explicit statement of support for the responsibility to protect by a U.S. official, a long-awaited change in the formal American position.[40] In a press briefing the following month,

Assistant Secretary of State for International Organizational Affairs Kristen Silverberg said, "making sure that we as a Security Council member always push the Council to follow through on its responsibility to protect citizens is a high priority for the Administration."[41]

Secretary of State Condoleezza Rice and other administration officials invoked the principle in discussions on the international community's responsibility in Darfur.[42] The United States has also supported efforts to include references to the responsibility to protect in Security Council resolutions, including the August 31, 2006, resolution authorizing a UN peacekeeping force for Darfur.[43] Yet the administration's statements on the applicability of the responsibility to protect in Darfur were not matched by an activist Darfur policy. Washington has been more effective than other permanent five (P5) members, but has not prioritized the issue in its relations with Beijing, which remains the main obstacle to strong Security Council action. Washington's involvement has also been episodic. One month after the World Summit, the Bush administration blocked a briefing to the Security Council on Darfur by the UN Secretary-General's top adviser on genocide prevention, who had just returned from a mission to the region. In August 2006, the United States supported efforts to replace the faltering African Union mission in Darfur with a UN force, but it did not put high-level diplomatic weight into securing troop contributions from other nations, as it routinely has done for other priority missions.[44] In May 2007, the administration moved to expand financial sanctions on Sudanese companies and individuals. This was a welcome effort, but one that would have been more effective if it was part of a coordinated response, either through the Security Council or with U.S. allies in Europe and elsewhere.[45]

More broadly, the United States has taken some important steps to improve its capacity to carry out the mission of stabilization and reconstruction, tasks also essential to a capacity for atrocity prevention. In August 2004 the administration created the Office of the Coordinator for Reconstruction and Stabilization (CRS), at the Department of State, with an assistant-secretary level "coordinator," with a direct reporting line to the secretary of state, at its head. The office was initially conceived to "serve as a sort of Joint Chiefs of Staff for the various agencies involved" in responding to crises.[46] The Defense Department approved Defense Department Directive 3000.05 in November 2005, formally elevating the mission of stabilization and reconstruction to place it on par with "war fighting."[47] In December 2005 the administration issued National Security Presidential Directive 44 (NSPD-44) to create a national architecture for stability operations, giving the secretary of state interagency leadership on the issue.[48]

These reforms are a welcome shift from earlier administration policy. They have the potential to back up the administration's rhetorical commitment to the responsibility to protect with actual capacity. Government-wide efforts, however, are suffering from a perceived lack of support at senior levels.

The administration's support for the responsibility to protect and President Bush's "Not on my watch" pledge have not been followed up with a formal strategy for implementation. Efforts by the National Security Council and the CRS to implement NSPD-44 hit bureaucratic roadblocks, and energy behind implementation has taken a back seat to the wars in Iraq, Afghanistan, and other higher order national security priorities. The CRS office faced turf battles with the Office of the Director of Foreign Assistance as well as regional bureaus at the State Department. The State Department has shown lukewarm support for the new office. The office has so far focused on situations in Haiti, Sudan, Cuba, Chad, and Nepal, providing election monitoring, support to peace talks, conflict assessments, and contingency planning. For the most part, it has not assisted efforts in Afghanistan or Iraq. Secretary Rice has said that she hopes the office will take the lead on the next nation-building effort, but that will require congressional support for a very substantial increase in funding that is highly unlikely to be approved.

Overall, the Pentagon has gone furthest in implementation. The Defense Department's QDR calls for deeper U.S. military involvement in nation-building. The QDR says the Defense Department "must become as adept at working with foreign constabularies as it is with externally focused armed forces, and as adept at working with interior ministries as it is with defense ministries—a substantial shift of emphasis."[49] In August 2006 the Pentagon proposed a significant reorganization, subject to congressional approval, of the Office of the Undersecretary of Defense for Policy. It would, among other things, establish an office for Global Security Affairs, headed by an assistant secretary of defense. The reorganization has been described as bringing a "key Defense Department office more in line with the growing emphasis on managing international military coalitions, equipping partner nations to fight terrorists, and managing the U.S. military response to a growing array of transnational threats."[50] It has the potential to intensify and better coordinate a focus on building competent indigenous forces, an opportunity enhanced by new leadership within the Army. These promising steps, however, are balanced by the military's concern that it lacks committed civilian partners, a worry reinforced by the uncertain future of stabilization and reconstruction efforts at the State Department.

Supporting peacekeeping and other capacities relevant to genocide prevention at the UN is a logical complement to the Bush administration's efforts to expand capacity in the United States. Recent studies by the U.S. Government Accountability Office (GAO) and RAND point to the cost-effectiveness and relative success of the UN in fulfilling mandates to stabilize and rebuild nations after the establishment of peace.[51] UN peacekeeping, however, is still in the very early stages of institutionalization. The Defense Department's 2006 QDR highlighted its readiness to assist: "The Department stands ready to increase its assistance to the United Nations Department of Peacekeeping Operations in areas of the Department's expertise, such as doctrine, training, strategic planning and management."[52]

This commitment has not been reflected in U.S. priorities at the United Nations. The United States has not made improving genocide prevention capacities a focus of its reform efforts. Concern about overstretching did not translate into financial backing in the 109th Congress to support the participation of other nations' troops in UN peacekeeping operations. The United States is roughly $600 million behind in payments for UN peace-keeping, reversing the excellent record of the Bush administration, which until recently had caught up on UN arrears accumulated during the 1990s.[53] Increases in operations in Darfur, Lebanon, East Timor, and the Democratic Republic of Congo are likely to increase the U.S. peacekeeping debt.

The administration has pledged to expand upon current efforts to train foreign troops, particularly in Africa, to conduct peacekeeping tasks, although the overall success of this effort is difficult to gage at this time. The Bush administration established the Global Peace Operations Initiative (GPOI) in 2004 to improve peacekeeping capacities throughout the world, with a focus on Africa. The goal is to train seventy-five thousand new peacekeepers over fifteen years; in fiscal year 2005, some fourteen thousand troops were trained under the program, including forces that were deployed to the African Union mission in Darfur.[54] Yet standards to measure the success of the GPOI program, including the number of trained troops that participate directly in peacekeeping operations, are not publicly available. Senate appropriators have expressed concern that the State Department, which administers the program, "has failed to demonstrate a requisite level of commitment to the program, instead viewing funds provided for GPOI as a funding source for other activities."[55] A plan proposed by the 109th Congress to shift the program to an account managed by the Department of Defense would bar ten countries from participating, including militarily capable states within Africa such as South Africa, because they have not agreed to grant immunity to the United States for prosecution under the treaty establishing the International Criminal Court (ICC).

Congressional division on the issue of improving capacities to conduct stabilization and reconstruction has complicated the administration's efforts. Senators Joseph Biden (D-DE) and Chuck Hagel (R-NE) championed the creation of the Office of Reconstruction and Stabilization at the State Department, and continue to support it. But there is resistance elsewhere. On the left is an unwillingness to give this office greater capacity as an indirect expression of disapproval of the administration's Iraq policy. On the right is long-standing disapproval of the nation-building mission on grounds that it diverts the military from its core, war-fighting mission. Public opinion in the United States exacerbates these challenges. The Iraq War has soured Americans on the muscular foreign policy they were prepared to support in the aftermath of 9/11.[56] To the degree that some kind of consensus had developed on genocide prevention, it is shallow and dissipating with every day of the Iraq War.

Recommendations to Implement the Responsibility to Protect

There are several steps the government and citizens can take to make good on the U.S. commitment to the responsibility to protect. The first would be to make "Not on my watch" formal U.S. policy. The administration should issue a presidential decision directive that operationalizes the concept. A presidential decision directive would identify the prevention of mass atrocities as an important national security interest of the United States, not just a humanitarian goal; outline the diplomatic and military steps the U.S. government is prepared to take; and develop a strategy for working with other leading democracies in the United Nations and with regional organizations as a foreign policy priority. The president should use the Office of Management and Budget effectively to line up support for this policy.

Secretary of State Condoleezza Rice should develop a program to institutionalize atrocity prevention into the normal work of the State Department. To that end, she should develop tailored strategies within the State Department for each of the countries that appears on the periodic CIA watch list to reduce risks in these specific cases, and work with U.S. allies and the members of the Security Council on rules of the road for international action in cases of humanitarian emergency. The secretary of state should strongly support the mission and activities of the Office of Reconstruction and Stabilization, lobby Congress to fully fund the activity, and invest in building an institutional capacity at the State Department for this critical mission. Civilians and NGOs should lobby Congress to fully fund and support the work of the office.

The secretary of defense should reaffirm support for fulfilling the recommendations of the 2005 Defense Department directive putting the stabilization and reconstruction mission on par with war fighting. Inadequate implementation of reforms elsewhere in the U.S. government is disappointing but does not change the importance of this mission, and is not a reason to hold back on the military's efforts to build U.S. and international capacity. With respect to U.S. forces, new leadership within the Army provides an opportunity to reinvigorate efforts to train and equip U.S. forces for the stabilization and reconstruction mission. To that end, the U.S. Army chief of staff should augment selected brigade combat teams to carry out the stabilization and reconstruction mission through added capacity, training, and doctrinal adjustments.

The United States should also make genocide prevention central to its UN reform efforts. In this vein, the United States should support an expanded role for the UN Special Adviser on Genocide, including additional funds and personnel for the office, and should support the discretionary authority of the special adviser to brief the UN Security Council. The special adviser can minimize controversy by reporting on regions of concern in an annual report, which would provide a baseline for other investigations.

The United States should also support steps to institutionalize peacekeeping at the UN. The first, and most basic, show of support would be for the administration to request and the Congress to support full funding for the U.S. share of UN peacekeeping operations. Increases in operations in Darfur, Lebanon, East Timor, and the Democratic Republic of Congo are likely to increase the U.S. peacekeeping debt. The United States has voted to establish or sustain each of these missions, and in doing so, has accepted a responsibility to support them financially.

The Department of Defense should fulfill the QDR commitment to support UN peacekeeping through selective participation in the UN command structure, including additional military planners at UN headquarters and at headquarters positions at UN operations in the field. The Department of Defense, working with the CIA and the Department of State, should develop a system of intelligence sharing that could assist the UN with immediate tactical needs. UN officials have said tactical intelligence could have yielded important information in UN operations in the Democratic Republic of the Congo and on the Lord's Resistance Army in Uganda. In addition to cell phone tracking information and tactical surveillance, UN officials cite the need for cartographic information.[57]

The National Intelligence Council should resume the practice suspended in 2001 of briefing the Department of Peacekeeping Operations and Security Council representatives on current and potential conflicts in order to assist the UN and representatives of the Security Council with contingency planning. Officials at the Department of Peacekeeping Operations have requested that these strategic briefings resume.

The United States should bring its participation in the voluntary UN Stand-By Arrangements system up to the standards of other militarily capable states, including Britain and Australia. Washington's nominal participation in the program sets a poor example for others and does little to enhance the UN's operational capability. The United States should provide detailed information about the logistical and other support it is prepared to make available and encourage active participation by other states.

The White House and Congress should support UN and international efforts to establish strategic reserves of forces designated by countries to be available for rapid deployment if authorized by the Security Council, and subject to the national decisions of each country. The forces would be trained to certain standards and take part in relevant exercises with one another. Contributing countries would receive modest payment to designate and train such forces, and a supplement when and if they are deployed. The major financial supporters of UN peacekeeping, particularly the United States and Japan, have traditionally opposed such efforts because of the expense. The unprecedented demand on America's volunteer army and on UN peacekeeping, however, should prompt a reassessment.

The United States should conduct a formal assessment of the progress and foreign policy contribution of the GPOI program, which has yet to be subjected to a systematic evaluation. What progress is being made toward the president's goal of training seventy-five thousand troops by 2015? Is this the right goal? Are U.S. and international efforts growing the available pool of troops for UN and other missions, and if not, what changes are necessary? On the basis of this assessment, Western governments should adjust and intensify their commitments to bilateral training initiatives.

Conclusions

In adopting the responsibility to protect in 2005, the United States accepted the principle that mass atrocities that take place in one state are the concern of all states. Yet agreeing on the principle of the responsibility to protect is not the same thing as acting on it. The inherent political barriers to implementing the responsibility to protect can delay urgent assistance, inject helpful precaution, or something in between. The lack of actual capacity—diplomatic, military, and otherwise—reinforces political barriers to effective action.

The United States and other economic and militarily capable states must take steps to bolster UN action and to be available when the UN is not. The United States has begun this process, through NSPD-44 and other initiatives, but these steps—though welcome—are not sufficient. The long-term goal is to avoid the stark options of "doing nothing" and "sending in the Marines." This requires establishing a pattern of early and effective international response at the first signs of concern. Universal adoption of the responsibility to protect has begun to remove the classic excuses for doing nothing in the face of mass atrocities. What is needed now is the capacity and political will to back it up.

Notes

* Lee Feinstein is visiting fellow in Foreign Policy at the Brookings Institution, and Erica De Bruin is a Ph.D. candidate in political science at Yale University, New Haven, Connecticut.
1. Clifford Krauss, "US Backs Away from Charge of Atrocities in Bosnia Camps," *New York Times*, August 5, 1992, http://query.nytimes.com/gst/fullpage.html?res=9E0CE4D81531F936A3575BC0A964958260.
2. White House, "Presidential Decision Directive 25: U.S. Policy on Reforming Multilateral Peace Operations," May 3, 1994.
3. U.S. Department of State, Cable No. 099440 to U.S. Mission to the United Nations, New York, "Talking Points for UNAMIR Withdrawal," April 15, 1994; U.S. Department of State, Cable No. 127262 to U.S. Mission to the United Nations, New York, "Rwanda: Security Council Discussions," May 13, 1994.
4. U.S. Department of Defense, Office of the Deputy Assistant Secretary of Defense for Middle East/Africa Region, "Discussion Paper: Rwanda," May 1, 1994.
5. William J. Clinton, "Remarks by the President to Genocide Survivors, Assistance Workers, and U.S. and Rwanda Government Officials" (Kigali Airport, Kigali, Rwanda, March 25, 1998).
6. U.S. Department of State, "African Crisis Response Initiative," fact sheet, May 2000.
7. See UN Doc. S/PV.3988 (1999) 2 and S/PV.3989 (1999) 6.
8. William J. Clinton, "Remarks by the President to the KFOR Troops" (Skopje, Macedonia, June 22, 1999).
9. Pew Research Center for the People and the Press, "Muted and Mixed Public Response to Peace in Kosovo," June 15, 1999.
10. Madeleine Albright, "Remarks," speech, Council on Foreign Relations, June 28, 1999.
11. Author's notes.
12. William J. Clinton, radio address to the nation, Washington, DC, March 27, 1999.

13. U.S. Department of State, "U.S. and NATO Objectives and Interests in Kosovo," fact sheet, Washington, DC, March 26, 1999.

14. See, for example, Kofi A. Annan, "Secretary-General's Annual Report to the General Assembly," September 20, 1999; Tony Blair, "Doctrine of the International Community" (speech, Economics Club of Chicago, Chicago, Illinois, April 24, 1999).

15. William J. Clinton, "Remarks to the 54th Session of the United Nations General Assembly," U.S. Press Release 59 (99), September 21, 1999.

16. Nicholas J. Wheeler, "*Legitimating Humanitarian Intervention: Principles and Procedures*," *Melbourne Journal of International Law and Politics* 2, no. 2 (2001): 550–68.

17. William J. Clinton, "*Remarks to the 54th Session of the United Nations General Assembly*," September 21, 1999.

18. Interview with Sam Donaldson, *ABC News This Week*, January 23, 2000.

19. Alex J. Bellamy, "*Whither the Responsibility to Protect? Humanitarian Intervention and the 2005 World Summit*," *Ethics and International Affairs* 20, no. 2 (2006): 143–69.

20. S. Neil Macfarlane, Carolin J. Thielking, and Thomas G. Weiss, "The Responsibility to Protect: Is Anyone Interested in Humanitarian Intervention?" *Third World Quarterly* 25, no. 5 (2004): 977–92.

21. White House, "National Security Strategy of the United States of America," September 2006, 14–15.

22. U.S. Department of Defense, "Quadrennial Defense Review Report (QDR)," February 6, 2006, 91.

23. National Association of Evangelicals, letter to President Bush, http://www.nae.net/images/darfurbush2.doc.

24. *Declaring Genocide in Darfur, Sudan*, H. Con. Res. 467, 108th Cong., 2d Sess. (June 24, 2004) and S. Con. Res. 124, 108th Cong., 2d Sess. (July 13, 2004).

25. Newt Gingrich and George Mitchell, *American Interests and UN Reform: A Report of the Congressional Task Force on the United Nations* (Washington, DC: U.S. Institute of Peace, 2005), 29.

26. R. Nicholas Burns, "On United Nations Reform," testimony as prepared before the Senate Foreign Relations Committee, Washington, DC, July 21, 2005, http://www.state.gov/p/us/rm/2005/49900.htm.

27. U.S. Department of State, "U.S. Priorities for a Stronger, More Effective United Nations," June 17, 2005, http://www.state.gov/r/pa/scp/2005/52982.htm.

28. Radzi Rahman, "Statement of the Chairman of the Coordinating Bureau of the Non-Aligned Movement at the Informal Meeting of the Plenary of the General Assembly Concerning the Draft Outcome Document," June 21, 2005, http://www.un.int/malaysia/NAM/nam210605.html.

29. Stafford Neil (chairman of the Group of 77), "Statement on the Draft Outcome Document of the President of the General Assembly for the High-Level Plenary Meeting of the General Assembly," June 21, 2005, http://www.g77.org/Speeches/062105.htm.

30. Government of China, "Position Paper of the People's Republic of China on the United Nations Reforms," June 7, 2005, 10–12, http://www.fmprc.gov .cn/ce/ceun/eng/xw/t199101.htm.

31. John R. Bolton, letter sent to UN member states conveying U.S. amendments to the section on the responsibility to protect of the draft outcome document being prepared for the September 2005 High-Level Event, August 30, 2005.

32. Ibid.

33. See, for example, Radzhi Rahman, "Statement by the Chairman of the Coordinating Bureau of the Non-Aligned Movement, June 21, 2005, http:// www.un.int/malaysia/NAM/nam210605.html.

34. These were the seriousness of the threat, the proper purpose of the proposed military action, whether means short of force might reasonably succeed in stopping the threat, whether a military response is proportional to the threat, and whether the intervention had a reasonable chance of success.

35. UN General Assembly, Sixtieth Session, *2005 World Summit Outcome*, UN Doc. A/RES/60/1, 2005, para. 138.

36. UN General Assembly, Sixtieth Session, *2005 World Summit Outcome*, UN Doc. A/RES/60/1, 2005, paras. 138–39.

37. Lee Feinstein, *Darfur and Beyond: What Is Needed to Prevent Mass Atrocities* (New York: Council on Foreign Relations Press, 2007).

38. The outcome document provides a more expansive range of actions than the ICISS, High-Level Panel, or even the Gingrich-Mitchell report provided.

39. The following analysis has informed the authors: Tod Lindberg, "Protect the People," *Washington Times*, September 27, 2005, http://todlindberg.net/?p =404.

40. John R. Bolton, "Challenges and Opportunities on Moving Ahead on UN Reform," statement before the Senate Foreign Relations Committee, October 18, 2005.

41. Kristin Silverberg, "U.S. Priorities to Strengthen the United Nations," on-the-record briefing, Washington, DC, December 20, 2005.

42. Condoleezza Rice, "Remarks at the United Nations Security Council Ministerial on Sudan," New York City, May 9, 2006; ibid., interview with Jon Karl, ABC News, Stellarton, Nova Scotia, Canada, September 12, 2006.

43. UN Security Council, Resolution 1706 (S/RES/1706), August 31, 2006.

44. Ibid.

45. White House, "Fighting Genocide in Darfur," fact sheet, May 29, 2007, http://www.whitehouse.gov/news/releases/2007/05/20070529-2.html.

46. National Defense University (NDU), "U.S. Support for UN Peacekeeping: Study on Possible Areas for Additional Assistance from the Department of Defense," October 12, 2006, 18.

47. U.S. Department of Defense, "Directive Number 3000.05: Military Support for Stability, Security, Transition, and Reconstruction (SSTR) Operations," November 28, 2005, http://www.dtic.mil/whs/directives/corres/pdf/300005p .pdf.

48. White House, "National Security Presidential Directive 44: Management of Interagency Efforts Concerning Reconstruction and Stabilization," December 7, 2005, http://www.fas.org/irp/offdocs/nspd/nspd-44.html.

49. U.S. Department of Defense, "QDR," 90.

50. "In Sweeping Overhaul, DOD Reorganizes Policy Office," InsideDefense.com, August 28, 2006.

51. U.S. Government Accountability Office, "Peacekeeping: Cost Comparison of Actual UN and Hypothetical U.S. Operations in Haiti," GAO-06-331, February 2006, http://www.gao.gov/new.items/d06331.pdf; James Dobbins et al., *The UN's Role in Nation Building: From the Congo to Iraq* (Santa Monica, CA: RAND, 2005).

52. U.S. Department of Defense, "QDR," 90.

53. Better World Campaign, "U.S. Funding to the United Nations System: Growing Arrears," May 2007.

54. Nina Serafino, "The Global Peace Operations Initiative: Background and Issues for Congress" (Washington, DC: Congressional Research Service, October 3), 2006, 4–5.

55. U.S. Congress, 109th Congress, 2nd Session, Senate Report 109-277, p. 92.

56. Pew Research Center for the People and the Press, in association with the Council on Foreign Relations, *America's Place in the World 2005* (New York: Pew Research Center, 2005).

57. NDU, "U.S. Support for UN Peacekeeping," 34.

12

Building Structures for Peace

A Quaker Lobby Offers
Strategies for Peacemakers

*Joe Volk and Scott Stedjan**

Is change possible? Can ordinary people influence the direction of history? Or are we just corks bounced here and there on a violent sea of human activity? Can we hope to influence the nation-state system to exercise the "responsibility to protect (R2P)" to help achieve the goal of human security? Some say that this ideal state is so unlikely as to be unachievable. However, an examination of the past few hundred years of history, war-torn though they were, suggests that it is possible to end genocide, crimes against humanity, and war crimes.

The Friends Committee on National Legislation (FCNL) is a nonpartisan Quaker lobby in the public interest. With offices on Capitol Hill in Washington, DC, FCNL's governing committee stakes out goals for change that might be achieved ten, twenty, or even a hundred years from now. Because our committee takes this long view, FCNL's goals are sometimes considered extreme when first put forward. Indeed, since the beginning of the Religious Society of Friends (called Quakers) during the bloody seventeenth-century civil war in England, Quakers have been a minority religious group, shunned, persecuted, and jailed for devotion to extreme ideals, such as

- religious freedom: rejection of the state-run church and exercising freedom of religion (extreme at the time, but later incorporated into our Bill of Rights);

- equality of women: treating women as equals of men and accepting that they might be ministers, too (extreme at the time, but later led to Quaker leadership in the movement for women's suffrage);
- abolishing slavery: holding that no human being can be owned by another human being; we were outlaws running the underground railroad to transport slaves out of bondage to free land (extreme and illegal at the time, but now slavery has been abolished and museums applaud the underground railroad).

Of course, we Friends were not alone in achieving these political changes. On the contrary, we participated in historic coalitions of conscience composed of members of virtually every faith community and many secular communities as well. We continue to seek participation in this coalition of conscience today. The history of the Quaker experience has been that we have often staked out new ground before anyone else is interested. Over time, our "extreme" ideas have gained wide acceptance. These innovations do not come into being through war, nor through the authority of established church or state, nor through popular acclaim. Rather, change comes through the power of love and the force of truth revealed by the voluntary risk-taking and suffering of many concerned and engaged people.

When the early antislavery activists first met in a printing shop in England, they debated whether to set their goal at abolishing slavery or whether they needed to be more practical by accepting that slavery would always exist but laws could be changed to prohibit the legal trade in slaves. Slavery was so common that people of that time could hardly imagine the possibility that slavery itself could be stigmatized and abolished. Today, regrettably, some slavery (e.g., in the sex trade) continues, but slavery has been largely stigmatized, prohibited by law, and exists primarily hidden from public scrutiny. Today we take for granted the abolition of slavery, something people just like us could not imagine three hundred years ago. This happened because groups of people staked out the goal, made strategies to reach the goal, and got to work implementing the strategy.

Today, the same kind of work needs to be done to create a strategy for the peaceful prevention of deadly conflict and for the protection of populations from genocide, crimes against humanity, and war crimes. We must succeed. The possibility seems remote, as remote as the possibility of free exercise of religion four hundred years ago, as remote as the possibility of the abolition of slavery three hundred years ago, and as remote as the possibility of women's suffrage one hundred years ago. But a saving remnant of our nation could help to brighten the prospects to make a world free of war and atrocity crimes. We are called not to despair, but to live in a world that is now-but-not-yet, and living in a now-but-not-yet world is how we will construct a sustainable peace.

The "How" of R2P

As the 2005 World Summit deliberations progressed toward adoption of the principles of R2P, Quakers experienced mixed feelings. We had hope that nation-states might now take steps to fulfill their obligations to protect the life, limb, and liberty of all their citizens or subjects, but there was also dread that R2P might be used by some nation-states to dominate others through war or the threat of war.

The human rights community has been a major force in discussions on R2P since the release of a report by the International Commission on Intervention and State Sovereignty (ICISS).[1] Many human rights advocates see R2P as a guiding principle that would enable enforcement of human rights and international humanitarian law when a state is unwilling or unable to enforce the law on its own. Enforcement of international human rights and humanitarian law is a laudable goal that Friends support, but the deliberations lack a parallel emphasis on the peace agenda. Indeed, some in the human rights community proposed to advance their important agendas through the use of military force.

In this circumstance, Quakers, who have long participated in movements for human rights and in on-the-ground humanitarian projects, experienced what one might call an "approach-avoid" conflict. Many Quakers did want to *approach* R2P because it seeks to uphold the dignity and value of every human being by stopping genocide or mass killings. This is a first responsibility for any nonviolent community. But the religious experience of Quaker communities, who have been persecuted for their beliefs, produced an *avoid* response to R2P. Quakers have experienced a profound and undeniable revelation that the means and ends are connected, which is to say that the means to an end will shape and form the end. Thus, when faced with suffering, Friends have sought to resist hate with love. As seventeenth-century Quaker James Naylor said on his deathbed after being beaten, robbed, and left in a field for dead, "There is a spirit which I feel, that delights to do no evil, nor to avenge any wrong, but delights to endure all things in hope to enjoy its own in the end. Its hope is to outlive all wrath and contention, and to weary out all exaltation and cruelty, or whatever is of a nature contrary to itself."

Thus it is not surprising that some Quakers view R2P with a level of uneasiness. The absence of a peace agenda means that most R2P dialogue has focused on whether, in seeking to stop atrocities, a state has a right to intervene in the affairs of another state. Questions of how to respond to acts of extreme violence receive much less attention. But for Quakers, questions of how to intervene are just as (if not more) important as the question of whether outside parties should intervene. When faced with terrified refugees, violated women, and brutalized children, the response of humanity must be to become engaged in protecting humanity. Yet Quaker values teach us that violent means do not achieve their objectives. Indeed, they often make the situation worse than if nothing had been done.

We approach the possible military interventions for R2P skeptically because of our beliefs, but also because of our experiences. Over the past few hundred years, Quakers have been witness to many wars and so-called low-intensity conflicts as they have ministered to victims of these deadly conflicts. Real-life experience in zones of deadly conflict has resulted in our relatively small community acquiring a knowledge and understanding of the root causes and complexities of conflict. We understand that the response to acts of violence will dictate the quality and duration of the peace that follows. Half of all postconflict regions fall back into violent conflict within five years because postwar policymakers act without taking the time to understand the dynamics of a particular conflict. Faulty analysis of the nature of conflict results in a failure to address the underlying causes and concerns. When unaddressed, the problems that led to conflict fester and create more conflict.

An effective response depends on using tools and techniques tailored to the specific circumstance in question. While some tools and techniques will be similar, each conflict requires a different response. Sometimes the drivers of a conflict can be removed, grievances can be assuaged, and disagreements can be reconciled. In others, hatreds have reached such a level of intractability that a conflict cannot be quickly resolved, only managed. For example, the conflict in Darfur, Sudan, is connected to a larger conflict in the country rooted in alienation of the entire periphery of the country and fueled by neighbors. Resolving this conflict will require a complex set of policy options that relate to not only the counterinsurgency campaign in Darfur, but also the rights of marginalized peoples throughout the Sahel.

At the same time, an effective response requires attention to timing. The international response must vary according to the stage of the conflict in question. The actions needed to stabilize a country in the process of transitioning into violence differ from the actions needed when a country is in the midst of widespread violence and grave human rights abuse. As Chart 1 illustrates, conflicts tend to go through an evolution, with stable peace giving way to structural violence, then erupting in overt violence and war, and over time, through a cessation of hostilities, and peace agreement, back toward resolution and reconciliation. Of course, not all conflicts follow this pattern—there may be multiple hills and valleys in a particular conflict and the hilltop may be a sharp peak or shaped like a seemingly endless plateau—but all conflicts tend to go through similar evolutions.

Chart 1

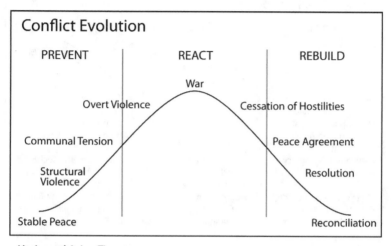

Horizontal Axis—Time
Vertical Axis—Level of Violence

The responsibility to protect calls for action across the entire conflict continuum. When governments are unable or unwilling to adequately protect their citizens, other nation-states have the responsibility to prevent, react, and rebuild (see Chart 2). Unfortunately, the ability to respond effectively is not constant along the entire evolution of a conflict. As violence increases, the number of actions that are available to peace-builders decreases. Thus the tools available to respond to situations of conflict or to mass human rights abuse decrease as the conflict evolution curve reaches its peak in the center. Or to put it another way, many tools and techniques of prevention and rebuilding exist, but tools of response are fewer in number.

Genocide and other terrible crimes against humanity can also occur in the absence of war between two or more armed adversaries. But even in the absence of armed conflict, these atrocities follow a similarly predictable evolution. Former State Department official Gregory H. Stanton argues that genocide is a process that develops in eight predictable stages: classification, symbolization, dehumanization, organization, polarization, preparation, extermination, and denial. The first stages build on each other and continue to operate throughout the genocidal process. At each stage, Stanton argues, preventive measures are possible.[2] However, the later the stage, the more costly and difficult such measures become.

Chart 2

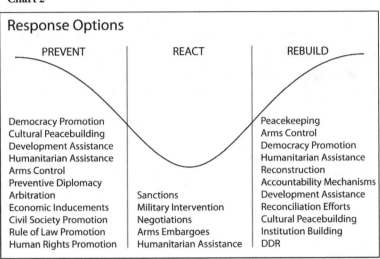

Response Options

PREVENT	REACT	REBUILD
Democracy Promotion		Peacekeeping
Cultural Peacebuilding		Arms Control
Development Assistance		Democracy Promotion
Humanitarian Assistance		Humanitarian Assistance
Arms Control		Reconstruction
Preventive Diplomacy		Accountability Mechanisms
Arbitration	Sanctions	Development Assistance
Economic Inducements	Military Intervention	Reconciliation Efforts
Civil Society Promotion	Negotiations	Cultural Peacebuilding
Rule of Law Promotion	Arms Embargoes	Institution Building
Human Rights Promotion	Humanitarian Assistance	DDR

Horizontal Axis—Time
Vertical Axis—Number of intervention options

The lack of tools for and difficulty of successfully responding to an ongoing crisis are illustrated vividly in the failure to bring sustainable peace to Darfur. The primary international initiatives intended to bring security to Darfur—the Darfur Peace Agreement (DPA), the African Union Mission in Sudan (AMIS), and the United Nations (UN)-African Union (AU) hybrid peacekeeping force—have all failed so far to stem the violence. The DPA, signed in May 2006 by one of the rebel groups in Darfur and the government of Sudan, collapsed while the ink was still wet. The overstretched and poorly funded peacekeeping missions find it extremely difficult to keep peace in a place where peace is elusive. While there has been ample political will, after five years the international community is still searching for a solution to the crisis.

Consider this unlikely parable from the world of advertising: A car manufacturer, let's call it, BigCar, wanted to get into the U.S. car market decades ago. They ran a compelling ad showing a brand new BigCar hitting an immovable concrete wall at sixty miles per hour. The narrator of the ad then says, "Look at the test manikins in that car. They're not injured, although the car is badly damaged. If you love your family, you'll buy a BigCar." Many saw that ad and felt compelled by love of family to buy a BigCar.

Some years later a different car manufacturer, let's call them "LittleCar," wanted to break into the market here with a smaller, less damage-resistant car. They copied the BigCar TV commercial. Actually used it and then added on their own tag line. They show the BigCar wreck, and they say if you love your family you'll buy a BigCar. Then they show a brand new LittleCar racing for that immovable wall. At sixty miles an hour, the announcer says: "or, you could buy a LittleCar, because we have a better idea . . . (the car stops). . . . Brakes!"

Think about it. Don't those TV car ads describe the international security policy we have had for decades and the alternative human security policy that we need now? The United States has and promotes a BigCar security policy. It's tough and durable; it can survive most "crashes," but wouldn't we be better off with a security policy that prevented crashes? Don't we need brakes?

Wrong Focus and Structures

Acknowledging that early action can prevent conflict, governments at the 2005 World Summit agreed that prevention should be the priority focus of international efforts to protect populations. However, seemingly preventable conflicts continue to proliferate, and the results of prevention, when tried, have been mixed.

The world has failed to take the necessary steps to organize itself in a way that would enable effective, peaceful prevention. The 2000 Brahimi Report on UN peace operations notes that effective crisis prevention is impeded by the "gap between verbal postures and financial and political support for prevention."[3] Western governments have invested hundreds of billions of dollars in the capability to fight and win wars, but little money or time in developing the skills, knowledge, and practical tools necessary to prevent deadly conflict. As a result, when policymakers look for tools to respond to wars and escalating conflicts, they find a toolbox with only one implement: a military hammer.

The United States in particular focuses on crisis management in the middle or late stages of a conflict, when the costs in lives and dollars are much higher and when the chances of success are more remote (see Chart 3). While State Department documents now claim that the "United States and our international partners share a commitment to preventing state failure and resolving violent conflict,"[4] rhetoric does not match reality. One need only examine federal budget outlays. While U.S. military budgets continue to grow, consecutive administrations and Congresses have allocated only minuscule amounts of money for such peaceful crisis-prevention tools as the development of U.S. diplomatic infrastructure, contributions to international organizations, and development assistance. This dearth of investment in "soft power" has left the United States with little capacity to respond to impending genocide, humanitarian crises, and failing states. When the United States does take action, the response is often too late, expensive, and ineffective.

Violence prevention and peace-building are civilian tasks and should be undertaken primarily by civilian government agencies and nongovernmental organizations (NGOs), in coordination with international institutions. But underfunded, overstretched civilian agencies are often incapable of adequately responding to imminent crises. In the absence of an alternative, the U.S. military, with its massive budgets and more than two million employees, often steps in to fill the void. After all, the military is the organization responsible for dealing with conflict when prevention fails and keenly understands the value of prevention. Military leaders often lament the failures of civilian agencies and Congress to invest in the tools and skills necessary for preventive action. As former chairman of the Joint Chiefs of Staff General John Shalikashvili said, "What we are doing to our diplomatic capabilities is criminal . . . by slashing them, we are less able to avoid disasters such as Somalia or Kosovo, and therefore we will be obliged to use military force still more often."[5]

But the U.S. government's focus on military solutions crowds out effective action for prevention of deadly conflict. The ICISS report and the consensus reached during the 2005 World Summit makes clear that international actors must exhaust prevention options before contemplating military intervention. But structures that would enable the use of preventive options do not exist, so military interventions are contemplated much too early. Budgets are limited, and the vast majority of funds are used to prepare for the worst-case scenario, leaving all actions short of last resort underfunded. As British Quaker Alan Pleydell has observed, "a major problem with 'last resort thinking', as with 'worst-case scenario thinking', is that it carries the risk of precipitating us towards actualizing the last resort option even in conditions short of the worst, and of numbing the potential for thinking through and practicing alternatives."[6]

The public dialogue surrounding R2P focuses on military intervention and the role of military force in stopping atrocities. But if the primary focus of R2P is prevention, the key question is not about military force; rather, it concerns the structure of responses to incipient crises. Focusing

Chart 3

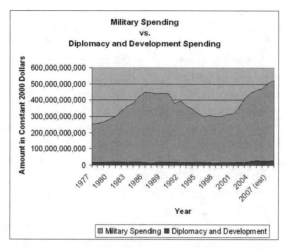

This chart shows U.S. military spending compared to diplomacy and development spending from FY 1977 to estimated levels for FY 2008. The figures are in constant 2000 U.S. dollars. *Sources: Public Budget Database* (http://www.whitehouse.gov/omb/budget/fy2008/db.html) and *Historical Tables, Budget of the United States Government, Fiscal Year 2008* (http://www.whitehouse.gov/omb/budget/fy2008/pdf/hist.pdf).

on the military portion of R2P limits the vital work of advocating for structures that could peacefully prevent deadly conflict and atrocities.

If rhetoric is to be transformed into an operational R2P policy, the United States will need to dramatically increase investment in the nonmilitary tools of statecraft. Just as governments require trained soldiers, guns, bombs, and tanks to perpetrate mass atrocities, nations and the global community must be equipped with the tools of peace-building to prevent war and manage conflicts nonviolently. Even if the U.S. government decided tomorrow to start preventing deadly conflict by nonmilitary means, it would fail for lack of trained personnel, funding, and effective programs. Unless the U.S. foreign policy toolbox is equipped with effective nonmilitary tools, military force will remain the instrument of choice. Or, to use a famous expression, "when your only tool is a hammer, every problem looks like a nail."

Building Structures to Make R2P a Reality

The responsibility to protect is first and foremost the responsibility of nation states and of the communities and institutions within them. At the same time, the 2005 World Summit made it clear that it is not only a national or local responsibility. Mass human rights abuses and deadly conflicts have ramifications for the international community as a whole and for individual states. Support from the international community in the exercise of the responsibility to protect by national or local communities is indispensable.

Probably no single government, however strong, can ever marshal the necessary resources and skills to prevent or stop mass atrocities alone. Thus the UN, as the only truly global institution, should serve as the central point for international prevention, protection, and rebuilding efforts in concert with a network of regional groups. The UN is not perfect; it has a mixed record of conflict management and must continue to improve its own prevention and response capabilities. But the UN is not a world government, and its effectiveness relies on the capabilities of individual states. Recognizing this, former Secretary-General Kofi Annan has called for the development of new capacities within national governments to undertake genuinely preventive actions in all stages of conflict, from latent tensions to hot wars to postconflict peace-building. In other words, nation-states should build structures to address the entire range of R2P: the responsibility to prevent, the responsibility to react, and the responsibility to rebuild.

As previously mentioned, the United States does not yet possess the nonmilitary capabilities necessary to put R2P into operation across the entire range of the conflict continuum. The U.S. government cannot, and should not, try to do everything on its own, but the United States, the richest nation in the world, has an opportunity to be a leader in the peaceful prevention of deadly conflict and mass human rights abuse. We at FCNL have defined ten steps the U.S. government could take to begin to establish an operational R2P capacity. The remainder of this chapter will focus on these specific steps.

Ten Steps for the United States to Become an R2P Leader

1. Reverse the militarization of foreign assistance.
2. Rejuvenate support for international law and diplomacy.
3. Make the State Department more operational.
4. Make available flexible funding sources.
5. Utilize special envoys.
6. Support and expand programs to deny combatants access to markets.

7. Better regulate the small arms trade.
8. Pay for UN peacekeeping.
9. Support the UN Peacebuilding Commission.
10. Expand disarmament, demobilization, and reintegration (DDR) and weapons destruction programs.

Reverse the Militarization of Foreign Assistance

The Pentagon has started, and hopes to expand, a $300 million pilot program to train and equip foreign military forces for counterterrorism and stabilization. This development is problematic because the Pentagon here assumes the roles formerly played by the State Department, and further asserts itself as the lead foreign policy agency of the United States. As long as the State Department remains weak in the U.S. foreign policy apparatus, nonmilitary means to prevent conflict will receive little support.

A more effective use of foreign aid is to use development assistance to prevent deadly conflict by supporting the creation of capable economic, political, and social infrastructures so the country in conflict can entice foreign investment, manage a transparent and open economy, and provide adequate education and health services.

For many countries, such infrastructure is unaffordable without international development assistance. The United States could be a considerable source of such assistance, but this would require a change in the size and composition of foreign aid. A shift should occur away from ineffective militarization of foreign assistance and toward a growth in structural prevention-based assistance. Infrastructure development and poverty alleviation is a long-term enterprise that requires donors to be patient. Thus structural prevention-based assistance is best provided through multilateral and independent agencies that are not unduly influenced by domestic short-term political and security concerns.

Rejuvenate Support for International Law and Diplomacy

The United States can also play an important role in promoting justice within societies through support of a stable international system. The foundation of such a system already exists in the form of human rights principles (both of its conventions: civil and political, and social and economic), international humanitarian law, diplomacy, international institutions, and arms control regimes. But the United States has much work to do before it can be considered a leader in this area. In recent years the United States has opposed numerous treaties that serve a structural prevention value, including the Rome Statute of the International Criminal Court (ICC), the Convention on the Rights of the Child, the U.K. initiative for an arms trade treaty, the Comprehensive Test Ban Treaty, and the Ottawa Mine Ban Treaty. The United States has a long history of ambivalence to the UN as an institution, with periods of relative cooperation and others of outright hostility. A period of relative cooperation would serve both global and U.S. security interests better than the current posture of hostility.

The United States also ignores international law when this behavior is deemed to best suit its national interest. However, treaty regimes and upholding of international law help reduce security risks by codifying norms of peaceful behavior, and these put in place a process by which disputes can be managed. Over the past sixty years, the UN has contributed significantly to reducing threats to global security. While there have been failures, the UN is the only place where all countries and peoples of the world can come together to create comprehensive solutions to their problems and build a framework for a more peaceful and just world. Increased support for international law and the UN, including full payment of dues, are essential components of structural prevention. Policymakers in the United States should accept and affirm the utility of treaties, international law, and diplomacy, and they should act accordingly.

Make the State Department More Operational

Prevention requires different skill sets in different situations. The State Department should have experts equipped to handle a variety of issues, including but not limited to land disputes, religious or ethnic strife, corrupt governance structures, political marginalization, and problems that arise from economic inequality. The State Department should be able to bring expertise to bear in emergency situations. With the exception of the U.S. Agency for International Development (USAID) employees and contractors providing foreign assistance, the State Department lacks sufficient expert diplomatic personnel to respond to conflict quickly. A delay of a few weeks, or even days, can be disastrous for direct prevention efforts. A rapid response corps of civilian experts in conflict prevention, mediation, public administration, and law could make the difference between brief instability and mass atrocity.

Recognizing the need for the State Department to increase its capabilities, Secretary of State Colin Powell established the Office of the Coordinator for Reconstruction and Stabilization (S/CRS) in July 2004. The goal of the S/CRS is to "lead, coordinate and institutionalize U.S. Government civilian capacity to prevent or prepare for post-conflict situations, and to help stabilize and reconstruct societies in transition from conflict or civil strife, so they can reach a sustainable path toward peace, democracy and a market economy."[7] More relevant here, S/CRS is also charged with developing a crop of prei-dentified experts in the area of conflict mitigation who can deploy rapidly to a crisis. This corps of civilians, similar in structure to the U.S. Army Reserve, would enable American civilians with skills in areas such as engineering, law, and public administration to use their skills to create structures of lasting stability in places where they are desperately needed.

By providing operational capabilities, S/CRS represents a major shift in how the State Department responds to crises. Since its creation, however, Congress has consistently underfunded S/CRS and the associated active response corps, even while offering rhetorical support for its mission. Without a financial commitment from Congress and the administration, the office will be unable to accomplish much.

Make Available Flexible Funding Sources

In addition to deploying civilian experts, the United States should be able to mobilize resources necessary for prevention. Crises do not allow the luxury of long-term budget planning, and administrations are forced to borrow money to pay for these necessary tasks. According to Secretary of State Condoleezza Rice, "very often, between budget cycles, we have to borrow money from accounts and then try to pay it back because things happen that we did not expect. I can give you many examples: Liberia, Haiti; positive examples like Ukraine. And we want to be able to be more responsive to those kinds of emergency situations."[8] A flexible funding source, such as the proposed Conflict Response Fund, would give the secretary of state the financial resources to respond quickly at the onset of a crisis. But the current foreign affairs budgetary process uses earmarks, which limits what the secretary can accomplish in a crisis. A special contingency fund would enhance flexibility, and flexibility is key to prevention.

Utilize Special Envoys

Another aspect of direct prevention is the ability to sustain high-level engagement in at-risk countries through the use of special envoys. Special envoys are typically eminent people respected by all parties in a conflict. Since special envoys report directly to the president, in the case of U.S. presidential envoys, or to the secretary-general, in the case of UN special representatives, they are able to use their stature to influence events more forcefully than the average negotiator. Envoys assist in creating political space for negotiations, participate in the negotiations, and help create peace processes. Recent examples of successful envoys include former senator John Danforth, whose mission to Sudan helped facilitate the Comprehensive Peace Agreement in Sudan, and Ahmedou Ould Abdullah, whose mission to Burundi helped keep the country relatively calm while neighboring Rwanda was engulfed in genocidal violence.[9] The fate of the missions of two envoys addressing the violence in Darfur, U.S. presidential envoy's Andrew Nastios and more recently Richard Williamson remain uncertain. Regardless of the outcome, U.S.-appointed presidential special envoys would still be welcome in many areas of conflict. But the success of special envoys requires speed. Andrew Natsios' mission to Darfur came after three years of violence and was then only appointed through much wrangling between the U.S. Congress and President Bush. It is clear that a presidential envoy that can bypass internal bureaucracy can produce a quick and more unified government response in situations where time is of the essence. The United States should use special envoys earlier and more often.

Support and Expand Focused Programs to
Deny Combatants Access to Markets

Once violence begins, the international community has a responsibility to deny combatants the means to continue their violence. This includes denying the global market to countries at war, thereby using economic pressure to stop the tools of war from entering a country. The UN charter gives the Security Council the power to place economic sanctions on states when such action is necessary to maintain or restore international peace and security. The imposition of sanctions, if applied wisely, can hasten the end of violence by restricting the economic and military means of continuing a conflict. Trade restrictions, embargoes on the import and export of certain goods, or the seizure of assets may compel combatants to stop violent acts and come to the negotiating table.

Sanctions may sometimes harm civilian populations more than governments. But not all sanctions miss their mark. So-called smart sanctions
focus on certain commodities, such as luxury goods, diamonds, timber,
drugs, oil, or weapons, which belligerents use either for war or to raise
money for war. Smart sanctions are designed to raise the cost of noncompliance to combatants while avoiding the general suffering that comprehensive
sanctions often create.

Unfortunately, there is no official global auditing mechanism to monitor
the implementation and enforcement of sanctions. Global Witness, a leading
NGO that works on the issue of conflict finance, notes that the implementation
of sanctions is watched over by a series of separate ad hoc, part-time com-
mittees nominated by the Security Council. Global Witness also found
widespread failure to impose secondary sanctions upon states that violate
sanctions.[10] The United States should work with its partners within the
United Nations to professionalize sanction monitoring activities. According
to Global Witness, "Expertise and speed of response are crucial to effective
sanctions (given that sanctions work best when targets are clearly defined
and decisively applied) to starve the conflict of revenues near the start
rather than later on, when conflict and economic networks have become
entrenched and the death toll has risen."[11]

Better Regulate the Weapons Trade

The United States could and should do more to deny combatants access to
the global arms market. On the books, the United States has arguably the
best weapons export control laws in the world. Over the last thirty years,
the United States has constructed a sophisticated export control legal system.
In theory, existing laws prohibit the transfer of weapons to any entity that
exhibits a "pattern of gross violations of internationally recognized human
rights." In practice, however, U.S. weapons routinely find their way to
regions of violent conflict and are routinely used to commit grave abuses of
human rights.

How does this happen? First, despite legal restrictions, almost half of the
total U.S. weapons sales went to countries plagued with ongoing conflict
and governed by undemocratic regimes with poor human rights records.
In 2003, $2.7 billion in weaponry went to governments deemed undemocratic
by the U.S. State Department's Human Rights Report, and another $97.4
million worth of weapons went to governments deemed to have "poor"
human rights records. The problem is that no U.S. law defines what exactly
constitutes a "pattern of gross violations of internationally recognized

human rights." Thus the weapons industry is able to follow the letter of the law while violating the spirit.

Second, once a weapon leaves U.S. soil, the United States no longer has control of it. Weapons transferred to one state can be illegally diverted or retransferred to another without U.S. knowledge. These weapons often end up on the black market, difficult to track or recover.

Additional national legislation to increase transparency and clarify existing law is necessary. But international controls are also needed, because the United States is not the only source of weapons to areas of armed conflict or human rights abuse. National initiatives must thus be complemented by the development of global agreements and by increased effectiveness of UN arms embargoes. This will ensure that the controls imposed by one state or region are not undermined by another state or region. Under the influence of the National Rifle Association and weapons industry groups, the United States has repeatedly blocked real progress on arms trade controls at the UN. In October 2006, the United States was the only country in the world to cast a vote against a UN resolution to start a process toward a global arms trade treaty. U.S. policy should change to put human rights and prevention of deadly conflict at the forefront.

Pay for UN Peacekeeping

Until the 1990s, UN and other multilateral peacekeeping missions were only used in the aftermath of a conflict to separate adversaries and prevent the recurrence of fighting. Largely symbolic, they did not use force, and their deployment rested on the consent of the parties to the conflict. But the failure of peacekeepers to protect civilians in Rwanda and Srebrenica has led to some changes. Peacekeeping mandates have progressively become more assertive, allowing peacekeepers to use deadly force to protect civilians. In addition, many human rights advocates are calling for the use of peacekeepers to forcibly pacify an area of conflict, with or without the consent of warring parties. This policy prescription is controversial, especially in the Quaker community, and will be the subject of debate for some time.

However, there can be little doubt that peacekeeping missions in the midst of war or grave human rights abuse are of value if they protect civilians, facilitate the delivery of humanitarian assistance, prevent war, and provide some security to open political space. The protection of so-called islands of civility, where carnage and the divisions that led to deadly conflict have not taken hold of the population, limits the lethality of a conflict and allows for the return of deliberative politics.[12] These protected islands can expand civility beyond their borders by expanding the protection activities of peacekeepers and by the population modeling an alternative way of life in the midst of war that may prove enticing to the warring parties. Peacekeepers can also be used efficiently to prevent a conflict from spreading, such as the case of the 1992 deployment of peacekeepers to the former Yugoslav republic of Macedonia, when violence was in danger of spreading there from other areas of Yugoslavia.

Deployed UN peacekeepers reached historically high numbers at the end of October 2006, with 80,976 military and police personnel and about fifteen thousand civilians serving in peace operations around the world. At the time of writing, the UN Department of Peacekeeping Operations is leading eighteen different missions in Africa, the Caribbean, the Middle East, Europe, and Asia.[13] While the United States has voted for the expansion of UN peacekeeping efforts in the Security Council, the United States has consistently failed to appropriate enough money to meet its obligations. In early 2008, U.S. arrears for UN peacekeeping stood at more than $1 billion. The problem is compounded by the U.S. law that limits the U.S. contribution to 25 percent of total UN peacekeeping costs, even though the United States is assessed at slightly over 26 percent. The United States should remove the cap on peacekeeping dues and fully pay its peacekeeping arrears as soon as possible.

Support the UN Peacebuilding Commission

The UN formed its Peacebuilding Commission in December 2005 to help states and societies manage the difficult transition from war to peace. The specific goal of the Peacebuilding Commission is to propose integrated strategies for postconflict recovery. Such strategies focus attention on reconstruction, institution building, and sustainable development in countries emerging from conflict. The commission brings together all the major actors in a given conflict to discuss a long-term peace-building strategy.

The Peacebuilding Commission is a welcome development, but it is off to a slow start. The UN's budget committee has already refused to approve funds from the organization's regular budget. The refusal has forced the commission to depend on "existing resources" and a peace-building fund composed of voluntary contributions from member states. The United States was instrumental in the creation of the commission and can help it to achieve its goals by annually providing a large portion of the funds necessary for its operation.

Expand DDR and Weapons Destruction Programs

Questions of how to address weapons and ex-combatants is a major aspect of rebuilding after a deadly conflict or mass human rights abuse. DDR programs are key to long-term peace-building efforts. Demobilization includes the dismantling of military units and the transition of ex-combatants from military to civilian life. After ex-combatants have been demobilized, most often by peacekeeping efforts, their reintegration into civilian life is necessary to prevent a new escalation of the conflict. As part of reintegration programs, ex-combatants may also require social counseling and incentives for returning to their communities and reestablishing civilian life. Ex-combatants will only put away their guns if they feel that they can find productive roles in peacetime society. But job creation proves very difficult in post-conflict situations. Expanding international development assistance, with a focus on creating economic infrastructure, can help create the conditions for reintegration.

Weapons collected in the aftermath of a peace settlement, if not quickly secured and destroyed, will often come onto the black market and be dispersed into the community, exacerbating instability and violence or fueling new conflicts. Destroying surplus, obsolete, or confiscated weapons ensures that they will not be illegally transferred and used to perpetrate violence in the future. Until recently, U.S. destruction of excess small arms and light weapons (SA/LW) had been largely an ad hoc effort. U.S. military forces frequently destroy arms seized or otherwise collected in military or peace-keeping operations. Starting in 2000, the Bush administration and members of Congress realized the importance and effectiveness of these efforts and decided to design and fund a more organized program for destroying such weapons. Since 2001, the budget has grown from $2 million to more than $47 million annually. Weapons destruction programs are a highly effective conflict resolution tool and should be expanded. The budget should be increased and the programs expanded to reach postconflict areas throughout the world. Given that destruction is relatively inexpensive (costing generally between US$1 and US$5 per weapon destroyed) and can generally be accomplished using locally available infrastructure and personnel, the weapons destruction programs offer large returns for a modest investment.[14]

Conclusion

At ceremonies and memorials remembering past atrocities, government leaders strongly assert the slogan "Never again!" as if they mean it, and they recount in moving rhetoric the terrible truths about the Holocaust, the killing fields of Kampuchea, Srebrenica, Rwanda, and other such unthinkable atrocities. But governments continue to provide insufficient resources to the problem. What can the average person make of this?

We heard a plausible explanation at an off-the-record interagency discussion with U.S. officials a few years ago. One official remarked that political will has to do with the personal courage of individual leaders of nations and states, but no matter how courageous, an official really cannot do much to respond to mass atrocities with an empty toolbox. Here is a close paraphrase: Our job as government functionaries is to create political will by ordering the right tools and getting those tools into the president's toolbox. If a president possesses the correct tools, he will be more likely to take timely and appropriate action.

Today, more than 40 percent of the federal budget goes to the military, and less than 1 percent goes to peaceful prevention of deadly conflict, with its usual share of atrocity crimes. Our country has the political will to make and win wars, but it lacks the political will to prevent or stop mass atrocities and genocide. Also today, the majority of casualties in war are civilians, whereas in the early twentieth century and before, the majority were combatants. The ability of the United States to win military victories does not protect civilians. An organized campaign, like the R2P coalition, could create a public demand for a new security system that protects civilians. Such a coalition of conscience could support government officials seeking to create the political will for R2P. If only 10 percent of the federal budget were spent on the peaceful prevention of deadly conflict, including the nonmilitary tools needed to exercise R2P, today's world of failed states and mass atrocities could be transformed into a world of stabilizing and developing states.

When it comes to R2P, war is not the answer. Prevention is a significant element of the answer, certainly more significant than military intervention. The true security of the world will depend on a popular movement that works strategically to demand that Congress create the nonmilitary tools for R2P to succeed. If the United States acquires the political will for R2P, the world will follow.

Notes

* Joe Volk is executive secretary of the Friends Committee on National Legislation (FCNL). Scott Stedjan is a senior policy adviser for humanitarian response at Oxfam America in Washington, DC.

1. The ICISS was established by the Canadian government to lead an international consultation process on the issue of international intervention in interstate conflict or humanitarian crises. Rather than focusing on the international community's

right to intervene, the report emphasized the responsibility of every state to protect its people and prevent violent conflict. The report is available at http://www.dfait-maeci.gc.ca/iciss-ciise/menu-en.asp.

2. Gregory H. Stanton, "Eight Stages of Genocide," 1998, http://www.genocidewatch.org/8stages.htm.

3. UN Security Council, *Report of the Panel on United Nations Peace Operations*, UN Doc. A/55/305–S/2000/809, August 21, 2000, http://www.un.org/peace/reports/peace_operations/.

4. U.S. Department of State, "International Partnerships to Build Peace," fact sheet, August 26, 2006, http://www.state.gov/s/crs/rls/71035.htm.

5. As quoted in Dana Priest, *The Mission: Waging War and Keeping Peace with America's Military* (New York: W. W. Norton & Co., 2004), 54.

6. Alan Pleydell, "Giving Meaning to 'Never Again:' The International Responsibility to Protect," *Committee for Conflict Transformation Support Newsletter* 31 (June 2006), http://www.c-r.org/ccts/ccts31/international-responsibility.htm.

7. U.S. Department of State, "About S/CRS," http://www.state.gov/s/crs/c12936.htm.

8. Secretary of State Condoleezza Rice, testimony, Senate Appropriations Subcommittee on Foreign Operations, May 12, 2005.

9. Michael Lund, *Preventing and Mitigating Violent Conflicts: A Revised Guide for Practitioners* (Washington, DC: Creative Associates International, 1997), http://www.caii.com/CAIIStaff/Dashboard_GIROAdminCAIIStaff/Dashboard_CAIIAdminDatabase/resources/ghai/toolbox1.htm.

10. Global Witness, *The Sinews of War*, January 11, 2006, 13, http://www.globalwitness.org/media_library_detail.php/480/en/the_sinews_of_war.

11. Ibid., 15.

12. Frida Berrigan and William D. Hartung, *U.S. Weapons at War: Building Peace or Fueling Conflict* (New York: World Policy Institute, June 2005).

13. UN Department of Peacekeeping Operations "United Nations Military, Police Deployment Reaches All-Time High In October," press release, PKO/152, November 10, 2006.

14. U.S. Department of State "Destroying Excess Small Arms: United States Policy and Programs," fact sheet, June 2, 2001, http://www.state.gov/t/pm/rls/fs/3767.htm.

13

Realizing the Responsibility to Protect in Emerging and Acute Crises

A Civil Society Proposal for the United Nations

*William Pace, Nicole Deller, and Sapna Chhatpar**

In 2005, 192 heads of state and governments, through the United Nations (UN), endorsed the responsibility to protect (R2P). In defining this principle, members of the UN not only accepted their individual responsibility to prevent and react to atrocity crimes, they also gave the international community, through the UN, the responsibility to help protect populations from genocide, crimes against humanity, war crimes, and ethnic cleansing (also referred to as atrocity crimes).

An effective system to protect populations from atrocity crimes requires a vast continuum of activities: preventive measures such as mediation and dialogue, effective systems of early warning to prevent escalation of crimes, a toolbox of measures to be applied when a crisis is escalating, capacity to use force as a last resort, and a framework for effective rebuilding. One book chapter cannot do justice to the entire range of UN programs, policies, and capacities that currently exist, or should be developed, to establish a comprehensive system of prevention, reaction, and rebuilding. Instead, this chapter focuses primarily on one critical element of this spectrum: the point at which warnings of a potential or existing crisis have been sounded.

This chapter surveys the existing UN policies and practices to respond when hostilities have escalated to the level where populations are at risk from genocide, war crimes, ethnic cleansing, and crimes against humanity. It offers guidance on what is needed for the UN to be better equipped to directly prevent and stop atrocity crimes. Finally, it demonstrates that the implementation of R2P remains a substantial challenge in the current deeply politicized UN environment.

Acceptance of R2P by the UN

When Kofi Annan recommended that states "embrace the 'responsibility to protect' as a basis for collective action against genocide, ethnic cleansing and crimes against humanity," he acknowledged the sensitivities surrounding the issue.[1] Two principal objections to R2P have persisted throughout the norm's development, and many expected that these would prevent its adoption in 2005.

First, when the idea of R2P was introduced in the International Commission on Intervention and State Sovereignty (ICISS) report, many governments believed that this doctrine was merely a rehashing of the debate over humanitarian intervention, a concept that had been rejected by large numbers of states. Second, UN members, particularly from the global south, saw in R2P an interventionist's charter that would be used by powerful states to wage war on weaker states. The political discourse on R2P began shortly after the September 11, 2001, terrorist attacks and continued during the lead-up to the invasion of Iraq in March 2003. At that time, it was nearly inconceivable that states would adopt the R2P principle.

These objections diminished during the World Summit negotiations. The draft text of the outcome document de-emphasized the role of the use of force, focusing instead on the role of the international community in assisting states and employing direct peaceful diplomatic and humanitarian measures to protect populations. The use of force was placed at the very end of a spectrum of measures to be adopted. This approach was guided by the secretary-general's formulation of R2P as an issue within the context of the freedom to live in dignity and not as an issue of collective security and the use of force, the framework in which the High-Level Panel had introduced R2P. Shifting the core of the debate on R2P away from use-of-force issues resulted in much stronger support within the General Assembly among governments from every region.

As to the perception that R2P was a northern agenda, southern leadership at the World Summit was central. Argentina, Chile, Guatemala, Mexico, Rwanda, and South Africa were some of the influential governments insisting on a meaningful commitment to R2P.[2] The leadership of these governments translated into the support of many other members from the global south.

A few vocal member states, however, remained steadfast in their opposition because they feared it would codify the right of major powers to intervene in the affairs of less powerful countries. Belarus, Cuba, India, Pakistan, Russia, and Venezuela were among the opponents. Some governments sought to remove all references to the concept of R2P. Others quietly expressed skepticism, saying that the proponents of the doctrine were fond of putting words on paper, but had not done enough in practice.

The supporters of R2P nevertheless succeeded in obtaining an endorsement of the concept in the 2005 World Summit Outcome document.[3] Although this adoption was hailed as one of the true successes of the summit,[4] the fact that it was negotiated with great haste as part of a broad package of reforms has left some of the UN membership, the vocal opponents and quiet skeptics alike, questioning what they agreed to and how it would be applied.

R2P Backlash?

As the UN began its post–summit follow-up, member states dedicated their efforts to the completion of other reform initiatives such as the creation of the Human Rights Council and the Peacebuilding Commission and pursued management reform. Questions of how R2P would apply to unfolding crises, or how the UN might better prepare itself to fulfill this responsibility were set aside.

The delays in trying to implement R2P within the UN system were as much a result of the political calculations of which reforms needed to be prioritized as they were a response to the almost immediate backlash against R2P that began to take shape within the UN membership. The reform initiatives had a polarizing effect among member states, solidifying the positions of the collective global south (often acting through the Group of 77 [G-77] voting block) against reforms perceived as entrenching northern governments' influence and power within the UN at the expense of the needs and goals of the south. The criticisms that had been set aside during summit negotiations, that R2P is an intervener's charter, a neocolonialist agenda, have thus reemerged with force. As this chapter points to the many opportunities within the discussion to further develop the concept of R2P, it also documents many of the ways that progress has been blocked as a result of these objections.

The challenge of overcoming these deeply rooted suspicions remains substantial. Following the success of other human security campaigns, support could be mobilized through a group of like-minded governments from all regions working in cooperation with international, national, and local civil society organizations. Supporters must ensure that R2P is not promoted principally as a use-of-force doctrine, but rather as a framework for the international community to enact a range of measures to avert and halt the most serious humanitarian crises.

How the UN Can Implement R2P
in Emerging and Acute Crises

The UN is an international organization that brings together all 192 "peace-loving" states in the world. Since its creation and to this day, the UN has six principal organs. For the purpose of this chapter, we will focus on the Security Council, the General Assembly, and the Secretariat.

The UN is not a single entity with autonomous decision-making authority. It functions as a forum for political decision making to address state behavior and as an operational entity providing direct services on the ground. Both of these roles are necessary for the protection of populations from mass atrocities. This section surveys many of the key political and operational bodies that must be called upon to implement R2P within the UN system.

As a forum for the deliberation of its member states, UN member states pass resolutions calling for the establishment of international policies and norms, and collectively address global issues and state behavior. This section assesses the roles of two principal deliberative bodies—the Security Council and the General Assembly, as well as one subsidiary organ to the General Assembly, the Human Rights Council.

This section also analyzes the ways in which the UN Secretariat should implement R2P. The UN Secretariat is the administrative arm of the UN, supporting the work of the political organs and seeing to the administration of their policies. Several departments and offices of the Secretariat, including the Department of Peacekeeping Operations, the Office of the High Commissioner on Human Rights, and the Office for the Coordination of Humanitarian Affairs, have various duties in monitoring, reporting, coordination, and policy development that are relevant to the implementation of R2P. The UN Secretariat is often a visible presence on the ground, but it does not have authority to shape state conduct.

Besides the above-mentioned intergovernmental bodies and the UN Secretariat, UN programs and funds, along with specialized agencies, play a role in providing direct services that can protect populations from mass atrocities. It is through these entities that the UN operates on the ground, delivering aid and assistance, building capacity, and providing training. A thorough review of the physical delivery of aid in conflict situations is beyond the scope of this chapter. Instead we focus on the processes of ensuring that the appropriate information is getting to the political actors with the authority to adopt specific measures targeting individual states or the international community as a whole.

The Role for UN Intergovernmental Bodies

The Security Council

Among the UN bodies, the Security Council has the widest range of measures at its disposal to react to an R2P crisis. Its decision-making process, however, is deeply political and so the council has historically been slow to react, particularly in situations of violence internal to one country.

Under UN charter Chapter VII, the council's ability to adopt enforcement measures hinges on its determination that a situation constitutes a threat to peace. Historically the council has not stepped in because of a reluctance to interfere with state sovereignty and because such situations were thought to be more appropriately addressed by the human rights bodies of the UN. When the council has taken up issues of violence against civil populations, it has generally been in the context of regional or cross-border security concerns that have come to the council's attention.

The World Summit Outcome document (paragraph 139) states that when a state manifestly fails to protect its populations from genocide, war crimes, crimes against humanity, and ethnic cleansing, the international community is "prepared to take collective action through the Security Council . . . including Chapter VII." With this language, UN member states accept in principle that atrocity crimes occurring wholly within a state can be considered as threats to peace, and once Chapter VII is invoked, the council may respond by adopting a range of measures. Those short of military force have included arms embargoes, travel bans, economic sanctions, and in the instance of Darfur, a referral to the International Criminal Court (ICC). The council may take military action to restore international peace and security if measures short of force would be or have proved to be inadequate.

The summit outcome document also makes clear that the council has a role to play in assisting states to comply with their responsibility to protect before a crisis has reached the level of a threat to peace. Paragraph 139 acknowledges the responsibility "to use appropriate diplomatic, humanitarian and other peaceful means, in accordance with Chapters VI and VIII of the

Charter, to help protect populations." This refers to, among other measures, the council's authority to investigate situations that might endanger peace and security and to work with appropriate regional organizations.[5]The summit document empowers the council to act, but it has taken only modest steps toward operationalizing this agenda and has faced considerable resistance in doing so.

The Security Council Affirms the R2P Norm

The first major post-summit initiative regarding R2P was aimed at gaining the express support of the Security Council for the norm. Negotiations on the subject faced more resistance than expected from Russia, China, and several nonpermanent members. In off-the-record conversations, some council members opposed giving more weight to the summit language on R2P, which they had only reluctantly accepted. Moreover, some council members believed that the Security Council was not the appropriate forum to "create" a new norm, and that further consideration of this issue should be decided by the General Assembly.

Notwithstanding the reluctance of some council members, and after several months of negotiation, in April 2006 the Security Council unanimously adopted Resolution 1674 on the Protection of Civilians in Armed Conflict. In operative paragraph 4, the Security Council "reaffirms the provisions of paragraphs 138 and 139 of the World Summit Outcome Document regarding the responsibility to protect populations from genocide, war crimes, ethnic cleansing and crimes against humanity."[6]

Challenges for the Council in Enforcing the R2P Norm

The council has now affirmed that a responsibility to protect exists, but it has not yet enforced it. The council referenced R2P in one country-specific resolution, in the preamble to the August 31, 2006, resolution calling for the rapid deployment of peacekeepers in Darfur. In this resolution, the council recalled the provisions of its Resolution 1674 with a specific reference to paragraphs 138 and 139 of the World Summit Outcome document. In theory, the reference to R2P in the Darfur resolution is a benchmark for the advancement of the R2P norm. In practice, it took another year before the peacekeeping force was authorized (on July 31, 2007, Resolution 1769), and yet another five months before the force actually reached Darfur, on January 1, 2008.

While several member states have discussed R2P in debates, the council as a whole has not invoked R2P to apply to any specific crisis. In January 2007, a double-veto of a Security Council resolution regarding widespread human rights violations in Myanmar suggests that the endorsement of R2P has not made the council more willing to address atrocities occurring within the borders of a state. Objections to council action included that the situation was the affair of a sovereign state, that the situation was not a threat to international peace and security, and that as a human rights matter, it should be taken up by the Human Rights Council rather than the Security Council. It may be that the Security Council does not consider the crimes that are occurring in Myanmar to be on the scale of those in Rwanda and Darfur. The vote on this resolution nevertheless raises the question of whether the council is retreating from the summit commitment.

The promise of R2P will have failed if governments begrudgingly admit that such a commitment exists, only to resist its application to specific conflicts. To ensure that R2P is properly invoked by the council, a clear framework is needed to determine how R2P should be applied to specific situations. The following are outstanding questions for the council to consider:

- Can the Security Council agree on a process for determining when a crisis has reached the threshold of crimes encompassed by the responsibility to protect (i.e., genocide, war crimes, ethnic cleansing, and crimes against humanity)? Could the council spell out the threshold of crimes, the character and scale of which would be cause for attention by the Security Council?
- Will the council recognize the role of other UN bodies or agencies in calling its attention to situations that should give rise to the council's responsibility to protect? This could include the Human Rights Council, the Office of the Special Adviser, or other offices described below.
- Will the council agree to establishing a monitoring and reporting mechanism for crimes fitting the responsibility to protect?[7]
- Can the council identify the spectrum of measures that could be applied, especially short of military force, to respond to an R2P situation?
- Will the council agree to be guided by use-of-force principles, as recommended during the UN reform process and in the ICISS report?

An additional challenge for the Security Council is, in the opinion of many UN member states, that this body is not the most legitimate one to decide when sovereignty must yield to the protection of civilians. The council has been accused of double standards and hypocrisy in how it enforces peace and security. As they have done in the past, the five permanent member states—China, France, Russia, the United Kingdom, and the United States—can block measures to address a situation in their territory or that of their close allies. Many opponents of R2P resist this principle for the reason that it will never be used to hold the influential accountable for their acts and that it will only apply to the less powerful.

For a large portion of the international community, deeper acceptance of R2P and of its operation by the Security Council thus depends on satisfactory reform of the Security Council, an issue that was left unresolved during the 2005 summit. The close relationship between R2P and Security Council reform was evident in earlier drafts of the R2P provisions of the summit outcome document that "invited" permanent member states to refrain from using the veto in cases of genocide, war crimes, and crimes against humanity. Although this language was rejected, the issue remains one of the proposed procedural reforms to the working methods of the Security Council.

The General Assembly

The General Assembly's Role in Establishing Global Norms

The General Assembly is composed of all the UN member states. While the Security Council is entrusted with the primary responsibility for maintaining peace and security on behalf of the UN, the General Assembly is the forum for elaborating norms. It is through this body that the principal human rights instruments of the past century were negotiated and adopted. The General Assembly also convenes world conferences that establish global norms. While these conference outcomes are not generally codified into international law, they carry significant political weight.

The General Assembly and the R2P Norm

The 2005 World Summit Outcome document is one example of a political agreement generated through the General Assembly negotiation process. In this instance, however, negotiations were not conducted through an extensive and transparent preparatory process. This process, with its vast agenda, extended over only a few months and was largely conducted behind closed doors by a few key member states. As a consequence, many member states opposed the inclusion of R2P on the basis that it had not been sufficiently considered by the General Assembly.

Taking these concerns into consideration, the summit outcome document includes a provision for the General Assembly to continue its deliberations on the concept: it "stress[ed] the need for the General Assembly to continue consideration of [R2P] and its implications, bearing in mind the principles of the Charter and international law." This language implicitly refers to Article 2.7 of the UN charter, which states that "nothing contained in the present Charter shall authorize the United Nations to intervene in matters which are essentially within the domestic jurisdiction of any state." Some member states would like an additional General Assembly resolution on R2P.

The General Assembly has not yet placed an R2P debate on its agenda, but this is now expected to take place in the 2008 to 2009 term. At the time of this writing, the contents and scope of the debate remain undecided. Supporters of R2P fear that a few focal opponents will take the opportunity to repudiate the agreement or limit its scope. The advancement of the norm is certainly not helped by such public declarations, yet the number of opponents is believed to be a very small minority. If the supporters are effectively mobilized, it is unlikely that a General Assembly debate would result in a resolution altering the R2P commitment.

Future Roles for the General Assembly
If the General Assembly becomes more inclined to work toward the operationalization of R2P, there are several initiatives for its consideration:

- Adopt a resolution on precautionary principles (right intention, last resort, proportional means, and reasonable prospects) that would guide the use of force in an R2P situation, as suggested in the ICISS report.
- Revise the Declaration on Principles of International Law Concerning Friendly Relations and Cooperation Among States in accordance with the charter of the UN (contained in General Assembly Resolution 2625) to include R2P language.
- In future instances with a risk of mass atrocities, pass resolutions calling for the international community to take action applying a range of diplomatic and political measures.
- If the Security Council fails to act on a situation of genocide, war crimes, crimes against humanity, or ethnic cleansing, consider a Uniting-for-Peace-style resolution to authorize force.

The Human Rights Council

Within the UN, the Human Rights Council (HRC) is the principal intergovernmental body responsible for promoting universal respect for the protection of human rights. The HRC must address situations of human rights violations, including gross and systematic ones—and therefore the crimes within the scope of R2P—and make recommendations thereon. Established on March 15, 2006, the HRC was created to replace the highly criticized Commission on Human Rights, which had served as the UN's primary human rights mechanism since 1946.[8]

The first years of the HRC were dominated by negotiations over its mandates and procedures, and the political issues that hampered the

Commission on Human Rights have remerged. If the HRC is able to move past this politicization, it could be an important focal point for R2P within the UN system. The three main features that could be activated to address R2P situations are the council's special procedures, the Universal Period Review (UPR) mechanism, and consideration in its regular or special sessions.

Special Procedures
Although the resolution establishing the HRC left undecided many important procedural matters, the General Assembly agreed to extend one of the most important features of the Commission on Human Rights: special procedures. Special procedures, which can be both thematic and country specific, allow the council to focus on special issues or conflict situations that may be of grave concern to the international community. The mandates of special procedures vary, but in general they allow the appointed individual (special rapporteur, representative, independent expert) or working group to undertake fact-finding missions to specific countries, issue communications and urgent appeals to governments, deliver press releases or statements, identify trends or emerging issues, contribute to the elaboration of human rights standards, and submit reports to the council, and in some instances the General Assembly. Special rapporteurs (or working groups) established under the special procedures can be effective tools for putting R2P into practice. They have direct access to first-hand information about crimes against humanity occurring within a state. Therefore they have a unique opportunity to speak out to HRC members and other member states, the secretary-general, the Security Council, or the General Assembly on the need for action. They can use diplomatic measures by providing technical advice and expertise to the country in question, or they can pursue a more outspoken approach by "naming and shaming" the country's authorities.

Universal Periodic Review
Universal periodic review (UPR) is another approach for the HRC to address governments' human rights records, including possible situations of genocide, war crimes, and crimes against humanity. The resolution establishing the HRC states that this body will undertake a UPR of the "fulfillment by each State of its human rights obligations" in a manner that ensures "universality of coverage and equal treatment with respect to all States."

Modalities and procedures for the UPR were finalized at the April 2008 inaugural session of the HRC. All member states will be reviewed within four years and the order of review is decided by the drawing of lots, keeping with the principles of "equal treatment and universality, and equitable geographic distribution." The council may also review the modalities and periodicity of the review after the completion of the first cycle (2011). The UPR cycle will occur three times per year until 2011, when all 192 UN member states will have been reviewed. As UPR will likely only target a country every four years, its ability to be used as a quick impact response or preventive measure for an emerging situation of mass violence will likely be quite limited.

Consideration in Regular or Special Sessions
One of the ways that the HRC has been able to address human rights concerns in country-specific situations is through regular and special sessions. The HRC meets regularly throughout the year, with no fewer than three sessions per council year, including a main session, for a total duration of no less than ten weeks. Under the agenda for regular sessions, the council can address emergency situations that require the attention of the council, such as those that would fall under R2P.[9]

Special sessions are also intended to respond to country-specific situations and typically involve urgent human rights violations. They can be convened at the request of any member state with one-third of the HRC's support. The use of special sessions is an important tool within the range of measures available for the international community to fulfill its responsibility to protect. As of May 2008, the HRC has held six special sessions. The first three sessions were directed at Israel for its actions in Lebanon and the Palestinian territories. The next two sessions bore a direct relationship to R2P. The fourth special session called for high-level monitors to assess the human rights situation in Darfur.[10] The high-level mission conducted its analysis through the framework of R2P.[11] The fifth special session focused on the situation in Burma/Myanmar following large-scale violence committed by the military government after nonviolent protests by civilians and Buddhist monks in response to increased fuel prices. The High Commissioner for Human Rights highlighted R2P in her address to this session.[12]

Early Assessment of the HRC
The HRC is undeniably off to a rocky start. Some of the early supporters of this institution now express their disappointment with its progress. Whether the HRC will agree on the remaining procedures and mechanisms, as well as ensure that those established serve their purpose, will serve as a strong indicator of whether the international community is prepared to put R2P into practice. Moreover, the HRC's ability to secure the cooperation of the state in question remains a political challenge.[13] The tension between respecting sovereignty and fulfilling the international community's responsibility to protect—even through noncoercive measures—exists for this new body just as it does for the Security Council and other UN actors.

The Role of the UN Secretariat

The UN Secretariat is the administrative arm of the UN, supporting the work of the political organs and seeing to the administration of their policies. The Secretariat, headed by the UN secretary-general, is made up of almost nine thousand international staff that answer to the authority of the UN rather than any single government. This section focuses on several of the key actors within this system that could be central to gathering and transmitting information about emerging crises. They are voices from within the UN system that can sound the alarm to mobilize the political actors to act.

The UN Secretary-General

The role of the secretary-general in advancing R2P is substantial. The position requires a commitment to strengthening acceptance of the norm, building UN capacity, and ensuring application when crises are occurring. The secretary-general may advance R2P through his administrative functions, such as offering his good offices and setting priorities for other UN offices or by acting as a moral authority, supporting the norm or calling for action during crisis situations. Often described as the "most impossible job,"[14] the secretary-general has to balance the needs of the member states, who tend to guard the exercise of their sovereignty, and the needs of the world's people, who may be suffering from the most heinous of crimes.

Administrative Functions
The secretary-general is the chief administrative officer of the UN. The UN charter requires the secretary-general to issue annual reports reviewing the organization's activities and outlining its future priorities. This is especially important in the implementation of R2P, as the secretary-general should advise and recommend how other UN agencies can implement R2P within their mandates.

The secretary-general may also propose strategies to be implemented by the UN system to address global issues and appoint advisers to assist in developing policies. In March 2006, former secretary-general Kofi Annan created a five-point action plan on the prevention of genocide, which included the creation of the Office of the Special Adviser for the Prevention of Genocide, discussed below.[15] Secretary-General Ban Ki-moon built on this strategy with the appointment of a special adviser on R2P, also discussed below.

The secretary-general's "good offices" are another potential operational tool for R2P when a crisis requires urgent attention. The secretary-general can use his good offices to privately mediate conflicts that may lead to genocide, ethnic cleansing, or crimes against humanity. Past examples of the use of good offices in situations of human rights abuses include the follow-up on the Arusha Peace Agreement and the role of a neutral international force in Rwanda, establishing dialogue and pressuring the government of Burma to respect human rights and political freedoms, and helping find a permanent solution to the conflict in the Darfur region. The secretary-general also has the ability to assign other senior officials to act as special representatives or envoys. For example, in December 2006, Kofi Annan and Ban Ki-moon agreed to appoint former president of the General Assembly Jan Eliasson as special envoy to Darfur.[16]

Finally, there is no question that the secretary-general is an appropriate authority to alert the international community to genocide, war crimes, crimes against humanity, and ethnic cleansing in crisis situations. Not only does Article 99 of the UN charter explicitly authorize the secretary-general to bring to the attention of the Security Council "any matter which in his opinion may threaten the maintenance of international peace and security," but Security Council Resolution 1366 (2001) enhances this preventive and early warning function by specifically inviting the secretary-general to communicate cases of serious violations of humanitarian law and human rights law that he or she deems to represent threats to international peace and security.

Acting as a Moral Authority
In addition to serving as the head of the UN Secretariat, the secretary-general can use his or her moral authority to call upon others to act on issues such as human rights, social and economic development, and humanitarian intervention.[17]The leadership of former secretary-general Kofi Annan in framing the debate and setting R2P as a priority for his agenda was crucial to the norm's acceptance. Annan's work on developing the norm is considered one of the most important achievements of his tenure.[18] He is described as having conducted "norm entrepreneurship"[19] on behalf of R2P. Secretary-general Ban ki-Moon has also committed to operationalizing R2P, including the appointment of a special adviser with a focus on R2P.[20] On July 15, 2008, the secretary-general gave a landmark speech on R2P; a first expression from the secretariat on what R2P is and is not, the challenges in advancing R2P and offering Ban's personal commitment to turn the concept into policy. This clarification provides authoritative answers to many difficult questions asked by both supporters and critics since the World Summit in 2005.

The authority of the secretary-general extends beyond leadership in developing policies and practices. He or she is able to publicly name and shame violator governments to influence their behavior or prompt the international community to react.

The Office of the Special Adviser on the Prevention of Genocide

From the Lessons of Rwanda: The Creation of a New Office

In April 2004, marking the tenth anniversary of the Rwandan genocide, secretary-general Kofi Annan launched an action plan to prevent genocide that included the creation of a new UN office: the special adviser on the prevention of genocide (SAPG). The SAPG was appointed with a mandate to

- collect information on massive violations of human rights and international humanitarian law of ethnic and racial origin;
- serve as an early warning mechanism to the secretary-general and through him to the Security Council;
- make recommendations to the Security Council on actions to be taken to prevent or halt genocide;
- liaise with the UN system and enhance its collective capacity to prevent genocide.[21]

The SAPG fulfills its early warning mandate by acting as a *focal point* for information found inside and outside the UN system. In particular, the SAPG, who formally received the "full support" of UN members in the World Summit Outcome document, has a mandate to bring R2P situations directly to the attention of the Security Council.

Early Activities of the SAPG

Juan Méndez, an Argentinean human rights lawyer, was appointed as the first SAPG in 2004. As a part-time position with only two staff members, the early activities were modest. Some of the notable events were two briefings to the Security Council, although the special adviser was denied a request to brief the council in 2005 following his second visit to Darfur. He transmitted confidential notes to the secretary-general on situations of concern, yet there is little indication how, if at all, the council considered these communications in its work.

When the secretary-general appointed Francis Deng, a Sudanese diplomat, scholar, and former special representative of the secretary-general on internally displaced persons as the successor to Méndez, changes were made to the post to enhance its effectiveness.[22] The post was elevated to full time, upgraded from an assistant secretary-general to an undersecretary-general, and "mass atrocities" was added to the title. The expansion of the title suggested a greater role in implementing a broader R2P agenda. The new title was dropped, however, once the UN budgetary committee began considering funding for the office.[23] Some member states were reportedly concerned that mass atrocities was a vague and broad term that would result in the special adviser interfering in the internal matters of a state.

The mandate of the office is undeniably politically sensitive. No country wants to be singled out by the UN as needing assistance in the prevention of genocide, a universally abhorred criminal act. For the special adviser to engage a country on preventing genocide, Special Adviser Deng emphasizes constructive engagement through a framework of "sovereignty as responsibility" as a means to build common ground and neutralize the controversy. For example, one early activity was a field mission to Kenya in response to the postelection violence in December 2007 that focused on assisting the state in the prevention of ethnically targeted violence against its populations.

Special Adviser with a Focus on R2P

In December 2007, secretary-general Ban Ki-moon noted his intention to appoint Edward Luck, an international scholar with expertise on the UN system, as special adviser on the responsibility to protect, with the primary roles of consensus building and conceptual clarity.[24] As with the appointment of Francis Deng, member states raised questions about this appointment in the UN's budgetary committee. Some UN member states raised procedural questions while others used this forum to assert that R2P was not an agreed-to concept.[25] The secretary-general ultimately removed "responsibility to protect" from the title, and Edward Luck is now a "special adviser" and his work is described as including the responsibility to protect.[26]

In the months following the appointment, this has proved to be a key role within the UN system for advancing R2P. The special adviser is helping to clarify the concept, as reflected in the secretary general's July 15, 2008, speech on R2P, and advancing the political dialogue among the UN membership. He is also working on improvements to the UN architecture. He and Special Adviser Deng are expected to form a joint office on genocide prevention and R2P, and are currently developing a plan to improve the coordination among the Office of the Secretary- General and UN departments for anticipating, preventing, and responding to R2P crises.

The Office of the High Commissioner for Human Rights

The Office of the High Commissioner for Human Rights (OHCHR) is the principal body within the UN Secretariat dedicated to the protection and promotion of human rights. Established in 1993, the office is headed by

High Commissioner Louise Arbour, who reports directly to the secretary-general.

Harnessing the Moral Authority of the High Commissioner for Human Rights

The high commissioner for human rights plays a critical role in the realization of the R2P principle. The high commissioner makes frequent public statements calling for urgent attention on specific human rights situations. Because the high commissioner has immediate access to information on the ground, he or she is well positioned to speak publicly about situations that have reached the R2P threshold of crimes. Moreover, the high commissioner engages in private diplomatic efforts with governments in an effort to strengthen national human rights protection. Should there be failures by a state to protect its population, the high commissioner can offer technical advice and assistance on how the government should reform its practices.

The OHCHR is tasked with several important responsibilities, including providing support for the high commissioner, human rights bodies, and organs, thematic and country fact-finding procedures, and technical cooperation and advisory services for governments. It also conducts field monitoring and reporting, and research and analysis for human rights mainstreaming. Structurally the Geneva office is broken up into five departments. The branches best suited to incorporate R2P into their work are the Special Procedures branch and the Capacity Building and Field Operations branch.

Operationalizing R2P Through OHCHR Field Operations

The Capacity Building and Field Operations branch is divided into five geographic teams. It monitors human rights abuses at the country level and provides support for fact-finding investigations. This branch also provides technical assistance and advisory services to governments requested through special procedures of the council or through offices of the Secretariat, including the Department of Political Affairs.

This branch offers three important roles with respect to R2P. First, information gathered by workers in the field could prove valuable in determining the gravity of crimes inside the state and assessing whether the situation has risen to an R2P threshold. In his report *Darfur and Beyond*, Lee Feinstein argues that this office is an "underutilized resource" for the prevention and deterrence of atrocities and notes that "Louise Arbour has proposed the early deployment of human rights officers to crisis situations to provide timely information and draw attention to situations requiring action."[27] Moreover, this branch could work with other UN offices, such as the SAPG, in recommending courses of action to respond to a crisis ranging from nonmilitary to military. Finally, this branch could also facilitate technical assistance to governments seeking help to prevent massive crimes from escalating.

Supporting the Work of the HRC Through the Special Procedures Branch

The Special Procedures branch provides key support for the HRC through its special rapporteurs, special representatives and experts, and working groups, each mandated by the council to address human rights violations, including conducting fact-finding investigations. As mentioned previously, the HRC may issue both country mandates and thematic mandates. Mandate-holders, who serve in their private capacity, are uniquely placed to serve as spokespersons for human rights crises and often issue urgent appeals to governments committing abuses. They also conduct country visits and provide reports and recommendations to the council. As these mandate-holders witness first-hand violations, their potential role as advocates for R2P is clear.

The OHCHR is regarded as a potential lead actor in the UN system to coordinate the implementation of R2P. It will face several challenges in playing this role, however. While R2P is a matter of human rights concern, it is also a matter of international peace and security. The work of the OHCHR on this subject must therefore link to the security architecture of the UN. Yet the OHCHR has limited access to the Security Council and its agenda. Moreover, there are questions as to the resources available for the OHCHR to play this role. The World Summit Outcome document doubled the UN funding for OHCHR existing and planned activities, but to further expand the OHCHR's activities so that the office can serve as a focal point for R2P will require additional resources.

Office for the Coordination of Humanitarian Affairs

The Office for the Coordination of Humanitarian Affairs (OCHA) is responsible for the coordination of the UN's humanitarian relief efforts. The office formulates policy and advocacy strategies, provides a media spotlight for conflicts and neglected crises, and offers guidance to member states on how to fulfill their protection responsibilities.

People at risk of genocide, war crimes, and crimes against humanity are a subset of the broader group of vulnerable populations to which OCHA attends, yet OCHA has not yet developed an appropriate framework to address their particular needs. OCHA can play an important role in ensuring that UN member states fulfill their responsibility to protect and also that the UN system does what it can to support member states in implementing their R2P obligations.

The Role of the Undersecretary-General
Emergency Relief Coordinator

The undersecretary-general for humanitarian affairs, who also serves as the emergency relief coordinator, is the chief spokesperson within the UN for humanitarian issues and could be a leading advocate for the UN's operationalization of R2P in addition to calling for action when an R2P threshold is reached.

The undersecretary-general for humanitarian affairs is the principal adviser to the secretary-general on humanitarian affairs. As the emergency relief coordinator, he or she is responsible for policy development, advocacy within the UN on humanitarian issues, and coordination of responses to humanitarian crises. The emergency relief coordinator could play an enhanced role by not only encouraging member states to fulfill their R2P obligations, but also advocating for the adoption of policies on R2P throughout the UN system. The emergency relief coordinator can also draw attention to crisis situations by calling on the international community to act.

Policy Development

At the field level and through the development of policy, OCHA could significantly contribute to the ways in which R2P is incorporated into the protection activities of the UN. OCHA works closely with member states, the secretary-general, the General Assembly, the Economic and Social Council (ECOSOC), and humanitarian organizations and academia to develop common policy positions based on human rights and humanitarian law.

One of the central projects of OCHA is the Protection of Civilians Project, which works to support the UN's diplomatic, legal, humanitarian, and human rights activities directed at the protection of populations during armed conflict. R2P addresses a subset of the crises that the protection of civilians agenda covers, namely genocide, war crimes, crimes against humanity, and ethnic cleansing. The R2P principles agreed to in the World Summit Outcome document also provide a normative foundation for work on the protection of civilians.[28]

By generating new policies, there are several different ways in which OCHA could take a more active role in operationalizing R2P. First, there is an institutional lack of understanding on how R2P relates to the protection of civilians agenda. OCHA could produce communications on this issue, which would be transmitted to all field officers, and could help other UN offices understand how R2P fits within their own mandates. OCHA's policy development branch could also play an important role in formulating guidelines for data collection on R2P crimes for UN field operations.

Field Operations
The Office for the Coordination of Humanitarian Affairs also has a crucial presence in the field. More than fifty field offices in forty countries provide information to a variety of UN agencies and international organizations through monitoring and reporting of humanitarian crises. Humanitarian coordinators, who are dispatched at the recommendation of the undersecretary-general/emergency relief coordinator in consultation with the Inter-Agency Standing Committee (IASC), are often the most senior UN humanitarian officials on the ground. Resident coordinators and humanitarian coordinators are well positioned to gather and disseminate information to other actors in the UN system, especially as it relates to genocide, war crimes, crimes against humanity, and ethnic cleansing. This information can then be transmitted to the emergency relief coordinator, who may wish to appeal to the government in question, other member states, or the secretary-general.

The Department of Peacekeeping Operations

The decision to use military force to halt genocide or other mass atrocities is at the end of the spectrum of measures that must be employed, and other chapters in this book discuss the role of the use of force with respect to R2P. Apart from the question of whether the use of force is appropriate, an issue germane to this chapter is how the UN's military apparatus is equipped to conduct R2P operations.

Within the UN, the Department of Peacekeeping Operations (DPKO) is the principal body that would operationalize the military aspects of R2P. UN missions have evolved in recent years from traditional peacekeeping, understood as a military presence to monitor or enforce a peace agreement, to incorporate a complex model of many elements—military and civilian—working together to build peace in the dangerous aftermath of civil wars. Historically, however, neither traditional peacekeeping nor the more complex operations have been used for the primary purpose of human protection.

While many of the mandates that are carried out by DPKO include civilian protection, none of the current UN peacekeeping missions is mandated with the primary purpose of preventing or halting crimes against a civilian population. There are many practical considerations about how the UN and other entities should be equipped to conduct a mission with the primary goal of human protection. One issue is whether the troops have the capacity to effectively conduct protective missions. Another consideration is how to prepare troops to conduct protective missions. Do troops have the appropriate training and instructions so that they are able to act most effectively for the purpose of protection? The scope of this inquiry extends beyond the overview provided in this chapter, although this subject has been studied in great detail by Victoria Holt and Tobias Berkman of the Henry L. Stimson Center. Their findings were published in *The Impossible Mandate? Military Preparedness, the Responsibility to Protect and Modern Peace Operations.*[29] This report highlights the gaps in preparedness of international organizations for missions or mandates relating to what they describe as "coercive protection." It makes recommendations for improving doctrine, rules of engagement, and training targeting national, regional, and international forces whose mandate is to protect civilians.

While R2P requires an emphasis on peaceful measures, there is growing recognition that international, regional, and national architectures must also factor in military strategies and doctrines for when prevention fails to protect populations.

Conclusion

The purpose of this chapter was to identify the key bodies, departments, and offices within the UN system that could best operationalize R2P in emerging and acute crises.[30] While our approach considered how each individual body should be tasked to further implement the norm, it is important to note that a coordinated and integrated system that incorporates the work of all UN actors would be the most effective way of stopping mass atrocities. Strengthening the offices and departments described in this chapter by improving their monitoring, reporting, coordination, and policy development functions as they relate to atrocity crimes could provide strong support for governments to take action, including through the Security Council, the General Assembly, and the HRC. It is through these intergovernmental bodies that political pressure will be garnered to prevent a crisis from reaching an acute stage.

As set forth in the World Summit Outcome document, these UN bodies, departments, and offices should enact all measures available, including a range of nonmilitary tools, from diplomatic to humanitarian. Through these peaceful measures, the UN can react earlier, before Security Council authorization for the use of force is required.

Civil society has a useful role to play in encouraging each of these bodies, departments, and offices to better integrate R2P into their mandates. Civil society organizations regularly consult with and provide recommendations to the secretary-general's special advisers, to the secretary-general, and to key staff from other UN departments on how to advance and implement R2P.

In addition to interfacing with the UN Secretariat and other bodies, civil society groups are engaging at the governmental level. Many civil society organizations consult with member states and their staffs in advance of relevant thematic debates or country-specific crises to see how language on R2P can be included or reinforced. This also involves monitoring debates in the General Assembly and Security Council.

Civil society members can contribute to greater understanding by the public, the media, and policymakers about the meaning of R2P and the types of situations in which it should apply. Civil society needs to hold governments accountable when R2P should be invoked and call attention to situations where it is misapplied by governments to serve their own political interests. Another related task for civil society is to identify the different measures—from nonmilitary measures to the use of force—that they would be willing to support in the event of an R2P situation. Finally, civil society needs to advocate for a coordinated system within the UN where each of its bodies feeds into the work of the others. Working with other civil society actors and pressuring governments to support the strengthening of these bodies, and the overall system, will be essential for the operationalization of R2P.

Notes

* William Pace is the executive director of the Institute for Global Policy in New York. Nicole Deller is director of programs for the Global Center for the Responsibility to Protect in New York. Sapna Chhatpar is project manager of the R2PCS program at the Institute for Global Policy.

1. Kofi Annan, *In Larger Freedom: Towards Development, Security and Human Rights for All*, UN Doc. A/59/2005, March 21, 2005, para. 135, http://www.un.org/largerfreedom/contents.htm.

2. Government statements from the debates leading to and through the 2005 summit are available at http://www.reformtheun.org/.

3. UN GAOR, Sixtieth Session, 8th plen. mtg., UN Doc. A/RES/60/1, para. 138, October 24, 2005.

4. Secretary-General's message, United Nations Department of Public Information, UN Doc. SG/SM/10671, October 6, 2006, http://www.un.org/News/Press/docs/2006/sgsm10671.doc.htm.

5. Measures under Chapter VI might include fact-finding missions and sending delegations of council members to potential crisis areas.

6. UN SCOR, Sixty-first Session, 5,430th mtg., UN Doc. S/RES/1674, para. 4, April 28, 2006.

7. A monitoring and reporting mechanism on R2P could be modeled on Resolution 1612, Children and Armed Conflict, which established a "systematic collection and channeling of information from the field through the relevant bodies in the UN system."

8. UN GAOR, UN Doc. A/Res/60/251, April 3, 2006, http://daccessdds.un.org/doc/UNDOC/GEN/N05/502/66/PDF/N0550266.pdf?OpenElement.

9. UN General Assembly, Sixty-second Session, Report of the Human Rights Council, UN Doc. A/62/434, December 7, 2007, available at http://daccess dds.un.org/doc/UNDOC/GEN/N07/622/01/PDF/N0762201.pdf?OpenElement.

10. UN Human Rights Council, Decision S-4/101, December 13, 2006.

11. *Report of the High-Level Mission on the Situation of Human Rights in Darfur Pursuant to Human Rights Council Decision S-4/101*, UN Doc. A/HRC/4/80, March 9, 2007, http://daccessdds.un.org/doc/UNDOC/GEN/G07/116/20/PDF/G0711620.pdf?OpenElement.

12. Statement by UN High Commissioner for Human Rights Louise Arbour on the occasion of the five-hour special session of the Human Rights Council on October 2, 2007.

13. For example, the government of Khartoum has refused to issue visas for the Human Rights Council's fact-finding team. See "UN Rights Team Halts Darfur Visit Over Sudan Visa Bar," Reuters South Africa, February 14, 2007.

14. Edward Luck, "The Toughest Job on Earth," *Washington Post*, October 8, 2006, B2; Shashi Tharoor, "'The Most Impossible Job' Description," in *Secretary or General? The UN Secretary-General in World Politics*, ed. Simon Chesterman (New York: Cambridge University Press, 2007), 33–46.

15. UN Secretary-General, "Secretary-General's Address to the Commission on Human Rights (As Delivered)," Secretary-General Office of the Spokesperson, April 7, 2004, http://www.un.org/apps/sg/sgstats.asp?nid=862.

16. UN Secretary-General, "Secretary-General Annan's Farewell Press Conference," Secretary-General Office of the Spokesperson, December 19, 2006, http://www.un.org/apps/sg/offthecuff.asp?nid=962.

17. Adekeye Adebajo, "Pope, Pharaoh, or Prophet? The Secretary-General after the Cold War," in *Secretary or General? The UN Secretary-General in World Politics*, ed. Simon Chesterman (New York: Cambridge University Press, 2007), 139–56.

18. Amin George Forji, "Adieu, Kofi Annan," *OhmyNews South Korea*, January 1, 2007.

19. Ian Johnstone, "The Secretary-General as a Norm Entrepreneur," in *Secretary or General? The UN Secretary-General in World Politics*, ed. Simon Chesterman (New York: Cambridge University Press, 2007), 123–38.

20. See, for example, "Secretary-General's message to UNU-ICG Conference on the Prevention of Mass Atrocities," October 10, 2007, http://www.un.org/apps/sg/sgstats.asp?nid=2787.
21. UN Security Council, *Outline of the Mandate for the Special Adviser on the Prevention of Genocide UN Security Council*, UN Doc. S/2004/567, July 13, 2004.
22. The decisions to strengthen the office were informed by the Advisory Committee on the Prevention of Genocide, established in May 2006 by the secretary-general at the suggestion of SAPG Méndez.
23. *Fifth Committee Takes Up Financing for Special Political Missions, Procurement Task Force; 11 General Assembly Texts with Budget Implications*, UN Department of Public Information, UN Doc. GA/AB/3832, December 17, 2007, http://www.un.org/News/Press/docs/2007/gaab3832.doc.htm.
24. Letter dated 31 August 2007 from the Secretary-General addressed to the President of the Security Council, UN Doc. S/2007/721, December 7, 2007, http://daccessdds.un.org/doc/UNDOC/GEN/N07/633/41/PDF/N0763341.pdf?OpenElement.
25. *United Nations Human Resources Structures Must be Adapted to Meet Growing Demands of Peacekeeping, Other Field Operations, Budget Committee Told*, UN Department of Public Information, UN Doc. GA/AB/3837, March 4, 2008, http://www.un.org/News/Press/docs/2008/gaab3837.doc.htm.
26. *Secretary-General Appoints Edward C. Luck of United States Special Adviser*, UN Department of Public Information, UN Doc. SG/A/1120, February 21, 2008, http://www.un.org/News/Press/docs/2008/sga1120.doc.htm.
27. Lee Feinstein, *Darfur and Beyond: What is Needed to Prevent Mass Atrocities*, Council Special Report No. 22 (New York: Council on Foreign Relations Press, 2007), 23.
28. UN Secretary-General, *Report of the Secretary-General on the Protection of Civilians in Armed Conflict*, UN Doc. S/2007/643, October 28, 2007, http://daccessdds.un.org/doc/UNDOC/GEN/N07/573/58/PDF/N0757358.pdf?OpenElement.
29. Victoria K. Holt and Tobias C. Berkman, *The Impossible Mandate?*, Annex 1 (Washington, DC: Henry L. Stimson Center, September 2006), http://www.stimson.org/fopo/pdf/Annex_1_The_Impossible_Mandate.Holt_%20Berkman.pdf.
30. Additional analysis on how the R2P relates to the UN Peacebuilding Commission, the International Criminal Court, and the proposal for a UN Emergency Peace Service (UNEPS) is available at http://www.responsibilitytoprotect.org.

14

Moving From Military Intervention to Judicial Enforcement

The Case for an International Marshals Service

Richard H. Cooper and Juliette Voïnov Kohler*

The international framework to prevent and react to atrocity crimes needs to be backed by tools that will ensure compliance with the global rule of law. Under the current institutional arrangements, the absence of a legitimate and effective collective enforcement mechanism within the United Nations (UN) to manage threats to international peace and security resulting from the commission of atrocity crimes is matched by the lack of a standing mechanism dedicated to ensure compliance with the International Criminal Court (ICC) statute.

In this chapter we offer a new paradigm for enforcement action aimed at ending atrocity crimes. We suggest moving from ad hoc, unilateral, and politically driven military interventions to sustainable and legitimate judicial deterrence and enforcement. At the heart of this approach is the establishment of a standing International Marshals Service (IMS) that is expected, first and foremost, to deter the commission of atrocity crimes. This police force will also increase the impartiality of investigations, help put an end to impunity, guarantee lasting respect for and enforcement of international justice, and will therefore contribute to the maintenance of local as well as international peace and security.

The Collective Use of Force to Protect Populations from Atrocity Crimes

The Collective Use of Force and the United Nations

The principle of the responsibility to protect populations from the most serious crimes of concern to the international community was unanimously endorsed by the international community during the 2005 UN World Summit and reaffirmed by the Security Council on April 28, 2006. This responsibility lies primarily with each individual state with regard to its population, with an emphasis on prevention. Each individual state has also accepted its responsibility to help other states protect their populations from atrocity crimes. The international community, through the UN, shares this responsibility to protect populations from atrocity crimes. In case national authorities manifestly fail to protect their populations and if peaceful means are inadequate, the international community, through the Security Council, may take collective enforcement action to protect populations from atrocity crimes, since these crimes then amount to threats to international peace and security.

The responsibility to protect (R2P) principle puts an emphasis on prevention, and rightly so. The use of force is confined to a "last resort" measure, in accordance with the principles enshrined in the UN charter. According to the charter, each member of the international community has conferred upon the Security Council the primary responsibility of ensuring international peace and security. A variety of tools are available to ensure that states do not breach international law and that if they do, compliance is restored. Diplomatic tools have priority under the charter, but enforcement approaches—sanctions or the use of force—are available if peaceful means fail to counter threats to international peace and security.

When it comes to applying such last resort negative incentives, the international community has resisted going beyond ad hoc responses. And if there are efforts to develop guidelines for the imposition of economic sanctions,[1] the use of force to stop atrocity crimes is only subjected to but one rule whose content is by nature evolving: the determination of a "threat to international peace and security" under UN charter Chapter VII. Recourse to the use of force to put an end to threats to international peace and security, including threats resulting from genocide, war crimes, and crimes against humanity, lacks an institutional enforcement framework to ensure that it is legitimate, coherent, and effective. Yet this framework should be established, because when it comes to atrocity crimes, it is probably the availability of "hard power" responses—including the use of force in extreme cases—that may have the greatest impact, both as a deterrent and as a reactive measure.

When they adopted the UN charter, the founding states expressed their willingness to create a tool that would effectively allow the Security Council to enforce its responsibility for the maintenance of international peace and security. Under Article 43 of the charter, all members undertook to make available to the Security Council armed forces, assistance, and facilities necessary for the purpose of maintaining international peace and security. These would be available to the Security Council on its call, should it decide that the existence of a threat to peace, breach of peace, or act of aggression required coercive action to be taken. Under such a scenario, the forces would come under the strategic direction of the Military Staff Committee composed of the chiefs of staff of the five Security Council permanent members (China, France, Russia, the United Kingdom, and the United States). In the 1950s, it became apparent that the arrangements under Article 43 would not materialize. And for the fifty years that the cold war lasted, the Security Council's ability to authorize or use coercive action was hijacked by the political opposition between the east and the west. This deadlock was finally broken in 1990 following the end of the cold war. For the first time in its history, the Security Council authorized the use of force under Chapter VII "to restore international peace and security" following the invasion of Kuwait by Iraq. Since 1990, the Security Council has authorized, or subsequently endorsed, the use of force under Chapter VII in several instances. In most of these cases, the use of force was requested or supported by the legitimate government of the targeted state—whether in charge or in exile. This type of intervention occurred in Liberia, Haiti, Sierra Leone, East Timor, and the Democratic Republic of Congo. In a minority of cases, the use of force was decided without the consent of the legitimate government, whether there was no clear authority in charge—like in Somalia—or whether the consent was not given at the time of the adoption of the resolution—like in Rwanda. On other rare occasions, a coalition of states used force to "restore peace and security" without a clear mandate from the Security Council acting under Chapter VII and without the consent of the targeted government, such as in Kosovo and more recently in Iraq. In all these cases—with the exception of the first authorized use of force against Iraq—humanitarian concerns were put forward as a key justification for the use of force: blatant and massive human rights violations amounted to a threat to international peace and security. Yet the international community did not intervene in a principled manner in order to prevent and stop all atrocity crimes. Genocide unfolded in Rwanda and Bosnia under the eyes of a rather passive international community before more robust action was taken. In Kosovo, it was argued that the military intervention actually made the human rights situation worse. And although some still believe that the 2003 invasion of Iraq was legal, few would argue today that it was genuinely driven by humanitarian concerns.

It should not come as a surprise that the UN legal and institutional framework has not easily adapted to the evolution of state practice since the end of the cold war. Although the international community has supported interventions based on humanitarian considerations, many governments, including permanent members of the Security Council, have repeatedly stressed the exceptional nature of such actions and pushed very hard to get the authorities of the targeted state to consent to intervention before going along with a resolution authorizing the use of force. Even the advocates of "humanitarian intervention" were long unable to agree on a framework that would provide legal clarity and certainty to this approach. And if the International Commission on Intervention and State Sovereignty (ICISS) put forward some guidelines regulating the use of military force for human-itarian purposes, the fact that then UN secretary-general Kofi Annan excluded these from the consideration of member states in the lead-up to the 2005 World Summit evidences that too many obstacles lie in the way of the elaboration of a more precise legal framework regulating such military action.

If progress has been made within the UN system to prevent and put an end to atrocity crimes, it has largely focused on a much-needed strengthening of peacekeeping operations. And these efforts are undoubtedly worthwhile: in the last decade, peacekeeping operations, together with peace-making activities, have fulfilled their promise to reduce conflicts and their usual share of mass atrocities.[2] Since 2000, peacekeeping operations have gone through several reforms that have focused on three aspects. First, the inter-national community has acknowledged the need to strengthen available capacities, including enhanced rapidly deployable capacities to reinforce peacekeeping operations in crisis, establishment of a standing police capacity,[3] and establishment of a strategic reserve. Second, there has been a loosening of the requirement that all the parties involved in a conflict situation consent to a peace agreement and to the deployment of peacekeepers: the deployment can occur on the basis of some kind of strategic consent for peace even if this leaves some players on the margins. And third, the limits on the use of force by peacekeeping forces have been revised: peacekeepers are no longer restricted in the use of force only in self-defense and are increasingly mandated to use force to protect civilians, particularly those under imminent threat of physical danger.[4] Today, many peacekeeping operations are "complex:" the UN operates in parts of the world where the states have collapsed or are severely weakened.[5] In these circumstances, the international community steps in and fills a sovereignty gap. Peacekeepers have to take the lead in offering protection to civilians, countering violent threats to peace by isolated peace spoilers, disarming and demobilizing combatants, and assisting in the reestablishment of the rule of law.

The efforts to strengthen peacekeeping are clearly necessary and very valuable. However, despite all the benefits they offer, peacekeeping approaches cannot be the sole means to provide the kind of physical protection called for by the R2P principle. First, the deployment of forces remains weakened by an institutional constraint: the consent of the states contributing the peacekeeping personnel and equipment. Second, the international community faces logistical constraints: even if troops and material are forthcoming, they must have the professional and technical capacity to counter military attacks against populations. These two issues are being tackled through the proposal to establish strategic reserves: "sitting, but ready to run"[6] military units whose deployment has been preauthorized by individual contributing states. A third constraint is that peacekeeping forces will only be deployed where there is a peace agreement that enjoys broad support. But peace agreements may well be concluded only long after atrocities have begun, and when concluded, they may also fail to stop atrocities, as the Darfur situation painfully reminds us. Finally, in situations that call for broader operations or where parties do not consent to the deployment of international forces, peacekeeping is not the answer.

Where Does the Collective Use of Force Stand Today?

The last decade has been witness to a number of initiatives to reinforce the authority and capacity of the UN to prevent and put an end to atrocity crimes. At the international level, the adoption of the soft law principle on states' responsibility to protect is by any account an historical step forward. However, the major stumbling blocks toward the establishment of a mechanism with the authority, the capacity, and the legitimacy to intervene against the will of the architects of hell on earth and protect populations from atrocity crimes have not yet been lifted. Based on their legal, political, and emotional understanding of their sovereignty, many states resist the adoption of a precise regulatory framework that will govern the collective use of force; resist empowering the UN with the capacity to deliver on its promise to protect populations from atrocity crimes; and resist entrusting the Security

Council with the duty to resort to the use of force—as a last resort—to protect populations from atrocity crimes.

Even in the United States, where the public still expresses strong support for sending troops to protect populations from atrocity crimes, history—the Vietnam debacle, the failed intervention in Somalia—lends support to the view that the Iraq War will, at least over the next decade, bar political leaders from sending American troops abroad to protect populations from atrocity crimes. The American political leadership's weakened appetite for military interventions combined with the world's widespread resentment over America's unilateralism call for a new approach to "hard power" answers to atrocity crimes. In this chapter we argue that the coming into existence of the ICC offers a unique opportunity to look at the issue of the collective use of force through new lenses: those of an international judicial process. A judicial approach to enforcement has the capacity to counter many of the objections raised by states, including U.S. political leadership, over the collective use of force. We also explore how a mechanism dedicated to the enforcement of the ICC mandate—an IMS—would not only deter the commission of mass atrocities but also ensure that justice is provided to victims and that perpetrators are held accountable.

The International Criminal Justice Approach to Atrocity Crimes

From Nuremberg to Rome and Thereafter:
The Birth of an International Criminal
Justice System Addressing Atrocity Crimes

Following World War II, the Nuremberg and Tokyo tribunals held for the first-time individuals—not abstract entities—personally responsible for grave abuses of human rights and humanitarian law. Fifty years later, the international community decided again to provide an international criminal judicial answer to atrocity crimes committed in the former Yugoslavia (International Criminal Tribunal for the former Yugoslavia [ITCY]) and in Rwanda (International Criminal Tribunal for Rwanda [ICTR]).

These ad hoc judicial responses to atrocity crimes led to the adoption, in 1998, of the Rome Statute of the ICC. The jurisdiction of the ICC is, for the time being, limited to genocide, crimes against humanity, and war crimes. Unlike the above-mentioned international criminal tribunals, the ICC is a permanent institution that was established by a diplomatic conference. The ICC can prosecute anyone, even a head of state or someone obeying a superior's orders, who commits (or attempts to commit, orders to commit, or contributes to the commission of) any of the crimes under its jurisdiction. The ICC can only deal with acts that occurred after June 30, 2002, and it can only do so if a case is not being or has not genuinely been investigated or prosecuted at the national level (complementarity rule). A case can be initiated through three different channels. A state party as well as the Security Council acting under Chapter VII can refer a situation. Moreover, the prosecutor may initiate an investigation *proprio motu*. In that case, a pretrial chamber must authorize the commencement of the investigation. When a situation has been referred by a state or when an investigation has been initiated by the prosecutor *proprio motu*, the court has jurisdiction if the crime occurred in the territory of a state party or if the crime was committed by a national of a state party. There are no such limitations in the case of a referral by the Security Council. Moreover, the Security Council, acting under Chapter VII, has the right to ask for the deferral, for a period of twelve months, of an investigation or a prosecution.

Since 1998, the international community has provided an international criminal justice response to mass atrocities through the creation of hybrid tribunals such as the Special Court for Sierra Leone, the Special Panels for Serious Crimes in East Timor, and the Extraordinary Chambers to try former Khmer Rouge leaders. Like the ICC, ICTY, and ICTR, these hybrid tribunals testify to the fact that the commission of atrocity crimes affects humankind in its entirety: criminal proceedings must comply with a minimum of international standards in order for justice to be delivered in a way that will satisfy victims, hold criminals accountable for their actions, and contribute to peace and stability at the local, regional, and global levels. Taken together, all these judicial efforts attest to the birth of a truly global international criminal justice system with the ICC as its centerpiece.

Enforcing International Criminal Justice: Lessons Learned from the ICTY and ICTR

To function effectively, international institutions rely primarily upon states' and other stakeholders' readiness to cooperate. Increasingly, however, the international community has endorsed the view that cooperation is best achieved when states or individual actors have clear incentives to do so. This is particularly the case when the benefits of entering or complying with an international agreement have to be weighed against its perceived costs. Such costs can be financial, such as those that might be induced by reducing greenhouse gas emissions. Yet these costs can be also be political; for example, when becoming a party to a treaty means that some decisions can no longer be taken unilaterally and are constrained by the terms of a treaty. Over the years, states have developed a broad range of tailor-made incentives to ensure compliance with specific international law instruments: positive or negative, soft or hard, preventive or reactive, or a combination of different approaches. When it comes to atrocity crimes, "the availability of effective legal institutions, creating the fear before the event, and the certainty after the event, that crimes will be prosecuted and punished,"[7] if necessary by resorting to the use of force, ensure that the international criminal justice system will have the desired consequences.

Both the ICTY and ICTR were established by the UN Security Council acting under Chapter VII. This means that each state is bound by the two Security Council resolutions.[8] To function effectively, the international tribunals need the states' cooperation at three levels: during an investigation (access to a country, access to information, and access to witnesses and documents since the tribunal has no *subpoena* power), to arrest indictees, and to execute sentences. In case of noncooperation, the president of the tribunal must report the matter to the Security Council. The fact that they are Chapter VII institutions gives both tribunals great authority, at least formally. In practice, however, cooperation with the ICTY and ICTR has not always been forthcoming. And despite the difficulties encountered by the tribunals, the members of the Security Council have shied away from their responsibility to enforce their mandates.

In its ten years of existence, the ICTY has met different challenges in the several areas over which it has jurisdiction: Bosnia and Herzegovina, Serbia, and Croatia. The level of cooperation has also evolved with the election of new governments more receptive to some of the demands of the international community.[9] Following the arrest of Radovan Karadzic in July 2008—thirteen years after his indictment—only one main indictee was still at large: Ratko Mladic.

Despite the ICTY prosecutor's repeated appeals to the Security Council for increased cooperation, this body has not used its power to enforce the mandate of the ICTY. At best, it "urged all States to cooperate fully with the ICTY."[10] The relative successes of the ICTY were achieved thanks to the support given by the United States and the European Union, which used their military, political, institutional, and financial leverage to obtain cooperation from states in the Balkans region. Yet even these tools know limitations. In her report to the Security Council on June 7, 2006, Carla del Ponte bluntly stated, "Since nobody else seemed to have the political will to locate and arrest them (*Mladic and Karadzic*), the Office of the Prosecutor would have no choice but to seek from the Security Council the powers to arrest fugitives wherever they were."[11]

Of course, everyone—including Carla del Ponte—knew that such a claim was wishful thinking. But with this statement, the ICTY prosecutor put her finger on one of the greatest institutional weaknesses of the current international criminal justice system: the lack of authority and capacity to arrest fugitives.

The achievements of the ICTR are generally considered to be far from satisfactory, an appreciation that can be explained by the amount of difficulties faced by the institution.[12] In January 2007, the prosecutor was still struggling to track and arrest eighteen indicted fugitives. The leaders of the Rwandan genocide were prominent politicians, members of the government, high-ranking military officials, journalists, high local authorities, and rich businessmen. Most of the powerful criminals managed to flee Rwanda and escape justice thanks to their influence and wealth. In other cases, the fugitives escaped to troubled areas beyond governments' control, for example, in the Democratic Republic of Congo (DRC).

Similar to the ICTY, the ICTR lacks its own enforcement power, and like the ICTY, repeated calls to the Security Council to enforce the states' duty to cooperate have been left unanswered. Unlike the ICTY, however, the ICTR does not have any powerful patrons in the Security Council.

At the very moment of their creation, the ICTY and ICTR were unfinished. Formally both institutions carry the political and legal weight of UN charter Chapter VII. In practice, however, both tribunals lack the necessary tools to deliver justice in the most effective manner. The two international tribunals have investigators, yet they do not have the power to arrest fugitives or to conduct activities without the consent of the concerned person or authority. The states' duty to cooperate is not backed up with any mechanism that provides appropriate incentives for compliance and tribunals have no way to enforce their mandate when such cooperation is not forthcoming.

The ICC and Enforcement

Contrary to the ICTY and ICTR, the ICC was not established through a resolution of the Security Council, hence the statute does not bind each and every UN member state. Like any other treaty, the statute binds only those states that are a party to it, a step that had been taken by 106 states as of July 22, 2008. Only two permanent members of the Security Council have ratified the statute: France and the United Kingdom. Russia has signed the statute and one can expect that it will, in time, become a party. China has neither signed nor ratified the treaty. The United States signed the statute and subsequently retracted its signature, a rather exceptional behavior. This is particularly troubling when surveys show that in 2002, 2004,

2005, and 2006 a large majority of Americans supported U.S. participation in the ICC.[13]

Part 9 of the statute contains detailed provisions on cooperation with states during the investigation and prosecution of crimes. State parties to the statute have the obligation to cooperate fully with the ICC. When a state party—or a nonparty state that has entered a cooperation agreement with the ICC—fails to comply with a request to cooperate from the ICC, the court is limited to making a finding of noncompliance and reporting it to the Assembly of States Parties (ASP), or to the Security Council if the case was referred to the prosecutor by the Security Council. The statute does not specify what kind of action the ASP may or should take in case of noncooperation, nor does it mention what the Security Council can or should do. The statute lacks any mechanism to react to noncooperation.[14] What the ASP will do is unclear. At the very least, it is able to name a non-complying state, hoping that official shaming will bring the state back into compliance. What the Security Council will do is also unclear. The precedents of the ICTY and ICTR show that this body has in the past been unwilling to intervene to enforce international justice.

This institutional weakness is highly regrettable: "enforcement remains the Court's Achilles' heel," and the ICC prosecutor "seems to be endowed with no more powers than any tourist in a foreign State."[15] This inability to enforce its mandate was acknowledged in a 2003 ICC informal paper. A group of prominent experts underscored that "The experience of the *ad hoc* Tribunals has proved that even with its far-reaching powers based on Chapter VII . . . the Prosecutor of the Tribunals have had to surmount reluctance and even opposition from some States in order to ensure their cooperation." The experts continued: "The Prosecutor of the ICC, whose powers are significantly weaker than those of his *ad hoc* Tribunal's counterpart, is likely to encounter similar unwillingness of States to cooperate."[16]

The first three situations being investigated by the prosecutor are Uganda, the Democratic Republic of the Congo (DRC), and Darfur, Sudan. All three investigations highlight the difficulties faced by the prosecutor: the lack of incentives to induce states to cooperate affects the work of the court; and in what appears to be a contradiction, the provision of such cooperation might actually not serve well the purposes of justice.

The situation in Uganda was referred to the ICC by the government of Uganda on December 16, 2003. On July 29, 2004, the prosecutor opened an investigation in northern Uganda. Warrants of arrest and surrender for five leaders of the Lord's Resistance Army (LRA) for war crimes and crimes against humanity were unsealed on October 14, 2005.[17] A cooperation agreement was signed between the office of the prosecutor and the

Ugandan government. The latter offers additional security to the ICC staff and provides enforcement capacity if needed. The prosecutor has also managed to secure, at least officially, the cooperation of Interpol, Sudan, the DRC, as well as the UN Mission in the DRC (MONUC)[18] toward the execution of the arrest warrants. As of July 22, 2008, no arrests had been made.

The situation in Uganda highlights two of the difficulties the ICC prosecutor's office is facing because it lacks a police force of its own. First, the fact that the ICC staff is protected by Ugandan forces—which is a clear form of cooperation by the Ugandan government with the court—may actually affect the independence and impartiality of the investigation, and thus its quality. This is particularly the case if witnesses have been the victims of atrocities committed by Ugandan troops. Second, the fact that the ICC does not have an enforcement mechanism means that it has to rely on the states' cooperation to execute arrest warrants. Despite these challenges, the ICC indictments, in themselves, seem to have had a clear impact on the peace negotiations conducted since 2006 between the government of Uganda and the LRA. On February 19, 2008, parties to the negotiations agreed that war crimes committed during the twenty-one-year-old conflict would be prosecuted in Uganda and not be the object of an amnesty.

On March 31, 2005, the situation in Darfur was referred to the ICC by Security Council Resolution 1593. On June 1, 2005, the prosecutor decided to open an investigation. On February 27, 2007, the prosecutor requested that Pre-Trial Chamber I issue summonses to appear for Ahmad Muhammad Harun, former minister of state for the interior of the government of Sudan and currently minister of humanitarian affairs, and Ali Muhammad Ali Abd-Al-Rahman, alleged leader of the militia/*Janjaweed* (also known as Ali Kushayb). The prosecution's application stated that there were reasonable grounds to believe that Ahmad Harun and Ali Kushayb bore criminal responsibility in relation to fifty-one counts of crimes against humanity and war crimes. On May 1, 2007, after having considered that there were reasonable grounds to believe that Ahmad Harun and Ali Kushayb would not voluntarily present themselves before the court, Pre-Trial Chamber I issued arrest warrants for both the minister and the leader of the militia. On July 14, 2008, the prosecutor presented evidence showing that Sudanese President Omar Hassan Ahmad Al Bashir committed the crimes of genocide, crimes against humanity, and war crimes in Darfur, and requested an arrest warrant.

The situation in Darfur highlights two of the difficulties encountered by the ICC in the execution of its mandate. In his second, third, and fourth reports to the Security Council, the prosecutor explained that the situation in Darfur was so volatile that investigative activities had so far taken place outside of Sudan, which constituted a "serious impediment to the conduct of effective investigations." The ICC attempted to overcome this difficulty by entering an agreement with the African Union, which had a peacekeeping force in the region—the African Union Mission in Sudan (AMIS). Yet even that peacekeeping force was not capable of securing stability and sufficient protection in Darfur. Despite the lack of effective investigations inside Darfur, the office of the prosecutor was able to register and document the commission of genocide, crimes against humanity, and war crimes.

The second obstacle to justice stems from the difficulties the ICC will encounter in apprehending Harun, Kushayb, and, if an arrest warrant is delivered, Al Bashir. The ICC has little leverage on the Sudanese government to obtain its cooperation, and this government has clearly stated that it will not cooperate with the court. Here again, the lack of effective legal institutions, creating fear before the event and certainty after the event that crimes will be prosecuted and punished, plays into the hands of indicted criminals.

The third situation we will consider is in the DRC. In June 2004, following a referral by the government of the DRC, the prosecutor opened an investigation for crimes committed since July 2002 throughout the territory of the DRC. At the operational level, the ICC has signed a cooperation agreement with the government of the DRC. The ICC also signed such an agreement with MONUC, which operates under a Chapter VII mandate. On March 17, 2006, following the issuance of a sealed warrant of arrest for the alleged commission of war crimes, Thomas Lubanga was arrested by Congolese authorities in Kinshasa and transferred to the ICC. Three other indictees—Bosco Ntaganda, Germain Katanga, and Mathieu Ngudjolo—were subsequently arrested and transferred to the ICC.

Just like in Uganda, protection provided to the ICC staff and witnesses by DRC military troops and MONUC has both advantages and disadvantages. Given the conflict situation in the northeast part of the DRC, the protection provided by MONUC to the ICC staff is absolutely "essential."[19] And even with that protection, investigating remains a great challenge. However, some DRC and MONUC troops have engaged in criminal conduct, and their presence around the ICC staff might well affect the quality of the prosecutor's investigation.

In conclusion, in fulfilling its mandate, the prosecutor must be guided by the general principles of independence, impartiality, and nondiscrimination. It is these principles that must govern the prosecutor's work for it to remain "judicial." If the conduct of an investigation is not independent, is not impartial, or is discriminatory, then no one can claim that justice is being delivered. Yet at the investigation level, witnesses and the ICC staff lack effective protection. This deficiency has been partly overcome by securing the cooperation of governmental or international forces. Such cooperation, however, bears certain costs and risks. The presence of governmental or international forces may affect the quality of the investigation in cases where the forces are associated with a party to the conflict or have themselves engaged in atrocity crimes. Moreover, the ICC runs the risk that such cooperation might simply not be forthcoming. Government officials might have a vested interest in an investigation and simply stall cooperation. Or there might be a conflict between peace and justice objectives. In that case, a country might decide to set justice considerations aside in the name of peace, a tactic Ugandan President Museveni seems to be using since he referred the LRA case to the ICC. Or the international forces might well be directed toward securing peace, at the cost of failing justice. Finally, there may simply not be any peacekeeping forces on the ground. And once an investigation is complete and arrest warrants delivered, how can the ICC make sure that indicted criminals are brought to justice?

The Case for an IMS

In the United States, the Marshals Service constitutes the enforcement arm of the federal courts. Although the service is part of the executive branch—the U.S. Department of Justice—marshals serve the judicial branch in a variety of ways. Among their many duties, they conduct certain types of federal investigations, ensure the safety of witnesses, protect the federal judiciary, and arrest more than half of federal fugitives.

Of course, there are limits to drawing a parallel between the domestic and the international levels. For example, the whole territory of the United States is under the authority of the federal government. At the international level, equally sovereign states form the international community and there is no superior authority that can be imposed upon states without their prior consent, with the exception of what the Security Council has the authority to decide under Chapter VII. Another difference between the domestic and the international levels is that judicial and enforcement authorities operate in contexts that may be very different. There is no war in the territory of the United States, but the three ICC situations we mentioned are conflict situations. This might not always be the case; as happened with the ICTY and ICTR, the ICC might be called to investigate situations in countries where stability has returned. Yet the need for tight security will almost always be higher at the international than at the federal level. Another difference is that U.S. marshals are not primarily responsible for investigating federal criminal offenses. This function is exercised by other bodies. At the international level, however, there is no other permanent institution besides the ICC, so the enforcement powers of an international police force would need to be extended to the conduct of all its investigations.

Characteristics of an IMS

In his first report to the UN General Assembly, the president of the ICC highlighted that the issue of cooperation during an investigation was a major concern for the ICC. He stressed in particular that the ICC lacks "a police force of its own." There are a variety of institutional possibilities for establishing an IMS that could perform, at the international level, tasks similar to those of a domestic judicial police force. Here we present what we feel would be the basic characteristics of an IMS. We also offer some options for its institutional structure.

The objectives of the IMS would be to deter the occurrence of war crimes, crimes against humanity, and genocide; to put an end to impunity for the perpetrators of these crimes; and to guarantee lasting respect for and the enforcement of international justice. The IMS would be the police arm of the ICC. It would work in cooperation with states and other actors. When authorized to do so, the IMS would have enforcement power in cases where state, intergovernmental, or individual cooperation cannot be secured. The IMS would serve the investigation mandate of the prosecutor. This includes ensuring the security of the ICC staff as well as the security of witnesses. This also includes securing access to countries, to documents, and to witnesses. The IMS would also execute orders and warrants issued by the Pre-Trial Chamber. The IMS would be a standing body staffed by five to ten thousand highly qualified individuals.

There are a variety of possible institutional arrangements for establishing, triggering, and operating an IMS. At one end of the spectrum, the service would primarily be an ICC institution; at the other end of the spectrum, the service would primarily be a UN body. Besides the ICC and the UN, regional and other organizations could have a role to play as well. Moreover, given that the pursuit of justice might very well occur within a conflict situation or within the context of peace-building efforts, institutional links would need to be formalized between the ICC and the actors in peace operations.

We offer two possible broad structural arrangements for an IMS: as primarily an ICC institution, and as primarily a UN body. In presenting such different options, we wish to emphasize how the choice of the institutional structure can impact the political nature of the service, its legitimacy, and its efficiency. We also point to some of the difficulties, and these are not minor by any account, that will need to be addressed before an IMS can be created.

An ICC IMS

Under the first option, the IMS would primarily be an ICC institution: the IMS is created by the ICC ASP, the staff is ICC staff, and the service is triggered by the prosecutor or the Pre-Trial Chamber and operates under the authority of the ICC. In order for the service to have enforcement power in any given state, the IMS would need to be called upon either by the UN Security Council acting under Chapter VII or by a regional organization under Chapter VIII. In that case, the Security Council or the competent authority of the regional organization would exercise the strategic authority over the police, while the ICC retained the operational authority.

The advantages of an ICC IMS are the following. First, it allows the ICC to have a standing police force to assist it in all investigations (security for staff and witnesses, thus guaranteeing the independence and impartiality of investigations). Second, the existence of a standing force already on the ground, even if it cannot directly exercise its enforcement power, would put pressure on states and other parties to cooperate. Third, if there is a need for enforcement action in a specific case, the request can be brought to the Security Council or the relevant regional organization, based on a preexisting memorandum of understanding between the ICC and the UN or the regional organization.

An ICC IMS would, however, face several challenges. The first cluster of constraints derives from the fact that the ICC statute is an international treaty. Establishing the service might require amending the ICC statute or adopting a protocol, which means establishing two categories of parties to the statute. Moreover, many ICC parties will resist the establishment of a force that could be given enforcement power by the Security Council. The second difficulty stems from the current structure and working methods of the Security Council. The five permanent members of the Security Council (P5) may resist allowing the IMS to enforce action on their territory or on the territory of their allies. They may equally resist a triggering mechanism that limits their discretionary power. These challenges might easily be exacerbated by the fact that thus far the United States, China, and Russia have not joined the ICC. A third drawback to having an ICC IMS is its cost: the ICC ASP, or to be more precise, those parties that ratify the amendment or become a party to the protocol, might not be ready to finance such an important standing police service.

These challenges can be overcome by making progress on two fronts. First, the working methods and the composition of the Security Council need to be reformed. Negotiations are currently taking place in order to make this body more representative and to ensure that the P5 do not use their veto in cases of genocide, crimes against humanity, and war crimes. We are not there yet, but these reform proposals must remain on the negotiating table. Second, there is at least one established strategy to induce all the parties to the ICC statute to accept an IMS, and that is to develop a comprehensive ICC statute noncompliance mechanism. This mechanism would offer both a facilitative and an enforcement response to noncompliance, thus building a compliance regime in which all the parties to the ICC statute—both developed and developing countries—would find acceptable.

A UN IMS

Under our second scenario, a UN IMS would be the enforcement mechanism for the Security Council in cases of atrocity crimes threatening international peace and security. This option would build on UN charter Article 43 and thus constitute a "baby step" toward a more comprehensive standing UN force such as the proposal for a UN Emergency Peace Service (UNEPS). The IMS would be created by a Security Council resolution, the staff would be UN staff, and the service would operate under the authority of the Security Council. Triggering the service would be the result of a regulated process similar to the guidelines for the use of military force proposed by the ICISS, with a specific role for the ICC prosecutor in order to guarantee the judicial nature of the process (a double-triggering function, for example).

The advantages of a UN IMS are twofold. First, the current non-ICC party status of the three Security Council permanent members is not questioned. Second, the establishment of a UN IMS offers an integrated approach to the maintenance of peace and security and the pursuit of international justice.

Just like an ICC IMS, a UN IMS faces several challenges. The first relates yet again to the current composition and working methods of the Security Council: many countries will resist empowering a nonrepresentative and overly political body with an enforcement mechanism, and the P5 will resist a triggering mechanism that limits their discretionary power just as much as they will resist allowing the IMS to enforce action on their territory or on the territory of their allies. The second difficulty stems from the fact that a UN IMS will be more disconnected from the ongoing investigative work of the ICC, especially at the field level. As its mandate would be limited to enforcement action, a UN IMS would not be in a position to provide day-to-day protection to ICC staff and witnesses. The third challenge is financial: here again, and just like any proposal to increase the UN budget, there will be resistance in the General Assembly Fifth Committee. These challenges can be partly overcome by reforming the composition and working methods of the Security Council and by adopting a UN-ICC memorandum of understanding to ensure that the work of the UN IMS is not disconnected from the ICC.

Conclusion

The individuals who plan and play a leadership role in the execution of genocidal acts and other atrocity crimes are encouraged by the lack of an effective international criminal justice system that will hold them accountable. The masterminds behind the genocide in Rwanda knew that if they slaughtered a handful of Belgian peacekeepers the international community would give them "carte blanche" to commit their heinous acts. When the LRA leaders were indicted by the ICC, they were suddenly willing to sit at the negotiating table in the hope of benefiting from an amnesty. Some even say that Al Bashir fears only one institution, the ICC, and the prospect of being indicted and brought to The Hague to face a trial. Potential individual accountability weighs very heavily in the decision-making process of individuals who might otherwise be tempted to commit atrocity crimes in order to achieve political and other gains. But the international criminal justice system is still in its infancy. It lacks the means to enforce its decisions, and because of this weakness, it does not have the greatest capacity to deter the commission of atrocity crimes. The current UN framework is also ill-suited to deter and react to the commission of atrocity crimes.

The institutional structure of the ICC and the UN must be built upon to allow the international community to live up to its responsibility to protect. The first step is for the United States and the other P5 countries to join the ICC. But the international community must do more. Taking a leadership role in establishing a standing IMS with the capacity to arrest indictees is the kind of bold step that is needed.

Aristotle rightly said, "It is in justice that the ordering of society is centered." And we concur with Carla del Ponte: "It is in international justice that the ordering of world affairs is centered, or rather, should be centered."[20] The unanimous endorsement of the responsibility to protect provides the opportunity to go beyond words and to empower the international community with the means to stop the architects of hell: not through the politically and morally sensitive use of military force, but through the enforcement of a legitimate international judicial process.

Notes

* Richard H. Cooper is founder of the General Welfare Group and convenor of the R2P Coalition in Oak Brook, Illinois. Juliette Voïnov Kohler is senior program officer at the Global Humanitarian Forum in Geneva, Switzerland. The views expressed in this chapter are those of the authors alone.

1. For an update on progress made so far, see the chairman's report on the 2002 to 2003 work of the working group, see letter dated December 19, 2003, from the Permanent Representative of Cameroon to the United Nations addressed to the president of the security council, UN Doc. S/2003/1197, January 22, 2004, http://daccessdds.un.org/doc/UNDOC/GEN/N03/670/83/PDF/N036783 .pdf?OpenElement.

2. Human Security Center, *2005 Human Security Report: War and Peace in the 21st Century* (Vancouver, Canada: Liu Institute for Global Issues, 2005), http://www.liu.xplorex.com/?p2=/modules/liu/publications/view.jsp&id=2067.

3. See the General Assembly resolution, *2005 World Summit Outcome*, UN Doc. A/RES/60/1, para. 92, October 24, 2005, http://daccessdds.un.org/doc/UNDOC/ GEN/N05/487/60/PDF/N0548760.pdf?OpenElement; UN Secretary-General, *Implementation of decisions from the 2005 World Summit Outcome for action by the Secretary-General*, UN Doc. A/60/430, para. 92, October 25, 2005, http:// www.un-ngls.org/UN-Summit-SG-Report-Implementation-N0554506.pdf.

4. UN Security Council, Resolution 1674, UN Doc. SC/RES/1674, para. 16. April 28, 2006.

5. Since 2003, complex peacekeeping operations have been launched in Burundi, Cote d'Ivoire, Haiti, Liberia, the Sudan, and the DRC. See Simon Chesterman, *The Use of Force in UN Peace Operations*, external study for the UN Peacekeeping Best Practices section, August 2004, http://smallwarsjournal .com/documents/useofforceunpko.pdf; Victoria K. Holt, *The Responsibility to Protect: Considering the Operational Capacity for Civilian Protection*, Discussion paper (Washington, DC: Henry L. Stimson Center, 2005), http://www.stimson.org/fopo/pdf/Stimson_CivPro_pre-pubdraftFeb04.pdf.

6. Jean-Marie Guéhenno, UN Undersecretary-General for Peacekeeping Operations, *Key Challenges in Today's UN Peacekeeping Operations*, May 18, 2006, transcript, Council on Foreign Relations, http://www.cfr.org/ publication/10766/key_challenges_in_todays_un_peacekeeping_operations _rush_transcript_federal_news_service_inc.html.

7. Gareth Evans, *Crimes Against Humanity: Overcoming Global Indifference*, 2006 Gandel Oration for B'nai B'rith Anti-Defamation Commission, April 30, 2006, http://www.crisisgroup.org/home/index.cfm?id=4087&l=1.

8. UN charter, article 25.

9. See the presentation by David Tolbert, deputy prosecutor of the ICTY, "Effective Apprehension of Indictees: Lessons Learned from the ad hoc and Hybrid Criminal Tribunals," *presented at the conference International Criminal Tribunals in the 21st century*, September 30, 2005, War Crimes Research Office,

American University, Washington College of Law. Audio recording available at http://www.wcl.american.edu/warcrimes/2005/criminaltribunals.cfm.

10. SC/RES/1166 (1998), http://daccessdds.un.org/doc/UNDOC/GEN/N98/131/ 78/PDF/N9813178.pdf?OpenElement; SC/RES/1329 (2000), http://daccesdds .un.org/doc/UNDOC/GEN/N00/773/49/PDF/N0077349.pdf?OpenElement; SC/RES/1534 (2004), http://daccessdds.un.org/doc/UNDOC/GEN/N04/286/ 29/PDF/N0428629.pdf?OpenElement.

11. Security Council, 5,453rd Meeting (AM), *Security Council Hears Briefings on Work of International Tribunals for Rwanda, Former Yugoslavia*, Department of Public Information, June 7, 2006, http://www.un.org/News/Press/docs/2006/ sc8740.doc.htm.

12. See the presentation by Hassan Jallow, chief prosecutor of the ICTR. See note 9.

13. In 2002, 71 percent of Americans said the United States should participate in the ICC. In July 2004, a Chicago Council on Foreign Relations (CCFR) poll showed that 76 percent of Americans support U.S. participation in the ICC. Also, "large majorities of the public (82%) and leaders (80%) favor the trial of suspected terrorists in the ICC." In September 2004, the Program on International Policy Attitudes (PIPA) found that 74 percent support U.S. participation in the ICC. In February 2005, CCFR/PIPA polls show that 69 percent support U.S. participation in the ICC. Finally, in May 2006, a PIPA/Knowledge Networks survey on "Americans on international courts and their jurisdiction over the US" shows that 74 percent of respondents said the United States should participate in the ICC.

14. There is one exception, however, in the case of a failed state. Under Article 57.3(d), the pretrial chamber may authorize the prosecutor to take specific steps to investigate within the territory of a state party that has not agreed to cooperation if the state is clearly unable to execute a request for cooperation due to the unavailability of any authority or any component of its judicial system to execute the request of cooperation.

15. Sarah B. Sewall and Carl Kaysen, ed., *The United States and the International Criminal Court: The Choices Ahead* (Cambridge, MA: American Academy of Arts and Science, 2000), 6, http://www.amacad.org/projects/iccarticle.aspx; Bert Swart and Göran Sluiter, "The International Criminal Court and international criminal cooperation," in *Reflections on the International Criminal Court: Essays in Honor of Adriaan Bos*, eds. Herman A. M. von Hebel, Johan G. Lammers, and Jolien Schukking (New York: Cambridge University Press, 1999).

16. ICC-OTP, *Fact-finding and investigative functions of the Office of the Prosecutor, including international cooperation*, Informal expert paper, 2003, http://www .icc-cpi.int/library/organs/otp/state_cooperation.pdf.

17. One of the indictees, Dominic Ongwen, has since been killed in battle.

18. On January 23, 2006, MONUC made an attempt to arrest LRA leaders in the northeastern part of the DRC, an ill-conceived mission that failed, leaving eight peacekeepers dead.

19. International Criminal Court, *Report on the Activities of the Court*, ICC-ASP -4/16, September 16, 2005, 9, http://www.icc-cpi.int/library/asp/ICC-ASP-4 -16_English.pdf.

20. Carla del Ponte, speech delivered during Justice in Pursuit of War Criminals forum, Kennedy School's Kokkalis Program on Southeastern and East-Central Europe, Harvard Law School's Human Rights Program, and Harvard's Center for European Studies, October 26, 2006.

Contributors

M. Cherif Bassiouni is a distinguished research professor of law at DePaul University College of Law and president of its International Human Rights Law Institute. He is also president of the International Institute of Higher Studies in Criminal Sciences in Siracusa, Italy, as well as the honorary president of the International Association of Penal Law, based in Paris, France. He has served the United Nations in a number of capacities. In 1999, Professor Bassiouni was nominated for the Nobel Peace Prize for his work in the field of international criminal justice and for his contribution to the creation of the International Criminal Court. Professor Bassiouni is the author of twenty-seven books and editor of forty-eight books, and the author of 240 articles on a wide range of legal issues, including international criminal law, comparative criminal law, and international human rights law.

Sapna Chhatpar Considine is a project manager for the Responsibility to Protect-Engaging Civil Society (R2PCS) project (www.responsibilitytoprotect .org) at the World Federalist Movement-Institute for Global Policy (WFM-IGP). The R2PCS project is currently leading efforts to build a global civil society coalition for the responsibility to protect. Previously, Sapna worked as legislative aide for a U.S. Congressman where she worked to mobilize congressional leaders against the war in Iraq. She has also worked for a civil rights law firm specializing in employment discrimination law. Ms. Chhatpar has a masters degree in international affairs, focusing on human rights, from Columbia University's School of International and Public Affairs and a bachelors in international relations from American University.

Richard H. Cooper is the convenor of the Responsibility to Protect (R2P) Coalition. He is also the founder of General Welfare Group LLC., a private merchant bank. Mr. Cooper is very active in philanthropy and community service. He is a life trustee of the Chicago Symphony Orchestra and serves on the Executive Committee and board of the Chicago Council for Global Affairs and the International Advisory Committee of the International Crisis Group.

Erica De Bruin is a Ph.D. candidate in political science at Yale University. She is a former research associate for U.S. foreign policy at the Council on Foreign Relations and for the Fellows Program at the New America

Foundation. Ms. De Bruin received her B.A. from Columbia University. Her research focuses on the causes of conflict, the conduct of war, and the evolution of the norms governing the use of force internationally.

Nicole Deller is director of programs for the Global Centre on R2P. From 2004 to 2007 she was senior program officer at the Institute for Global Policy, where she headed the Responsibility to Protect-Engaging Civil Society project. As research associate for the Lawyers' Committee on Nuclear Policy and the Institute for Energy and Environmental Research, she was the principal editor and coauthor of *Rule of Power or Rule of Law: An Assessment of U.S. Policies and Actions Regarding Security-Related Treaties* (2003). Ms. Deller received her Juris Doctorate from New York University School of Law and served as chair of the International Security Affairs Committee of the New York City Bar Association (2004 to 2007).

April Kanne Donnellan joined Global Philanthropy Partnership as executive director in 2005. She previously served as program director of the Chicago Council on Foreign Relations (now the Chicago Council on Global Affairs). Prior to that, Ms. Donnellan was a Foreign Service officer with the U.S. Department of State completing assignments in Port Louis, Mauritius, and Washington, DC. She served as staff assistant to the assistant secretary for international organization affairs, and as a sanctions/peacekeeping officer covering the Middle East and Africa, where she earned a Meritorious Honor Award for her work implementing multilateral sanctions. Ms. Donnellan, a former term member of the Council on Foreign Relations, is a graduate of Georgetown University.

Aaron Dorfman is the director of education at American Jewish World Service (AJWS). Aaron has worked in Jewish education and social justice for fifteen years and holds a masters in public policy from the Kennedy School of Government at Harvard University and a certificate from the Pardes Institute of Jewish Studies in Jerusalem.

Gareth Evans has been, since January 2000, president and chief executive of the Brussels-based International Crisis Group. A member of the Australian Parliament for twenty-one years, Gareth Evans was one of Australia's longest serving foreign ministers. Gareth Evans has won numerous international awards and has written or edited nine books. I 2000–2001 he was cochair, with Mohamed Sahnoun, of the International Commission on Intervention and State Sovereignty (ICISS), appointed by the government of Canada, which published its report, The Responsibility to Protect, in December 2001.

Lee Feinstein is visiting fellow in Foreign Policy Studies at the Brookings Institution. A former senior Defense and State Department official, he was the national security director for Hillary Clinton's campaign for president when he wrote his chapter. Mr. Feinstein received a Juris doctorate from the Georgetown University Law Center and an M.A. in political science from the City University of New York, and is a member of the New York and Washington, DC, bars. He has taught international law and politics as an adjunct professor at George Washington University's Elliott School of International Affairs and the City University of New York.

Susan E. Mayer is a professor and dean of the Harris School of Public Policy at the University of Chicago. She has published numerous articles and book chapters on the measurement of poverty, the effect of growing up in poor neighborhoods, and the effect of parental income on children's well-being. Ms. Mayer is a member of the Board of Directors of Chapin Hall Center for Children and the General Accounting Office Educators' Advisory Panel. She has been a member of the National Academy of Sciences Committee on National Statistics Panel to Review U.S. Department of Agriculture's Measurement of Food Insecurity and Hunger, and the Committee on Standards of Evidence and the Quality of Behavioral and Social Sciences Research.

Ruth W. Messinger is the president and executive director of American Jewish World Service (AJWS). Prior to assuming her position at AJWS in 1998, Ms. Messinger was in public service in New York City for twenty years. She served twelve years on the New York City Council and eight years as Manhattan borough president, and was the first woman to secure the Democratic Party's nomination for mayor in 1997.

Since 1994, **William Pace** has served as the executive director of the World Federalist Movement-Institute for Global Policy in New York. In 1999, Mr. Pace served as the secretary-general for The Hague Appeal for Peace civil society conference, a monumental gathering for peace in the city of The Hague, Netherlands. In 2001, Mr. Pace was awarded the William J. Butler Human Rights Medal from the Urban Morgan Institute for Human Rights for being one of the "cardinal figures in the creation of a permanent International Criminal Court." Mr. Pace is the author of numerous articles and reports on international affairs and UN issues, multilateral treaty processes, and NGO participation in international decision making.

Mary R. Page is director of the Human Rights and International Justice area in the Program on Global Security and Sustainability of the John D. and Catherine T. MacArthur Foundation. She joined the foundation in

1990 as a program officer in the Program on Peace and International Cooperation, where she had responsibilities for grantmaking in the areas of conventional arms policy, Middle East regional security, and U.S. military production and budgets. In 1998 she became associate director of the U.S. Interests and Responsibilities area, working on public deliberation and the role of the United States in international affairs. Ms. Page was engaged in research and development of computer-assisted instruction programs at Stanford University, mathematics education research and teaching at the University of Chicago, and English composition and early childhood education at Holt, Rinehart & Winston publishers, where she was a senior editor. She has consulted on projects in African education, mathematics for limited English speakers, and U.S. public opinion and foreign policy.

Samantha Power is the Anna Lindh Professor of Practice of Global Leadership and Public Policy, based at the Carr Center for Human Rights Policy, where she was the founding executive director (1998–2002). She is the author of *Chasing the Flame: Sergio Vieira de Mello and the Fight to Save the World* (Penguin Press, 2008), a biography of the UN envoy killed by a suicide bomber in Iraq in 2003. Her book *"A Problem from Hell": America and the Age of Genocide* (New Republic Books) was awarded the 2003 Pulitzer Prize for general nonfiction, the 2003 National Book Critics Circle Award for general nonfiction, and the Council on Foreign Relations' Arthur Ross Prize for the best book on U.S. foreign policy.

Kenneth Roth is the executive director of Human Rights Watch, a post he has held since 1993. Human Rights Watch investigates, reports on, and seeks to curb human rights abuses in some eighty countries. From 1987 to 1993, Mr. Roth served as deputy director of the organization. Previously he was a federal prosecutor for the U.S. Attorney's Office for the Southern District of New York and the Iran-Contra investigation in Washington, DC. He also worked in private practice as a litigator.

David Scheffer is the Mayer Brown/Robert A. Helman Professor of Law and the director of the Center for International Human Rights at Northwestern University School of Law. He teaches international human rights law and international criminal law. He was previously the U.S. Ambassador at Large for War Crimes Issues (1997–2001) and led the U.S. delegation in UN talks establishing the International Criminal Court.

As executive director of Amnesty International USA from 1994 to 2006, **William F. Schulz** headed the American section of the world's oldest and largest international human rights organization. He is currently a Senior Fellow at the Center for American Progress in Washington, DC, and an adjunct professor at the Wagner School of New York University. Dr. Schulz is the author or contributing editor of four books on human rights and is regularly quoted in the *New York Times* and other national publications.

Adele Simmons is vice chair of Chicago Metropolis 2020 and president of the Global Philanthropy Partnership. Mrs. Simmons was president of the John D. and Catherine T. MacArthur Foundation from 1989 to 1999. Since leaving the MacArthur Foundation, Mrs. Simmons has been spending part of her time strengthening the infrastructure of global philanthropy through work with the Chicago Global Donors Network, the World Economic Forum, the World Bank, and the Global Fund for Women. She serves on a number of boards, including the Chicago Council on Global Affairs, the Synergos Institute, the Field Museum, the Union of Concerned Scientists, and the Environmental Defense Fund, and she edits a bimonthly newsletter, *Global Giving Matters*, for the Synergos Institute.

Scott Stedjan is a senior policy advisor for humanitarian response at Oxfam America in Washington, DC, specializing in humanitarian and conflict issues. Scott contributed to this book in his previous capacity as legislative secretary for peaceful prevention of deadly conflict at the Friends Committee on National Legislation (Quakers), where he worked from 2002 to 2007. At FCNL, Scott lobbied the U.S. Congress and executive branch on conflict prevention and the arms trade, and served as national coordinator of the U.S. Campaign to Ban Landmines. He holds a master of science degree in human rights from the London School of Economics and Political Science.

Juliette Voïnov Kohler is senior program officer at the Global Humanitarian Forum in Geneva. She edited and contributed to this book in her former capacity as deputy convenor of the R2P Coalition. Previously, she worked for the Federal Department of Foreign Affairs of Switzerland. Dr.Voïnov Kohler is the author of *Le Mécanisme de Contrôle du Respect du Protocole de Kyoto à la Convention-Cadre des Nations-Unies sur les Changements Climatiques: Entre Diplomatie et Droit* (Schulthess, 2006) and coauthored *The End of Exceptionalism in War Crimes—The International Criminal Court and America's Credibility in the World* (Harvard International Review, August 2007).

Joe Volk is executive secretary of the Friends Committee on National Legislation (FCNL). Joe Volk has more than three decades of experience working for peace and social justice. He played key roles in founding the Iraq Working Group and the Arms Transfer Working Group, and has served as a leader in the Washington Interreligious Staff Committee. He has lobbied Congress to support peaceful prevention of deadly conflict, nuclear disarmament, peace in Iraq, and many other issues.

Herbert F. Weiss is emeritus professor of political science at the City University of New York (CUNY), Senior Fellow of the Ralph Bunche Institute for International Studies (CUNY), and senior policy scholar at the Woodrow Wilson International Center for Scholars in Washington, DC. He has been a student of political developments in the Congo since 1959. His study of the independence struggle, *Political Protest in the Congo*, won the Herskovits Prize of the African Studies Association (U.S.) and was republished in French under the title *Radicalisme Rural et Lutte pour l'Independence au Congo-Zaire*. Professor Weiss has been a consultant of the United Nations, USAID, the World Bank, and various NGOs dealing with the Congo and, more generally, with political protest, democratization, and elections in Africa.

Index

p. 12.   " mature world " ...

p. 40   " developed state "

Jus Cogens ... ->
compelling law
peremptory Norm

p 28 -

p. 46